HOLDING THE GROUND: THE NATIONALIST PARTY IN NORTHERN IRELAND, 1945-72

Ashgate

Aldershot • Brookfield USA • Singapore • Sydney

Holding the Ground:
The Nationalist Party
in Northern Ireland, 1945-72

BRENDAN LYNN

Ashgate

Aldershot • Brookfield USA • Singapore • Sydney

© Brendan Lynn 1997

Published by
Ashgate Publishing Limited
Gower House
Croft Road
Aldershot
Hants GU11 3HR
England

Ashgate Publishing Company
Old Post Road
Brookfield
Vermont 05036
USA

British Library Cataloguing in Publication Data
Lynn, Brendan
   Holding the ground : the Nationality Party in Northern Ireland,
   1945-72
   1.National Parliamentary Party - History 2.Northern Ireland
   - Politics and government
   I.Title
   324.2'41'0983

Library of Congress Cataloging-in-Publication Data
Lynn, Brendan.
   Holding the ground : the nationalist party in Northern Ireland,
   1945-72 / Brendan Lynn.
     p.   cm.
   Includes bibliographical references.
   ISBN 1-85521-980-8
   1. Political parties--Northern Ireland--History. 2. Northern
Ireland--Politics and government. 3. Nationalism--Northern Ireland.
I. Title.
JN1572.A979L96   1997
324.2416'083'09--dc21
                                             97-7846
                                             CIP

ISBN 1 85521 980 8

Printed in Great Britain by Galliard (Printers) Ltd, Great Yarmouth

Contents

Abbreviations

AOH	Ancient Order of Hibernians
APA	Anti-Partition Association
APL	Anti-Partition League
CAB	Cabinet (file)
c.	column(s)
CDU	Campaign for Democracy in Ulster
CnaP	Clann na Poblachta
D.E. Deb.	Dail Eireann Debates (followed by volume and column numbers)
DHAC	Derry Housing Action Committee
FF	Fianna Fail
FG	Fine Gael
FOI	Friends of Ireland
FU	Fianna Uladh
H.C. Deb.	Parliamentary Debates, (UK) House of Commons (followed by volume and column number)
H.C. Deb.(NI)	Parliamentary Debates, (NI) House of Commons (followed by volume and column number)
HCL	Homeless Citizens League
H.O.	Home Office (file)
INTO	Irish National Teachers Organisation
IUA	Irish Union Association
IRA	Irish Republican Army
LLI	Labour Lawyer Inquiry
MP	Member of Parliament (the term applies to both the Stormont and Westminster Parliaments)
NCCL	National Council of Civil Liberties
NCU	National Council for Unity
NDP	National Democratic Party
NICRA	Northern Ireland Civil Rights Association
NILP	Northern Ireland Labour Party
NLN	National League of the North

NPF	National Popular Front
NU	National Unity
PD	Peoples Democracy
PP	Parish Priest
PRONI	Public Records Office of Northern Ireland
RLP	Republican Labour Party
RUC	Royal Ulster Constabulary
SDLP	Social Democratic and Labour Party
SF	Sinn Fein
SPA	Special Powers Act
SU	Saor Uladh
TD	Teachta Dala (Member of the Irish Parliament)
UIA	United Ireland Association
UIL	United Ireland League
v.	volume

Acknowledgements

I would like to begin by thanking all the staff from the School of History, Philosophy and Politics at the University of Ulster at Coleraine, and in particular Professor T.G. Fraser for all his advice and encouragement throughout my research. Furthermore, I wish to express my gratitude to the library staff at the University of Ulster, Queens University Belfast and the Linen Hall Library in Belfast. In addition I am extremely grateful to the staff of the Public Record Office of Northern Ireland for their co-operation in assisting research. A special word of thanks must be given to those who made themselves available for interview and who proved to be an important source of material. I would also like to place on record my gratitude to the McAteer Family who not only allowed me access to their father's papers but, who took time to assist me in anyway they could. Finally, to my family and in particular my mother, this book is dedicated to them for giving me a second chance and having faith when I had none.

Foreword

History is sometimes said to be the story of the victors. This may perhaps explain why, amid the profusion of books written about the Troubles in Northern Ireland and the events leading up to them, there has until now been a notable absence of any serious consideration of the post-World War role of the Nationalist Party. But this is to deprive the account of one half of its drama. The period of 1945-1972 in Northern Ireland cannot adequately be understood without a proper assessment of the part played by those anti-partitionist politicians who, in Eddie McAteer's words 'down through the years kept a flame alive'. The fact that in the end they were tossed aside and other forces took their place does not mean that they deserve to be rubbished by the historian or disposed of in a footnote.

In picking the subject for his PhD thesis and in subsequently turning it into a book, Dr Brendan Lynn has made certain that such figures as Cahir Healy, Eddie McAteer, Paddy McGill and James Doherty will in future be given their due, though no more than their due for this is far from being an uncritical account. As Dr Lynn explains, the fact that the Nationalist Party never really solved the problem of organising itself means for the researcher that there is a great shortage of party records. This has not fazed the author who has shown how much can be distilled from memoirs, interviews, pamphlet literature like that famously preserved in the Linen Hall Library in Belfast and the local press. And he has also clearly established what some of us who were present at the end of the 1960s was, among a great many other things, a revolution against the Roman Catholic political establishment.

The civil rights campaign was at once narrower and deeper than the Nationalist stand. By its emphasis on British civil rights, it turned its back, for the time being, on anti-partitionist principle. But in its readiness to face open confrontation it affronted basic Nationalist instincts of respectability. In this respect John Hume's electoral victory over Eddie McAteer in the Stormont contest of February 1969 was, as the author presents it, a defining moment.

I was first made aware that politics in Northern Ireland were not like those of the rest of the United Kingdom when as an Oxford undergraduate in the late 1940s I listened to several speeches by the Labour MP Geoffrey Bing, who was attempting at the time to make public opinion alert to future troubles that were lying in store unless remedies were imposed in sufficient time by Westminster. But, although there was a Labour Government, he could get nowhere in the Commons because questions affecting Northern Ireland were instantly ruled out of order on the ground that they were related to matters that had been transferred to Stormont. When I was in Northern Ireland for *The Economist* in 1959 the dying embers of the IRA's border campaign had not been entirely extinguished and the frustrations of politicians who preferred to represent their people peacefully but at the same time did not want to appear to be recognising the legitimacy of the state were palpable. In a long interview with Cahir Healy he laid out for me the history of his dilemmas in a manner that was instantly recognisable in Dr Lynn's thorough and authentic account. It was a sad, but not an ignoble, story that came to be described later as one of 'intermittent and erratic abstentionism' (Jonathan Bardon, *A History of Ulster*) or one of 'timorous attendance' (Austin Currie, quoted by Lynn).

In 1969 and subsequent years when I was in the North for BBC Television the Nationalists may no longer have been the principal players but they had played their part (and in Eddie McAteer they still had a notable coiner of quotable comments). I was privileged to discuss Dr Lynn's work with him on two occasions during its progress and it gives me great pleasure to salute its appearance in print.

Keith Kyle
Visiting Professor of History, University of Ulster

Notes on Terminology

In the text a number of terms are used which may need some explanation. The phrase 'minority community' refers to the catholic/nationalist population within Northern Ireland.

The terms 'nationalist' and 'nationalism' (lower case) have been used to describe all shades of nationalist opinion in Northern Ireland, irrespective of individual political affiliation , whilst the term 'Nationalist' (upper case) applies specifically to, or members of the Nationalist Party. A similar distinction has also been applied to unionist politics: 'unionist' and 'unionism' (lower case) refers to all shades of unionist opinion, whilst the term 'Unionist' applies specifically to, or members of the Unionist Party which governed Northern Ireland, throughout the period dealt with in this book. On occasions 'Stormont' has been applied to describe the Unionist government which administered Northern Ireland.

With reference to the use of the phrase 'Six Counties' this applies directly to those counties which made up Northern Ireland after the Anglo-Irish Settlement of 1921. Likewise the term '26 Counties' describes those counties which formed the Irish Free State in 1921 and which later became a Republic in 1949.

Introduction

For almost 50 years the Nationalist Party was regarded as the principal political organisation representing the interests of the minority community in Northern Ireland. Yet in spite of this fact little detailed research has ever been done on the party and only in recent years has this begun to be rectified chiefly through the publication of *Northern Nationalism: Nationalist Politics, Partition and the Catholic Minority in Northern Ireland, 1890-1940* by Eamon Phoenix. As the title of this important study suggests, this only takes the story up until 1940, and hence a very important but largely forgotten period has still to be explored. In particular what were the events and developments which affected the party in the post-war period up until the impact of the rise of the Civil Rights movement in the 1960s?

This period after all was the era in which the Unionist ascendancy at Stormont seemed most secure and when it was at the height of its power and control over Northern Ireland. The Ireland Act 1949 had further strengthened the province's position within the United Kingdom and successive Westminster governments continued to exercise extreme caution about involving themselves in what were seen as the internal affairs of Northern Ireland. Within the province itself the supremacy of the Unionist Party, with its unassailable majority at Stormont, guaranteed there would be few threats to their grip on power. What dangers there were, were quickly dealt with and none ever posed a major risk. From 1956-1962 the Irish Republican Army (IRA) launched a campaign, but it was largely confined to the border areas, and after an initial burst of activity it petered out and finally the IRA itself was forced to call a halt. In political matters the only apparent danger to the Unionist Party appeared to come from the rise of the Northern Ireland Labour Party (NILP), when it won four seats in working class areas of Belfast at the 1958 general election. Yet by the time of the 1962 election, although it polled a record number of votes, the surge from Labour had been checked and no further seats were lost. Instead three years later at the next general election the tide was turned and the Unionists regained two of the seats it had lost seven years earlier.

1

This was, therefore, the harsh reality which faced the Nationalist Party in trying to provide a constructive and constitutional opposition. It was in the unenviable position of being confined to eternal opposition with little or no prospect of ever achieving power. This was largely due to the fact that, as Donald Horowitz suggests, the province is a prime example of where ethnic conflict dominates the nature of political debate and divisions. According to Horowitz:

> Where conflict levels are high ... ethnic parties reflect something more than affinity and a vague sense of common interest. That something is mutual incompatibility of ethnic claims to power. Since the party aspires to control the state, and in conflict prone polities ethnic groups also attempt to exclude others from state power, the emergence of ethnic politics is an integral part of this political struggle.[1]

Furthermore Horowitz concludes that such a situation will ultimately lead to a position where:

> An ethnically based party derives its support overwhelmingly from an identifiable ethic group ... and serves the interest of that group. In practice, a party will serve the interests of the group comprising its overwhelming support or quickly forfeit that support.[2]

It therefore, stands to reason that in the period dealt with in this book, what is of interest is not simply the perennial struggle with Unionism; rather it is the contest within its own community that the Nationalist Party had to face, in order to maintain its position as the recognised leader of Northern nationalists.

In trying to trace how successful the party was in facing this challenge the most immediate quandary one comes across is that although the term Nationalist Party is used, in reality for long periods of time there never was such a thing as, a properly co-ordinated and constituency based Nationalist organisation. This means in effect that there are no records as such and no one single source where one can find out about the problems and difficulties faced. Consequently, it comes as no great a surprise to discover that there is a shortage of secondary material dealing specifically with the Nationalist Party. As a result the bulk of the research has been concentrated upon a number of basic primary resources which are available and which enable one to begin to get an insight into the issues that were being raised. The private papers of politicians such as Cahir Healy, Eddie McAteer and Anthony Mulvey were therefore of great assistance, as was the *Irish News*, which remained the only daily newspaper aimed solely at the nationalist community in the province. Finally, important insights were gained into the political developments of the time through a number of interviews with people, many of whom had been involved at some point with the party and its activities.

How successful, therefore, was the Nationalist Party in meeting the various challenges it had to face? The main difficulty that was to confront it was the party's inability to find what Phoenix describes as 'some middle course between constitutional opposition and negative abstention'.[3] Certainly this was something that failed to be done in the years following partition when it proved impossible to get the supporters of both these views to work together in order to create a 'political force', capable of providing 'the growing demand of the Catholic community for clear political direction and constitutional redress of their grievances'.[4] The basis of the problem lay in whether or not by taking their seats in a Northern Ireland parliament Nationalists would be effectively recognising the permanency of partition. By 1925 Joe Devlin was convinced that the only option was to take their seats as, 'permanent abstention means permanent disfranchisement, and to any such policy, leading as it would to helplessness, confusion and failure, I could not give the slightest countenance'.[5] On the other hand for Nationalists in the border areas expecting the Boundary Commission to approve their transfer to the Free State such a step was rejected out of hand as it could easily damage the claims they had made to the above body. However, the leaked publication of the Commission's report put paid to such aspirations and left them facing the 'reality of lasting partition'. It left 'Republicans in the border constituencies of Fermanagh, Tyrone, Derry and South Down a dilemma: should they persevere in a negative policy of non-recognition of the Northern government, or should they follow Devlin's lead of constitutional resistance'.[6] After much deliberation and spurred on by De Valera's decision to lead his Fianna Fail (FF) party into the Dail, finally by the end of 1927 those MPs from the border areas including Cahir Healy, John McHugh, Alex Donnelly, T.J. Harbinson and John H. Collins took their seats alongside those already in attendance. The attitude, however, of this group of ten MPs remained defiant and was summed up by the maiden speech of Patrick O'Neill, MP for Down. He declared that he represented 'a large majority ... (who) did not expect to be anything more than temporarily under the jurisdiction of this House, and, consequently did not desire to be represented in it. Whilst they had been forced to accept the situation as it is', they remained 'in strong opposition to this parliament'.[7]

For Healy the next vital step to take following their entry into parliament was to try and draw the 'Devlinites and his own supporters' together as he was only too aware of the fact that the 'Northern Ireland state was a fait accompli, and that if they were to advance their position, their only course was to establish an effective organisation'.[8] Behind the scenes Healy worked to bring this to fruition and finally in May 1928 the National League of the North (NLN) was launched at a convention in Belfast. Amongst its aims was to work for the 'National Unification of Ireland' and along with what Phoenix describes as a 'radical and thoughtful' political programme, hopes were high that it could provide an organisation in which all shades of nationalist opinion could work. As the *Ulster Herald* was to declare it was time to 'bury deep all the bitter memories and march forward to victory'.[9]

Yet right from the outset it was evident that the NLN would struggle to achieve its goal of binding Northern Nationalists into 'a political force capable of achieving reforms'.[10] The problem was that as Healy was to conclude at one point 'there are people who would object to join(ing) Joe Devlin in heaven'.[11] Such people could never forgive Devlin and his supporters, mainly from the East of the province, for their decision to 'acquiesce in the exclusion, albeit as a "temporary" expedient, of a six county bloc from the jurisdiction of a Home Rule parliament, as the only means of achieving self-government for nationalist Ireland'.[12] This was clear from the fact that apart from Healy, Alex Donnelly and John Collins, few of the 'old pro-treaty Sinn Fein section ... played little part in the organisation of the League', and as a result 'its Central Council was dominated from the outset by old Devlinite and Hibernian (Ancient Order of Hibernians, AOH) elements'.[13]

To add to the difficulties facing the NLN was the growing realisation that in spite of all the best efforts of Devlin and his colleagues in parliament, they appeared powerless to prevent what was seen as further attacks on the nationalist minority. A further example of this concern came with the abolition of proportional representation for future parliamentary elections in Northern Ireland by Sir James Craig and his government in 1929. Certainly by 1932, as Phoenix shows, the feeling had grown amongst Northern Nationalists that the parliament that they sat in had become in essence a

"Protestant Parliament" for a "Protestant State".[14] Even for Devlin the frustration proved too much and in May 1932 after a row with the Speaker he withdrew from the House, accompanied by his colleagues, and he never personally returned. In any case for many Nationalist MPs such as J.H. Collins and Joe Connellan, who had been elected MP for South Armagh in 1929, Devlin's strategy of parliamentary opposition had never been their favoured option and in all probability they must have welcomed the developments of May 1932.[15]

As the NLN continued to struggle to achieve its objectives there remained a considerable body of opinion which continued to call for a policy of strict non-recognition. This group was headed by men such as Eamon Donnelly, a former republican/abstentionist MP for Armagh and FF activist, and pockets of 'anti-treaty Republicans', such as the Nationalist Defence Association (NDA) founded by Peadar Murney and Patrick Lavery in the Newry and South Armagh area, which had campaigned against any recognition of the Northern parliament.[16] The increasing drift towards abstention was to be illustrated at the general election in Northern Ireland which was held in November 1933. In South Armagh the NLN's nominee was defeated by an abstentionist candidate; in Central, Devlin's majority was cut to just under 3,000 by a republican prisoner; and in South Down De Valera was nominated and returned unopposed as MP by local nationalists. Such results only seemed to indicate that the disillusionment of Northern Nationalists had shattered the 'fragile unity' established by Devlin and Healy.[17]

If anything in the years ahead these divisions widened even further and numerous examples bear this out. After Devlin's death in January 1934 it proved impossible for anyone to emerge as a figure who could bring the different Nationalist factions together. For instance Healy 'with his Sinn Fein background and Fianna Fail orientation made him suspect amongst the Hibernian elements'. Whilst T.J. Campbell, who had succeeded Devlin as MP for Central and who had his own leadership ambitions, was seen as a 'moderate Redmonite ... and (his) rigid attendance and parliamentary etiquette ruled him out as a unifying influence'.[18] Then in November 1935 the holding of a Westminster election brought about a debacle in the constituency of Fermanagh-Tyrone, where the two sitting Nationalist MPs, Cahir Healy and Joe Stewart, were forced to withdraw their nominations in the face of Republican threats to stand against them. In the end a last minute compromise prevented a split in the vote whereby two "non-party candidates", Anthony Mulvey and Patrick Cunningham, were nominated as Abstentionists.[19] As for the attitude of Nationalist MPs to the Northern Parliament, a policy of 'qualified abstention' had been proposed and according to the *Irish News* this meant they would only attend on occasions to make a 'statement on National policy or exposing a public grievance'. Other than that 'it is understood, they are not likely to be heard very often'.[20] However, even this line did not hold and different MPs began to take different attitudes. In April 1934 Alex Donnelly withdrew completely and a year later Hugh McAleer, MP for Mid Tyrone followed suit. Eventually only T.J. Campbell and his colleague from Belfast, Richard Byrne, MP for Falls, attended on any kind of a regular basis.[21]

Thus the period up until the outbreak of war continued to be a time when the ever present question of abstention prevented Nationalists in the province from working together. In 1936 an attempt was made to revive the ideas of the NLN with the creation of a new body, the Irish Union Association (IUA), at a convention in Omagh in June. As with the NLN, it was hoped that the IUA would 'consolidate the entire strength of the anti-partition elements in the Six Counties', but it appears as if this goal was still unattainable. For instance it never attracted Campbell or Byrne to its ranks as both were wary of any involvement with the elements in it who continued to favour abstention. They therefore continued to maintain their own political machine in the Belfast area. It comes as no surprise to find that just over a year later Healy was suggesting that the IUA be allowed just to simply fade away. In October 1937 he was approached by Paddy Maxwell, the new MP for Foyle, to help call an "Ard Feis" of the IUA. Healy, in reply dismissed the idea pointing out that as so few areas had been organised it was not worthwhile going to such trouble. In any case he argued that any attempt to decide upon an agreed policy would 'only stir up dissension ... which we can ill afford to do at present'.[22]

Similar problems were to arise with the creation in 1937 of the Northern Council for Unity (NCU) by supporters of abstention such as Mulvey, Murney and Eamon Donnelly who had now become a Fianna Fail TD. The NCU had been formed to campaign in favour of the application of De Valera's new Free State constitution over the whole of Ireland. As part of this the NCU called for Northern Nationalists to be allowed to take their seats in the Dail and as an election in Northern Ireland approached they called for a complete boycott of the poll. For those MPs like Healy still trying to pursue the policy of "modified abstention", the suggestion of the

NCU was dismissed out of hand. The reason for this was simple as they believed that total abstention was no longer a viable option following the Representation of the Peoples Act 1934. This particular piece of legislation had been introduced by the Northern Ireland authorities following the success of De Valera and other abstentionist candidates at the election in 1933. It required any prospective candidate to sign a declaration requiring them to take their seats if elected. Once again, however, an election merely highlighted the deep divisions which continued to exist. In three Nationalist-held constituencies local selection conventions refused to nominate candidates and the seats were lost, with Mourne and South Down falling to the Unionists, and South Armagh to the NILP. After the election in one last attempt to unite Nationalists in a new campaign against partition Healy approached the NCU with a proposal to create a "National Council". The offer, however, was refused when the NCU made it clear that 'full blooded non-recognition of Stormont ... (was) a prerequisite for any cooperation'.[23]

It was left to De Valera to take the initiative and in 1938 he launched his own anti-partition campaign aimed specifically at influencing public opinion in Britain on the issue. Under the banner of an "Anti-Partition League" speakers both from FF and Northern Nationalists like Healy and Mulvey, were sent to speak at public rallies throughout Britain. The campaign soon faltered, however, in the face of a renewed IRA bombing campaign and the simple fact that instead of changing public opinion it merely stiffened British attitudes towards partition.[24]

As the outbreak of war approached in 1939, it was evident that the split in Northern nationalism was as wide as ever it had been. Yet, however, as Phoenix suggests it was at this point that developments began to occur which were to have important long-term consequences. The threat by the British authorities to introduce conscription to the province managed to unite Nationalist opinion, along with De Valera, in a way which had not been done for years and a successful campaign was fought against the proposal. Even though this temporary alliance was to break up shortly afterwards it certainly gave renewed hope to Healy. With war imminent he believed that the 'need for Britain to secure both Irish and American support' could open 'a possible avenue to Irish unity'.[25] As he informed Eamon Donnelly, 'England must have America in any difficulties that arise. That is our main lever ...'.[26] He therefore shared De Valera's view that a solution could be obtained through 'the larger general play of English interest'.[27] Even though these hopes were not immediately realised, of crucial importance was the fact that the 'incipient alliance between the main two sections of northern Nationalism, and their continued reliance on De Valera, was to form the basis of a new united anti-partition movement in 1945'.[28]

If this new attempt was to be successful however, it was going to have to overcome the fact that the Second World War had radically altered the status of Northern Ireland, so far as the British government was concerned. The province could not simply be regarded any longer as an unimportant backwater but one of crucial strategic importance to Britain. Its contribution to the war effort was widely acknowledged and contrasted with that of De Valera's policy of neutrality. All of this was clearly illustrated by Winston Churchill's radio broadcast on 13 May 1945 when he spoke of the danger German U-Boats had posed to Britain's survival during the war:

> We had only the North-Western approach between Ulster and Scotland through which to bring in the means of life and to send out the forces of war. Owing to the actions of Mr de Valera ... the approaches which the Southern Irish ports and airfields could so easily have guarded were closed by the hostile aircraft and U-Boats. This was indeed a deadly moment in our life, and if it had not been for the loyalty and friendship of Northern Ireland we should have been forced to come to close quarters with Mr de Valera or perish for ever from the earth. However with a restraint and poise ... we left the de Valera government to frolic with the Germans and later with the Japanese representatives to their heart's content.[29]

Undoubtedly therefore, the position of Northern Ireland within the United Kingdom had been strengthened and thus, Nationalists in 1945 were to begin their campaign in a much weaker position. The test that now faced them was whether they could successfully rise to this considerable challenge.

Notes

1.   D. Horowitz, *Ethnic Groups in Conflict*, (London, 1984), p.294.
2.   Ibid., p.291.
3.   E. Phoenix, *Northern Nationalism: Nationalist Politics, Partition and the Catholic Minority in Northern Ireland, 1890-1940*, (Belfast, 1995), p.374.
4.   Ibid., p.362 and p.345.
5.   *Irish News* 24 March 1925, quoted by E. Phoenix, 'Introduction to the Healy Papers, Part 2: The Nationalist Party in Northern Ireland', (PRONI, D.2991), p.1.
6.   Phoenix, 'Introduction to the Healy Papers', p.2. Plus Phoenix, *Northern Nationalism*, p.338.

7. H.C. Deb, (NI), 7, c.43-44, quoted by Phoenix, *Northern Nationalism,* p.342.
8. Phoenix, 'Introduction to the Healy Papers', p.4. Plus, Phoenix, *Northern Nationalism,* p.345.
9. Ibid., pp.352-361.
10. Ibid., p. 362.
11. C. Healy to Canon Eugene Coyle, 7 May 1928, D2991/B/9, Healy Papers, and quoted by Phoenix, *Northern Nationalism,* p.358.
12. Phoenix, *Northern Nationalism,* p.391.
13. Ibid., p.362 and p.371.
14. Ibid., p.368.
15. Ibid., pp.367-371.
16. Ibid., pp.340-361.
17. Ibid., p.372.
18. Ibid., p.374.
19. Ibid., p.381.
20. *Irish News* 24 March 1933, D2991/DS, Healy Papers.
21. Phoenix, *Northern Nationalism,* pp.377-386.
22. Healy to P. Maxwell, 15 October 1937, D2991/A/48/C, Healy Papers, quoted by Phoenix, *Northern Nationalism,* p.382.
23. Phoenix, *Northern Nationalism,* pp.382-387.
24. Ibid., pp.387-388.
25 Ibid., p.390.
26. Healy to E. Donnelly, 22 June 1939, EDP, quoted by Phoenix, *Northern Nationalism,* p.455.
27. Healy to E. Donnelly, 15 March 1940, EDP. Plus Jonathan Bowman, *De Valera and the Ulster Question 1917-1973,* (Oxford, 1982), p.108, quoted by Phoenix, *Northern Nationalism,* p.455.
28. Phoenix, *Northern Nationalism,* p.390.
29. C. Eade (ed.), *Victory: War Speeches by the Rt. Hon. W.S. Churchill O.M., C.H., M.P.,* (London, 1945).

1 1945-1949: Post-war Reappraisal, Stormont, Westminster and the Anti-Partition League

In the introduction reference was made to the fact that since partition Northern Nationalists had found it difficult to maintain any kind of a unified political organisation, and therefore, as Paddy Maxwell MP for Foyle had pointed out in 1941, one could not talk of a 'Nationalist Party in the North in the sense in which parties are understood in other places', and that only on 'any matter of vital National importance (do) all Nationalists come together'.[1] This policy had succeeded in avoiding the splits that had destroyed Devlin's National League of the North and the Irish Union Association, but had left a position where anti-partionists had no single political body to represent them. However, as the Second World War came to an end there was a growing realisation that this would have to change as the ending of hostilities might present an opportunity when the whole question of partition could be reopened.[2] If this were to occur it would be vital that Northern nationalists were prepared. This was going to have to involve all shades of opinion coming together to ensure that Nationalists were returned to all seats, both at Stormont and Westminster, where they stood a chance of winning. In addition some kind of agreement would have to be reached to avoid the old abstentionist/attendance split from re-emerging. Even as Sir Basil Brooke, the Prime Minister of Northern Ireland, sought the dissolution of a Stormont parliament that had been sitting since 1938, there were already indications that preparations were already underway in many constituencies, 'Nationalists have been devoting considerable attention to the election so far as it will effect constituencies in which they are directly interested. The necessary arrangements are being made and meetings will be held shortly'.[3]

11

Across the province election conventions began to meet and select candidates. These were normally called by a parish priest who then sent out invitations to attend to the local clergy, public representatives and two delegates from every parish in the constituency, who were, chosen at a local meeting. From reports in the *Irish News* the mood at these gatherings appears to have been eager and optimistic. A good example of this was in Mid-Derry, where a meeting in Maghera to select a candidate for the seat, which had been allowed to remain vacant since the death of George Leeke in 1941, was attended by delegates from all over the constituency. Father R. Walsh who presided, spoke of the 'enthusiasm' displayed and 'hoped it was a portent of the resurgence of Nationalism in the constituency and throughout the six Counties'.[4]

This mood also appears to have been perfectly summed up by the decision of the delegates to chose a candidate, Eddie McAteer, who was entering the political arena for the first time. He had been born in Coatbridge, Scotland, in 1914 but had lived in Derry since an early age, when his father had moved to the city to find work. After attending the Christian Brothers school in Derry, McAteer had sat the entrance exam for the British Civil Service and after recording the sixth highest mark, he took up a post in the Inland Revenue department. By 1945, however, he had tired of this job and had left to establish his accountancy practice in the city. As for his political beliefs and objectives, McAteer's family background in many ways epitomised the dilemma that always existed for Northern nationalists. In 1936, along with his father and three brothers, he had been arrested on arms charges after a police raid on the family home in William Street. Subsequently his brother, Hugh, took personal responsibility for the weapons found in the search and the charges against the rest of the family were dropped. Sentenced to a lengthy prison term, Hugh later became commander-in-chief of the IRA and in 1943 achieved some notoriety with his successful escape attempt from Crumlin Road jail in Belfast. Although he was to remain close to his brother, Eddie McAteer always rejected the use of force and differed from Hugh on his 'concept of the way to Irish unity'. Throughout a political career which was to last for some 25 years and which included five years as leader of the Nationalist Party, Eddie maintained that only a patient, peaceful and constitutional approach would eventually lead to reunification.[5]

Across the province the emphasis everywhere appeared to be on the need to stress the common ground that existed between nationalists and to avoid the disharmony that had been a common feature throughout the 1920s and 1930s. The best and simplest way to do this was by pointing out that although they differed on various subjects they did share a common objective: namely an independent 32 county Republic. At the meeting that selected James McGlade as Nationalist candidate for Falls, T.J. Comerton praised the decision of the Republican Party, which had campaigned for Eamon Donnelly in 1942, not to nominate anyone. He also stated that they deserved credit for their recommendation to their supporters to refrain from voting for 'any candidate who did not subscribe to the principles of sovereign independence for the 32 counties of Ireland'.[6] Later he praised:

> The sacrifice which they have made ... [is a] measure of their contribution towards unity among Northern Nationalists. That gesture has not been lost upon us ... They stand they say, for the sovereign independence of Ireland. Well so do we ... We have never compromised and we shall never compromise that inalienable right, but until right has been conceded it is idle and mischievous, as we now see and as Republicans see, to allow ourselves to be divided ... Let us all unite ... We shall allow no man or party to jeopardise or undermine that unity ... A new spirit of resurgence has been born in the North ... It will be the duty of our leaders to harness that tide to the accomplishment of the national objective.[7]

In the constituencies of South Down, Mourne and South Armagh, abandoned in 1938, it was important to convince the electorate that they had a duty and an obligation to come out to vote and return Nationalist representatives once again. At his nomination for Mourne, James McSparran KC made it clear that he was standing to dispel the view 'amongst those various groups of Unionists who fondly imagined Nationalists were incapable of unity' and to try to ensure that they would not be represented in 'Stormont or elsewhere by representatives who ... acquiesced in the insufferable injustices inflicted on Nationalists in the six Counties'.[8] In South Armagh the claim was made that 'Labour had no national policy and therefore no right in a Nationalist constituency', and that it was essential that every vote be registered to show 'to the world that there was virile opposition to the dismemberment of their country'.[9] Similarly, at election rallies throughout South Down Peadar Murney the Nationalist, candidate spoke of the 'duty of every lover of Ireland to vote in the coming contest as a protest' against partition.[10]

Less time and attention were spent on the question of whether

Nationalist representatives would be returning as a body after the election to take their seats. The problem that this issue continued to pose can be seen in a report in the *Irish Times* which referred to the fact that:

> party leaders desire that Nationalists elected should not disenfranchise his constituents by abstention ... (they) argue that partition apart, there is domestic policy to be considered and so the place for members is at Stormont to support the leaders ... Die-hard abstentionists argue to sit at Stormont is tantamount to betrayal. I will be surprised if Mr T.J. Campbell is able to win over all Nationalists.[11]

Not surprisingly, therefore, at many selection conventions it was decided to postpone any decision until after the election was over and this was agreed to in Foyle, East, West and Mid Tyrone. The only area to make a positive decision was in Fermanagh where the convention there passed a motion recommending that Cahir Healy, their candidate for South Fermanagh, should abandon abstention from Stormont.[12] Even by 1945 Healy could be classified as a veteran with his political connections dating back to his involvement with the establishment of Sinn Fein (SF) in Fermanagh after Arthur Griffiths had launched the organisation in 1905. His prominent position as one of the leading spokesmen of SF in Northern Ireland had led to his arrest and detention by the Stormont authorities in 1922. This however, had not deterred him and after partition, he had continued to pursue his political beliefs and, had been returned unimpeded as Nationalist MP for South Fermanagh, as well as representing the Fermanagh-Tyrone seat at Westminster from 1922-1924 and again from 1931-1935. During the Second World War he had again been detained by the British authorities between July 1941 and November 1942. According to the then Home Secretary, Herbert Morrison, his detention had been due to the fact that he had been 'recently concerned with the preparation or instigation of acts prejudicial to the public safety or defense of the realm'.[13]

In addition, the delegates at the Fermanagh conference went further and urged that the joint Fermanagh-Tyrone convention, which was to be held shortly to select nominees for the forthcoming Westminster election, should also call for the ending of the boycott of the Imperial parliament.[14] Elsewhere, however, there appears to have been little comment on this subject other than to repeat that nothing would be decided until after the election. But on occasions different speakers outlined their preferences at various election rallies. In Derry, Healy stated that the question would be decided upon by a 'democratically convened convention' once the results were known and that whatever was decided upon the public representatives would abide by it. At this stage what was more important was to preserve the unity amongst Northern nationalists that 'they had not had since 1926' and to preserve a 'united front' in their attempts to secure a united Ireland.[15] Others, like McAteer, took a different view and declared support for a return to Stormont because since Nationalists were limited to constitutional methods and also in 'their choice of weapons', they must be prepared to 'play their opponents at their own game', namely the 'Parliamentary game of obstructing and annoying them as much as possible'.[16] But it was to be McGlade who most strongly advocated a return to parliament:

> We have had enough of divided counsels during the war years; we have had enough of abstentionism, we have decided to let no more Nationalist seats go to the board ... I hope that never again will the Savories and Littles (two Unionist MPs) be permitted to get away scot free with the lies and slanders they have uttered against this country during the war years ... Now when politics are at a turning point in England, and when so many of our people in Britain and America have the power to influence elections, now is the time for us to bring our case before the tribunal of public opinion overseas, and by every constitutional means in our power to remove for all time this terrible curse of contention and friction.[17]

When nominations closed on 4 June Nationalists had already secured six seats where no one had stood against them: Healy in South Fermanagh, McAteer in Mid Derry, Thomas J. Campbell in Central, Joe Stewart in East Tyrone, Alex Donnelly in West Tyrone and Michael McGurk in Mid Tyrone. This left contests in Mourne and South Down against Unionists, and in Foyle, South Armagh and Falls against candidates representing various strands of the Labour movement. As campaigning got underway the most frequent call was for every nationalist voter to use his vote 'as an emphatic protest against the present Government of the six Counties'.[18]

In addition a call began to be made for Northern Nationalists to take the lead in establishing an organisation after the election, as mentioned by Eamon Donnelly in 1944. He had suggested the creation of a body in which all political parties could come together in order to form a united front on the issue of partition. At a rally in Derry Maxwell called for the establishment of an 'Anti-Partition Council' encompassing not only people in the North but also from the South.[19] If this body were going to stand any chance of succeeding it was going to be very important that Nationalists had the support of their Belfast constituencies. With Campbell returned unopposed in Central, the vital contest was to be in Falls where McGlade was faced with two opponents who had both stood in earlier elections as Nationalists but who now went under the Labour banner. The problem facing Nationalists in Belfast was that since partition they had been engaged in a battle for control of the Catholic working class with the labour movement. It appears that as long as Devlin remained at the head of the Nationalist organisation in the city they could count on continuing support in such areas. In an interview Harry Diamond spoke admiringly of Devlin's genuine concern for the interests of ordinary people which won him enormous respect and gratitude. However, after Devlin's death he believed that the control of the Nationalist organisation in the city had fallen into the hands of men who were involved in politics for selfish reasons such as pursuing their own business interests, particularly those involved in the licensed trade. As a result, he had drifted away from the Nationalists and had stood against Campbell in the Central by-election in 1934.[20]   Such a view, that Nationalists had ceased to represent the interests of the working class, was to appear throughout the campaign in Falls and was one the party wished to discount, given the obvious strength of potential nationalist voters in the city.

The attempt to re-establish Nationalist credibility in the city had been begun by Campbell, who on accepting the nomination for Central had made it clear that he was standing on a wide-ranging programme that not only called for the ending of partition but also included a social programme to tackle poverty. There were promises to work toward the establishment of a better health care system, a demand for a major slum clearance programme and for a fair system of social welfare benefits.[21] But this did not prevent Diamond and John Collins in Falls from launching attacks on what, and for whom, Nationalists stood. According to Collins, his decision to stand was based on the need to prevent the area from being 'represented by men who would deny the raising of the standard of life for the working class' and who 'oppose the right of workers to increased wages'. He pointed to the involvement of McGlade, a local publican, in a recent industrial dispute by barmen for better wages and alleged he had opposed any such rise.[22] Later he would return to this subject and accuse Nationalists of being 'nothing ... more than a trade organisation seeking a place at Stormont in the interests of their business organisation'.[23]

Meanwhile, Diamond, who had recently returned from England, linked up with Republican elements to create the Socialist Republican Party that was to campaign for a united Ireland based on Socialist principles. He considered the contest between Collins and McGlade as a split in the Nationalist camp and tried to concentrate on emphasising the policies of his new party.[24] Yet, on occasions, he also attacked his opponents, accusing the 'so called Nationalist Party' of being a 'middle-class party' and having 'no regard for the full rights of workers' and alleging that Collins had changed the 'colour of his coat' to suit his 'immediate surroundings'.[25]

The charge that Nationalists had become a mere 'business organisation' was obviously something that could not go unchallenged. At a rally for McGlade, which to show the significance of the contest in Falls to the Nationalist Party, was attended by McAteer, Campbell, Senator Thomas McAllister, Senator Joseph Maguire and Senator James Lennon, this accusation was strenuously denied. On the charge that their organisation was controlled by the licensed trade Campbell pointed out that at the convention that had selected McGlade 'less than a dozen' of those present had any connection with that trade. In any case, he argued, that those involved in such a business were their 'own kith and kin', who had been forced into that particular trade because every other 'avenue of business' had been closed to them due to their religion. He also argued that 'members of it were true Irishmen and there were very few trades ... that had contributed more generously to charity than the licensed trade'.[26]

McGlade himself also replied to the charge by denying the accusations made against him by Collins that he had opposed a rise in the wages of Belfast barmen and stated that, had it not been for himself, there would have been no machinery in place for barmen to negotiate with their employers. His only part in the recent dispute had been to represent the employers on the arbitration tribunal and he wanted it made known that he 'Never had ... any dispute with his employees, nor had his people before him' and that an agreement drawn up 'with the unions in 1939 during his period of Chairmanship of the Licensed Vintners Association had been loyally observed ever since'.[27]

For Nationalists it appears that Collins was seen as their main opponent and they responded to his jibes with their own attacks on his character. On 6 June Senator McAllister accused him of abandoning the Nationalist cause years ago for his own benefit:

> The diabolical partition of their own country came about, and division and disillusionment took hold on their people, it took the staunchest hearts to

stand up to it, and when Mr Collins thought the Nationalist cause was in jeopardy he walked out ... to the Labour movement, and now he had deserted that movement and somersaulted into an organisation born and created by Mr Collins.[28]

In addition to answering such claims, the Nationalist message in Falls was very much along the lines of that being pushed in the other contested constituencies, namely the importance of unity amongst themselves and of having their candidate elected. Senator Lennon pointed out that only by returning McGlade could the people of Falls be guaranteed a seat on the Anti-Partition Council that was to be set up after the election.[29] At the same rally McAteer spoke of the fact that disunity in their ranks had frustrated them from achieving their goal and that now in 1945, 'a year in which lay much hope for gaining that cherished ideal', splits had appeared again as could be seen in the opposition to McGlade. He appealed for everyone to support the Nationalist candidate:

> I seriously considered for a long time before I decided to enter party politics, and I made my decision for one reason only ... that I firmly believed that in joining the Nationalist Party I had joined the party with the broadest platform embracing as it did of Irishmen of all shades of opinion, and the party in which lay the only hope for the unity of our country ... Only by uniting could they succeed, and it was only by unity under the Nationalist banner that the Falls Division could send a representative to the Council of Irishmen which would strive for the ending of partition.[30]

The summer of 1945 also saw a Westminster election with polling day set for 5 July. For Nationalists, their interest, as it had been for the seats at Stormont, was concentrated on areas where their candidates stood a good chance of being elected. As a result their immediate priority was to retain the twin constituency of Fermanagh-Tyrone which returned two MPs. The last time the seat had been fought in 1935 both Nationalists and Republicans had nominated candidates. At the last moment, in order to avoid a split in the vote, both sides had agreed to stand aside and allow Anthony Mulvey and Paddy Cunningham to go forward as Unity candidates standing on an abstentionist ticket. Once again the question was going to be whether this policy was going to be continued or whether it was felt the time was right for these MPs to make an impact in Westminster. The Fermanagh convention on 29 May had selected Healy as their candidate and had also recommended that abstention from both Stormont and Westminster be abandoned.

But, as the convention to select the nominees for the seat was fixed for 8 June in Omagh, the *Irish News* was reporting that despite the decision reached in Fermanagh there was still considerable support in Tyrone for abstention to be retained.[31]

The convention met on 8 June in Omagh when Mulvey and Cunningham were again chosen to contest the seat. On the question of whether, if elected, both men would take their seats, the decision was taken to re-convene another meeting after the result to decide. The gathering finished with all the main speakers appealing for unity in the constituency and for everyone to come out and vote to ensure that Mulvey and Cunningham were successful.[32]

The attempt to draw all anti-partition forces together was maintained by the decision of Nationalists to fight the Derry constituency, their candidate Dr D. Cavanagh pledged himself to 'unite all forms of Nationalist opinion under one banner' in their campaign to end partition.[33] As in the Stormont campaign emphasis was to be placed on the need for unity and loyalty to their demand for a united Ireland. For example, McAteer argued that the:

> people of Northern Ireland had slept too long since the Civil War. They had accepted dictation, gerrymandering and insults of every kind. Now that day had passed ... In this election there could be no question of disunity or any room for conflicting opinions ... If you have any nationalism at all there can only be one cause for you ... vote for Dr Cavanagh. Every effort should be put into the fight, because it actually amounts to ... a plebiscite on the question of Partition.[34]

Other speakers were also keen to point out the possibilities opened up by the end of the Second World War. At a meeting in Dungannon, Mulvey called for 'quick and decisive action' to be taken at home and abroad to let the rest of the world 'know of the grave injustices' which they were having to endure.[35] A few days later he stressed that in 'the present position of world affairs and when the rights of small nations would come into the spotlight' that 'it was more necessary than ever that Fermanagh and Tyrone be retained for the nation'.[36]

The first election results announced were those for Stormont and according to the *Irish News* these had produced a 'Nationalist Comeback' and showed that 'while Unionists have been forced to retreat, a virile Nationalism continues to advance'.[37] This belief seems to have been based on the victories of McSparran and Murney in Mourne and South Down respectively and, in Foyle and South Armagh where Nationalist candidates were also successful. But in Falls, Nationalists suffered a major setback that illustrated their continuing decline in Belfast, with their candidate trailing badly in third place. However, the new Nationalist MPs were eager to look for positive aspects and for McSparran these could be found in the fact that the elections had shown that 'when people were united there were no bounds to the progress that can be made'.[38] This point seemed to be reinforced when the Westminster results were announced and these showed that they had held onto Fermanagh-Tyrone and had cut the Unionist majority in Derry from around 25,000 to 2,653. (See Appendix 3: Election Results 1945-1949).

According to Maxwell these results and in particular the result in Derry was a:

> magnificent demonstration on their determination to see that the Border was removed as soon as possible. During recent years they had been on the defensive. Now they had gone over to the offensive ... They had achieved ... something precious ... They had achieved unification of the people and had shown that they had their feet on the same road until ... their goal ... freedom, unity and independence of the whole country was achieved.[39]

What was now going to be needed was a new organisation to enable Northern Nationalists to maintain the unity they had achieved and to launch a new anti-partition campaign. At the Fermanagh-Tyrone convention on 8 June the delegates had passed a resolution calling for the 'establishment of a united organisation for the entire partitioned area and the framing of an effective policy to undo partition'.[40] Now, argued Mulvey, was the perfect time for the 'initiation of a movement to bring the injustice of partition to the world' and it was up to them in Northern Ireland to launch it.[41] A few days later in Belfast a meeting of all Nationalist MPs agreed to call together a convention at the earliest possible moment to put this into effect.[42]

But, before this could be done the question of whether Nationalist MPs would now take their seats in both parliaments had to be settled. On 17 July MPs and Senators met before the opening of the new Stormont parliament and, although the press statement merely noted that they had agreed on several important matters and would hold further discussions,[43] the following day saw them enrol and take the Oath to enable them to take part in the proceedings, and over the next few weeks men like Campbell and McSparran began to do so. Finally, the whole question appears to have been settled at the re-convened Fermanagh-Tyrone convention on 10 August. By 113 votes to 23, Mulvey and Cunningham were instructed to take their seats at Westminster, and by 93 votes to 16, Stormont MPs were also directed to abandon abstention.[44]

The reason behind this change in policy can be found in the press statement released by Mulvey and Cunningham when they arrived at Westminster and made it clear they had come:

> to forward the claims of the Irish people for the unity and sovereignty of the Irish nation, unnaturally divided twenty years ago ... During the lifetime of the last Parliament, we, in accordance with the wishes of our constituents, abstained ... as protest against the existing position. We believe in the present changed political circumstances in Britain our policy can be best served by attendance.[45]

What seems to have brought about this change was the return of the first majority Labour government. This was significant in that Labour had been opposed to partition and, at a special conference in London on the subject in December 1920, had called for:

> an immediate election, by proportional representation, of an entirely open Constituent Assembly, charged to work out, at the earliest possible moment, without limitations or fetters, whatever constitution for Ireland the Irish people desire ...[46]

In addition, some encouragement was also taken from a highly critical report by the National Council of Civil Liberties (NCCL) in 1936 on the use of the Special Powers Act in Northern Ireland as it had been made up of 'many Labour stalwarts including two present Cabinet Ministers (Bevin and Pethwick-Lawrence)'.[47]

However, if a new anti-partition campaign were to be launched to take advantage of what appeared to be an excellent opportunity, then some kind of a centralised organisation was going to be needed to link the various strands together and to unite all public representatives in one unified body. Such a plan had already been discussed and McSparran gave it further impetus when he stated that now Northern Nationalists had come together it was essential to create an 'organisation representative of all Nationalists of the Six Counties', and that it should have 'a central office to which people could send their grievances and if possible have them remedied'. If this was done he was hopeful that they might be 'able to better their conditions to some extent'.[48] Finally, at a meeting of all Nationalist MPs and Senators it was agreed to summon a province-wide convention for 14 November in Dungannon with the:

> primary purpose to promote a united effort to consolidate all Anti-Partition forces in the Six Counties and to launch an organisation of the people as a democratic body, having for its objects, the independence of Ireland, the well being of all the people, the fostering of an Irish outlook ... and the promotion of co-operation among all creeds and classes.[49]

Although invitations were sent out to all 'Nationally minded groups' and public representatives to attend Diamond refused claiming he could not take part in what he considered to be a 'purely sectarian manoeuvre'.[50] Nonetheless, on 14 November up to 480 delegates and public representatives plus all the Nationalist MPs and Senators met and agreed to create the 'Irish Anti-Partition League' (APL). A fund was opened to launch the new body and over £1000 collected and a Standing Committee appointed to begin the task of establishing the IAPL.[51] This met for the first time a week later and was pleased to report that there 'was a general feeling' that the chances of it 'achieving ultimate success' was 'much brighter than those of any previous organisation in the North' because it had been formed from 'all shades of anti-partition feeling'.[52]

The type of organisation founded and its objects and goals can be seen in the pamphlet, *The Irish Anti Partition League: Constitution and Rules*. The objectives of the APL were to be achieved by various means and these included:

> organisation of the people of the six Counties as a democratic body; an appeal to the people of the Irish race at home and abroad for moral and material support to help in the solution of the partition problem; truthful and reasoned propaganda through the press and other agencies ...; attention to Voters registration and to parliamentary and local elections.

Concerning the internal set up the foundation of the movement was to be the local district club with each having its own committee and officers elected annually. Its role according to the rules was to 'endeavour to carry out the policy of the organisation; to promote peace and harmony in the district; and to strive to discourage sectarian bigotry'.[53]

Above the district club was to be the Area/County Committee that was to consist of two delegates elected by each club within its boundary. The governing body of the APL was to be the Standing Committee which was to consist of all the MPs and Senators along with three representatives from each of the six counties plus three from Belfast and Derry City. It was to have total control of policy and the League's activities such as the publication of pamphlets and the work of local clubs and district committees.

However, the new organisation was immediately plunged into a crisis that not only threatened to reopen old divisions but also highlighted how delicate a coalition of groups it was to be. A few weeks after the meeting in Dungannon, Campbell resigned his Central seat to take up the offer from the Northern Ireland authorities to become a County Court Judge.[54] In addition, Healy was to be fiercely attacked for a call he had made at Stormont pledging Nationalist support if the government sought to withhold some of its Imperial Contribution in order to improve living conditions in Northern Ireland.[55] In an editorial the *Derry Journal* criticised both men:

> What Mr Healy, and each and every member of the Nationalist Party in Stormont including Mr T.J. Campbell, was categorically pledged to do was to pursue the cause that the latter has now abandoned for a Stormont judgeship and, that the former seems prepared to reverse to bolster up Stormont's Partition policy by British grants.[56]

Once again the old question of how far Nationalists could co-operate with the Stormont authorities without being seen to be bolstering partition had been reopened and McAteer appears to have caught the mood of many when he warned, 'We are faced at the close of 1945 with the acutest problem we have ever faced the problem of purging our ranks of the risks of defections for high places'.[57]

Few were prepared to defend Campbell publicly although Rev C. Byrne PP in Omagh, who had presided over Nationalist conventions in Tyrone that summer, in a private letter to Healy did illustrate the dilemma faced: 'if he (Campbell) didn't accept it, the Government would make strong propaganda out of this, as the denial of distributive justice is one of our grievances'.[58]

Meanwhile Healy received support from both McAteer, who denied he had meant him when he had referred to the "purging of our ranks", and from his fellow MPs and Senators who in return accused the *Derry Journal* of being part of an effort to wreck the APL.[59] This in turn was rejected in an editorial by the paper and instead it urged the organisation to look at itself:

> the insinuation that this organ ... is out to wreck the APL is worse than ridiculous, the prompt defection of that leading member – if not the leader of the Nationalist Party from the League with which his name had been linked – has been a let down of the Dungannon Convention which can scarcely be laid to our charge. As to that, it would seem that the party which has sat on judgement of us might do well to look at itself.[60]

But still the whole furore over Campbell did not end and Murney announced in a letter to the *Irish News* that he intended to disassociate himself from the Nationalist Party at Stormont as a protest at its failure to express 'unqualified condemnation' of Campbell's actions.[61] In an attempt to draw an end to the incident McSparran, in reply to Murney, made it clear at meetings of APL executive and of party members at Stormont only Murney had advocated the issuing of a statement regarding Campbell. Others were keen to avoid the situation that was now being suggested by Unionists and sections of the Dublin press; that once again the anti-partition forces were split. It was now a time, he argued, for all sections to work together under the auspices of the APL to secure a united Ireland.[62]

In spite of these setbacks steps began to be taken to establish branches of the League across Northern Ireland. At this point it is important to highlight as McAteer was to comment in 1949, that the APL was not a 'political movement in the ordinary sense of the word', rather it was to be 'a common platform of all who believed in the unity of the country'.[63] This was a point that was to be made again by speakers at meetings held early in 1946. For example, McSparran declared that if they could manage to create 'some sort of a compact, cohesive body under some responsible leadership' they could then be in a position to let the rest of the world know what was happening in Northern Ireland, and so claimed Canon Coyle, 'shame England before the world into removing this blot'.[64]

Throughout 1946 there is extensive coverage in the *Irish News* of the efforts made to establish the APL across the province and it reported the formation of branches in places as far apart as Ballymena, Crossmaglen, Enniskillen and Derry City. By the end of the year a full-time organiser, Sean O'Gallagher, had been appointed and up to 40 clubs established.[65] The problem at this point is in trying to evaluate the strength of the APL and how successful it had been in its attempt to 'mould all national minded people together',[66] since the *Irish News* paints a picture of an organisation that was thriving. The first area of concern that one can identify is that there were still problems over Campbell's resignation. These appeared to centre on rumours that he was by no means the only figure in the League who was, or had been, willing to accept a job from the Stormont authorities. In a letter to Mulvey, the Rev Thomas Maguire PP, Maguiresbridge, who had long been active in anti-partition politics and who was later to be a frequent correspondent with Healy, alleged that McSparran too had been offered a Judgeship, and had only refused it on the grounds that it was 'not sufficiently remunerative'.[67] Whilst not directly answering Maguire's claims, McSparran denied that the APL was simply made up of 'lawyers looking for jobs', and that nothing would 'prevent members of our party from putting ... the real aims and objects of our party', and those of ordinary nationalists calling for the end of partition.[68]

This then leads onto the question of how successful the League had been in establishing itself as an effective force across the province. In particular a question mark hung over its strength in Belfast. Despite the fact that Campbell had resigned his Central seat in December there appears to have been a reluctance to take any steps to move the writ for the by-election. Conlon outlined the frustration that this was causing:

> It is hard to understand the attitude of the Belfast people to the Central Election. I mentioned it to McSparran at the meeting thinking he would put it to the meeting for discussion. Instead he told me to let it sit. It may be strategy and it may be fear, I don't know which. At our meeting everyone was emphatic it should be fought but equally pessimistic it would be lost.[69]

In the end Conlon did not move the writ until 21 June and in the contest that followed no Nationalist candidate was nominated and their last parliamentary seat in Belfast was fought between Victor Halley, Socialist Republican and Frank Hanna, NILP. Thus the city which had been a party stronghold under Joe Devlin's leadership was now virtually abandoned and the Nationalist Party now became largely confined to rural areas West of the Bann.

Evidence of further difficulties facing the League can also be found in a series of letters between Maguire to Mulvey during 1946. In June Maguire confessed:

I do not know what to do about starting the League here. I know it is not going to make a hit anywhere because there is no real enthusiasm behind it or in it ... Is there no hope for a policy on Partition? ... Remove the Border is not a policy – nor any shadow of one. Where is the use ... in stating Remove the Border-people are sick of this – show them how and they will sit up and listen.[70]

A few weeks later he wrote to Mulvey asking him to attend a public meeting he was trying to arrange not to form a branch of the League but to try to 'arouse the drooping spirits'.[71]

Equally revealing was Conlon's correspondence to Mulvey regarding the attempts to hold a nationalist rally in County Down, to protest at the proposals by the Boundary Commission to create two new Westminster constituencies. He confessed, 'Enthusiasm is lacking in almost any political subject in the North and I doubt if any but a few old campaigners will turn up at all'.[72] In addition, as the year progressed, in spite of all the appeals for unity, the APL was being forced to defend itself from the accusation that it was not making any progress. At a meeting, in Newcastle McSparran attempted to answer the League's critics by arguing that at least it was trying to do something worthwhile and warned that if nationalists remained divided and apathetic, 'they would remain in the position ... they had been for centuries'.[73] Later, he also defended their presence at Stormont by pointing out that as long as they had to remain under the control of Stormont it was 'necessary that they should do their best to make life tolerable for the people they represent'.[74]

However, as the APL had always made clear, the work in Northern Ireland was just one part of its strategy and as Canon Coyle stated at one of its rallies early in 1946, 'Through the IAPL, we can with the hope of God, unite the Irish race at home and abroad and bring all freedom loving people to our side', and so make the question of partition 'a living issue that must be dealt with'.[75]

At meetings across the province, McSparran and other speakers had made it plain that it was up to them to convince Britain that it was in its interests to leave Ireland and that this required an anti-partition campaign of world-wide proportions. By the summer of 1946 the executive of the League was according to press reports, already in contact with interested parties in Great Britain and the United States. Healy too had drawn attention to the importance of engaging the help of Irish Americans by claiming that if they could be properly organised they could form such an important political force that the American government could not ignore.[76] Conlon, acting as Secretary of the APL, had already sent an appeal to America:

> We suggest that all Irish American Societies do what we have succeeded in doing at home – form one broad platform ... When you achieve this ... call an Irish Race Convention of such dimensions that it would of itself attract world attention ... Our organisation would then send you a delegation of speakers, who would be capable of telling Irish Americans and the whole world just what partition means ... Such a Convention and such an exposition of English craft and guile would, we believe, have the most telling effect on world opinion.[77]

As for activities in Britain the League's first foray was to send Lennon, McAteer and McSparran to a rally in Birmingham on 5 July. The message they delivered was for Irish exiles to assist their campaign by spreading 'our gospel to every English man and woman', in order to convince them that they had a duty to right the 'wrong perpetuated on Ireland ... and that Ireland ... be given the right to govern her own destiny'. In addition it was made clear that they were hopeful that Attlee's government would move on partition:

> We think that possibly the British Government now in control of affairs in Britain, for whom the Irish were the spearhead at the last general election may, perhaps consider it an opportune moment to weigh up the expediency of maintaining a government in Northern Ireland which detests the very name Labour.[78]

But, as Rees illustrates, the possibility of Labour either taking a 'cognisance of the minority's grievances', or even considering altering the constitutional position, was never a real possibility. Attitudes towards Ireland in Britain had been affected by the war: not only did it feel it owed an enormous debt of gratitude to the North for its assistance to the war effort but the conflict had also shown its continuing strategic importance. There was also the fact that De Valera's actions in remaining neutral, and his visit to the German Embassy in Dublin to offer condolences on the death of Hitler, had angered many. Not surprisingly, there were many members of the new cabinet, like Herbert Morrison who had served in the wartime government, only too anxious and determined to defend the existing relationship with

Stormont. The cabinet's policy towards Ireland was to be drawn up by Viscount Addison, the Dominions Secretary, and relied heavily on an earlier document, *The Irish Question in 1945,* written by John Maffey, Britain's representative in Dublin. In his memo to the Cabinet, Addison noted that due to the war 'that never in our history have we been in such a strong position in relation to world opinion so far as Ireland is concerned and Eire's position has never been weaker'. He also noted the 'strong if latent feeling of resentment' against Eire in Britain and warned that any government could create major problems for itself if it attempted to drastically alter the existing policy of 'distant relations with Eire'. The Cabinet met and accepted Addison's proposals and made it clear that it would move very cautiously on Irish affairs and would seek to improve relations with Eire in less controversial areas such as trade 'without any ostentation'.[79]

Although the prospects of immediate action by the Labour government appeared remote the League had taken some encouragement from the establishment of a 'Friends of Ireland Group' (FOI) amongst Labour MPs at Westminster. In November 1945 Mulvey had received a letter from Harry McGhee, one of its founders telling him of the new group and the appointment of Hugh Delargy as secretary and Richard Stokes and himself as treasurers.[80] A week later McGhee wrote to Mulvey informing him that he wanted to see the two organisations work together in the hope that 'our joint action will result in solving some of the outstanding difficulties'.[81] From the League's viewpoint it appears that the hope was that this group of MPs could keep alive the issue of Northern Ireland at Westminster. This was to be done by providing the FOI with evidence of serious malpractice by the Stormont authorities. For example in the Mulvey Papers there are frequent requests from men like Geoffrey Bing, the leading left-wing lawyer and MP, seeking material on such matters as discrimination and other examples of alleged wrong doing.[82]

Even though, as Rees highlights, both governments in Belfast and London were alarmed by the activities of the Friends of Ireland, it was not long before tensions between it and the APL arose.[83] These were to centre on the fact that the FOI had very limited aims and objectives. Not only was it to remain a very small grouping amongst Labour MPs but as Purdie points out, there were contrasting views as to how partition should be solved.[84] Whilst the League sought the creation of an independent 32 county Republic, the Friends, according to its chairman, Dr H.B. Morgan, saw their initial goal as 'to try to restore friendly relations between ... Britain and

Ireland' and not necessarily to intervene on the question of partition.[85] He later stressed that this improvement would be achieved over a long period and that the FOI was a 'movement which began quietly and will grow and become more effective as the years go on'.[86] Early in 1946 Victor McEntee and Fred Longden, two members of the group, visited Dublin and made clear that although both of them supported a united Ireland, they believed that the Labour government had more pressing problems to deal with, and therefore there would not be a quick end to partition. As the London correspondent of the *Irish News* was to comment:

> The conclusion one reaches is that 90% of the Labour Party are overwhelmingly in favour of a united Ireland, but except among the actively pro-Irish there is little realisation of Britain's responsibility for Partition and no recognition that the quick and right way to end Partition is by action on the part of Britain ... There are dozens of suggestions put forward ... Being Labour ... naturally they lay most stress as does the Friends ... on strong Trade Union and Labour party organisations on each side of the border which would eventually coalesce by reason of common interests and common objectives.[87]

All this leads on to the question of how much the APL can be blamed for misreading or simply overestimating the intentions of the Labour government. It had to try to negotiate a delicate path of not raising hopes, but at the same time needed to give reasons for people to join and support it. That people were already aware that little hope of progress could be expected can be seen by attacks on Labour policy by the *Irish News*. As early as October 1945 an editorial referred to the decision of the British Home Secretary, Chuter Ede, to allow Stormont to retain the Residence Permits Order and sarcastically suggested that 'Stormont may yet erect statues to some of Britain's Labour Ministers'.[88] However, this did not prevent speakers at APL rallies from arguing that the Labour Government could be forced to change its mind. At the formation of a branch in April Healy predicted that, if sufficient pressure could be brought to bear, the British government could be persuaded to move on the Irish question. A few weeks later he pointed to the recent aviation agreement between the British and Irish governments as an example of the changing mood in London towards Ireland.[89] Another speaker at Lisnaskea argued that Labour had shown little sympathy for Stormont and that the 'Tories in the Six Counties were beginning to realise that when it suited England she would remove Partition, whether they liked it or not'.[90] McAteer also pointed to the fact that 'They had in power in England a Government of working men who had been persecuted by Toryism just as much as the Nationalists of Northern Ireland', and as a result he was 'confident that they would listen with sympathy when the claim of a united Ireland was made to them'.[91] He then followed this by arguing that if the British government's policy towards India and Egypt could be changed then it could be possible to force a similar shift with regard to Ireland. But he stressed that if Northern nationalists remained divided then they would be simply ignored and that Ireland would be placed at the bottom of the pile of 'problems the British Government had to solve', but if they remained united they could force the government into making it a priority.[92]

Yet by the end of 1946 it was becoming increasingly obvious that the expectations raised by the return of Labour to power the previous year had been misplaced. As Maguire informed Mulvey:

> If things are as bad as a Manchester Irishman told me in regard to the British Labour Party the sooner that you and Cunningham raise a racket at Westminster and shake the dust off your boots the better for the unity of Ireland. He says there is not one of them serious on the Partition issue because they see no reason to raise any disturbance where things are getting on nicely.[93]

As a result, while the League concentrated on organising itself in Britain, more and more attention was paid to the importance of the Irish vote and in particular the possibility that it could be used to influence a Labour government. At a meeting in Glasgow in December one of the speakers estimated that some five million people of Irish descent lived in Britain and, that if this group could be properly organised then it could assert considerable political pressure.[94] This was followed by an article in the *Irish News* referring to the work carried out by McGhee and other members of the Friends of Ireland that had identified some 75 constituencies where the Irish vote held the balance of power. According to Delargy it was up to the Irish to mobilise this support in order to convince the Labour government to change its policies towards Ireland.[95] Conlon concurred with this assessment and suggested:

> The Irish vote which is the one weapon we have abroad must be consolidated. The Irish population in Britain have in their hands a weapon which can twist the tail of the British lion and make it do what Ireland wants to do.

When we have organised the Irish vote here we can bring pressure to bear on the Labour Government ... If I thought any other weapon would be more successful at this time I would not be here preaching this gospel ... But those who know best amongst us have consented that this should be the weapon in this particular age and we agree for the time being.[96]

In order to assist this effort, the League's executive intensified its efforts in Britain and delegations were dispatched to assist this process. In November Stewart was present at a gathering in Birmingham which saw the creation of a central body to co-ordinate activities on the mainland.[97] Yet, in the midst of all this activity it was Healy who struck a pessimistic note on the chances of their successfully organising the Irish vote in Britain, as the work was being done by a small group of enthusiasts. He confessed to Mulvey 'I don't know if there is anybody behind the Anti-Partition League besides these boys'.[98]

By the start of 1947, relations between the APL and the Labour government were on the verge of collapse and the League increasingly saw it as an enemy rather than as a potential ally. In March McSparran posed the question 'What has the Labour Government done for us'? For him the answer was nothing: there had been no change in its policy towards Irish unity and more significantly nothing had been done to remedy the abuses inflicted on them by the Stormont authorities. He warned that if they could not persuade them to change their minds the only alternative was to threaten them, and the only way to do that was through the Irish vote.[99] As Healy pointed out, there were now up to two million Irish voters in Britain and if these 'could be used as Parnell utilised the Irish vote in his day they could make Partition a real live issue in Britain'. Furthermore, he cautioned the Labour party that there was no reason why Irish exiles should necessarily vote for them unless they believed it would 'fulfil its old promises and give to the Irish people the right of saying how they wished to be governed'.[100] This was to be a point taken up by other speakers at rallies in Britain and they made it clear that unless Labour paid more attention to their demands it ran the risk of losing up to 75 constituencies. To back up this claim, Conlon gave an example of recent events in Glasgow where he alleged that two Labour councillors had lost their seats on the city council due to their reluctance to co-operate with the anti-partition movement.[101]

But, instead of any signs that Labour was concerned by this apparent threat and prepared to listen to APL, the indications were that not much was going to change. In February the *Irish News* reported that in response to the ongoing anti-partition campaign a new British Foreign Office document was to be released that repeated the claim that there was no obligation on the British government to end partition and that the decision alone rested with the majority of the people of Northern Ireland. This seemed merely to confirm that 'no matter what Government comes to power in England the old imperial British attitude to Ireland will never change'.[102] Further dismay greeted the introduction at Westminster of a Northern Ireland Bill that had been drawn up to relax certain restrictions placed on Stormont under the Government of Ireland Act 1920. Although, as Purdie points out, it was 'a fairly technical piece of legislation' for the APL, it was an attempt to 'buttress partition at the expense of the British taxpayer' and 'the first step taken by any British Government to perpetuate the partition of our country'.[103] In order to try to defeat the Bill, the League attempted to appeal over the heads of Labour leaders to ordinary party members. For example, Mulvey requested that a call should be made to ordinary party members that they insist that the Bill should be withdrawn because it would destroy Labour's claim to be the 'sponsors' of democracy'.[104]

But the Bill also presented the League with a rare opportunity to work closely with the Friends of Ireland and MPs from the group successfully drew up an amendment to the Bill that would allow for a full discussion on the way Northern Ireland was governed.[105] In June Bing wrote to Mulvey asking him to meet, in order to have, 'a short preliminary discussion on tactics'.[106]

As the debate on the Bill approached the APL was keen to emphasise that it had been a major boost to their campaign in Britain. At meetings on both the mainland and in the province itself this message was repeated and, as Father Donnelly commented at Lisnaskea, 'the spotlight of truth and justice was being pressed upon the six Counties and people were waiting to see the reaction to the promised debate'.[107] A report in the *Irish News* highlighted the mood and declared it would take place:

> in an atmosphere one would not have dared to hope for a few months ago and which a year ago would have been inconceivable. The problem of Northern Ireland, instead of remote, has come right up into the limelight, and it looks like staying there even after today's debate.[108]

Undoubtedly this debate was an important event since it was a rare occurrence for Northern Ireland affairs to be raised at Westminster as, it had become an accepted practice that issues dealing specifically with the province were considered to be the sole responsibility of Stormont. This, according to Purdie, allowed Mulvey and Friends of Ireland members such as Bing to make detailed speeches 'listing complaints about abuses of power by the Unionists and discrimination against the minority. As a result they tended to range over the 30 years of Unionist rule and much of the evidence was anecdotal'.[109]

Although the Bill was passed McSparran urged people not to consider the debate a failure and instead to look at the fact that for the first time many people had heard about the problems nationalists had to endure in the North. In addition, it showed how far the Labour party had gone in betraying the Irish who had done so much to help it into power:

> not a word of sympathy had been uttered or helpful action taken by the Labour Government to alleviate the conditions of their people in the Six Counties. Half of their politicians consider it more appropriate to lavish praise ... on a reactionary group who were the most bitter enemies of the Labour Party in the British Empire today ... he could see no logical reason why the Labour Government should seek to bolster up the Northern Ireland regime in the manner they had done in recent times.[110]

The final insult for the APL came later in the year when Chuter Ede, the British Home Secretary, made a customary visit to Belfast. At the request of their MPs and Senators, a meeting was arranged with him to raise such issues as the Special Powers Act (SPA), the misuse of the Residence Permits Order, the alleged tampering of mail and the electoral system in Northern Ireland. But the meeting was to prove a disaster and McAteer was to tell Rees that on his arrival Ede informed the delegation that he could only spare them six minutes.[111] The League responded by releasing a press statement, later issued to all branches in Britain and Ireland as a pamphlet, which castigated Ede and the whole Labour government:

> The attitude of Mr Chuter Ede is in accord with that of other prominent Labour Ministers on this and other matters affecting our country in general and the minority in this area in particular. After two years of experience it is now abundantly clear to us that the present Labour Cabinet or a majority of its Ministers are quite definitely opposed to the introduction of any measure to end Partition[112].

A warning from the APL now went out to the leaders of the Labour party that their attitude towards Ireland ran the risk of seriously damaging their future electoral prospects. Whilst Labour MPs like Delargy, who were sympathetic to a united Ireland, appealed for patience and argued that the party was gradually being won over to their view, the opinion of men like McAteer and McSparran was that Atlee's government had had enough time. In Derry, McAteer warned that the attitude of Cabinet Ministers towards Ireland ran the risk of them losing five million Irish votes at the next election.[113] A few weeks later, in spite of a call from W.D. Griffiths, MP for Moss Side, that they should 'not despair of the Labour Party', McAteer called on ordinary members of the party to take steps to get rid of those who were preventing the problem of partition from being solved.[114] By November, McSparran was accusing Labour of treating Northern nationalists with complete 'contempt' and that no Tory Home Secretary had ever shown the same 'hostility' to them as Ede had. Their patience had finally run out and they had been left with no alternative but to call on the 'exiles to act as emissaries', and 'to cast their vote only for the party willing to undo partition'.[115] Finally, Healy appealed for the APL in Britain now to make the Irish question such a 'big' issue at the next general election that it could not possibly be ignored.[116]

Within Northern Ireland the League had continued to try to expand its organisation. The difficulty was in preserving the enthusiasm and support it had managed to generate when there seemed be no evidence of progress towards the ending of partition. Thus, what one finds is that a great deal of emphasis was placed on the positive results it believed it had achieved. A good illustration of this would be the League's first annual convention held in Dungannon on 11 April 1947 which attracted 146 delegates and representatives from 63 branches in the North. In his address as Chairman, McSparran spoke of the success the League had had in just over a year in overcoming despair and apathy, and in creating an organisation in which people of different political persuasions could work together under a common banner. New hope had been created and although he, admitted that immediate redress of their grievances was unlikely, they could take comfort from the fact that the League had succeeded in ensuring that the crimes committed under partition were no longer hidden from the rest of the world.[117] What was needed most of all, people like McAteer suggested, was that if the APL got the support of all 'nationally minded people' within Northern Ireland it would undoubtedly achieve results.[118]

Yet, in spite of such appeals evidence continues to emerge that the

League was still facing major obstacles. It had succeeded in holding its first major rally in Belfast in January and had according to the *Irish News* established branches in various parishes across the province, but the APL had still not been able to prevent the decline in the fortune of Nationalist politics in the city. At the 1946 Belfast Corporation elections Nationalists had retained four seats: Alderman J. Boyle and Councillor J.A. McGlade in Smithfield; and Councillors P. Gregory and J. Hopkins in Falls. However, early in 1947 J. Boyle, a political veteran of Devlin's United Irish League and National League of the North and more recently a member of the APL, died. At the subsequent by-election the Nationalist candidate was opposed by two Labour opponents and, in spite of appeals for the electorate to remain loyal to the national cause, was pushed into second place. (See Appendix 3: Election Results 1945-1949).

A further problem facing the League was that in spite of the continuing attempts to portray itself as an organisation open to all, and representing different political views, it appears that it was still coming under attack from Republican elements. For instance Conlon confessed that one of the main obstacles facing the APL was:

> the attitude of certain people in the North of Ireland who had withdrawn into a shell of political self righteousness ... and whose sole contribution to national endeavour was to sneer at the APL and say it was controlled by the Hibs or that it was a renewal of the old Nationalist Party.[119]

This can also be seen by the need of Nationalists MPs to defend their continuing presence at Stormont and Conlon denied that by doing so they were 'co-operating with the Northern Government and perpetuating Partition'.[120] Instead, as McSparran argued, they continued to attend as, 'so far as the position with Stormont was concerned most people would recognise that anti-partitionists were in a small minority and could not achieve a great deal. But they could prevent greater harm being done'.[121]

As disillusionment had set in over the lack of progress by the Labour government in Britain, the APL began to show an increasing awareness that their campaign could well have an impact in the Free State. According to John Bowman, De Valera's 'failure to make progress on Partition rendered him vulnerable to his republican critics'.[122] The most significant figure to emerge was Sean MacBride, a former Chief of Staff of the IRA and who had in recent years acted as lawyer for a number of IRA prisoners. MacBride had launched a new political party Clann na Poblachta (CnaP), in July 1946, which not only advocated radical 'left-wing economic policies' but whose outline of provisional policy called for a more strident anti-partition campaign. These were to include such measures as:

> (1) The opening of the Dail to the elected parliamentary representatives of the people of the Six Counties; (2) Utilisation of the fullest of the propaganda and diplomatic means available to Government ... (5) Taking such other national and international action as may be expedient.[123]

Since its launch the new party had gradually attracted more support and by 1947, after gaining two by-election victories, appeared to be a serious threat to Fianna Fail. To try to halt its progress De Valera decided to call an early general election for February 1948.[124] This prospect attracted the attention of the APL and at the monthly meeting of the Executive in December it was decided to draw up a list of questions to put before prospective TDs, to discover their views on how to end partition.[125] Conlon also made it clear that the 'League was going South to bring to the people there the true state of affairs here, some of whom seemed to have forgotten that here in North they were rebels before the people in the South'.[126]

This was followed by the decision to hold an anti-partition rally in Dublin attended by around 6-7,000 people on 25 January. The speeches concentrated mainly on their reasons for coming to the South and McSparran noted that their main aim was to try to obtain assurances that after the election the new government would be prepared to give assistance to the APL, by way of finance and propaganda. Whilst McAteer stressed they were determined not to become involved in day-to-day politics in the Free State, he attacked the way in which political parties had treated the issue of partition. He accused them of turning it into a 'political football' at election times and then quietly forgetting about it. What the League wanted to do, he stated, was to reawaken the interests of ordinary people and to seek the assistance of every individual in the South.[127]

With polling day set for 4 February, the APL published the responses of the different parties to two questions they had asked: 'Is your party prepared ... to ... assist ... the APL ... end Partition' and, if so, would it provide 'financial assistance and state sponsored propaganda'? The response, according to McSparran, was disappointing and he regretted 'that certain parties do not think it expedient to provide the assistance asked for'. Although CnaP promised to implement the proposals they had already made and the Labour party to give any assistance needed, both major parties were a great deal less reticent. FF merely reiterated that a united Ireland was its primary purpose and that it would work with any group seeking to achieve their goal, whilst Fine Gael (FG) repeated that it stood for unification.[128] Nonetheless, at the next monthly meeting of the League's executive, it announced itself well satisfied with the success of the recent meeting in Dublin and plans were drawn up to extend the organisation throughout the Free State.[129]

When the election results were announced, De Valera's gamble had failed to work and with FF short of an overall majority he was faced with the prospect of sharing power in order to form a government. But 'to the astonishment of all beholders' an inter-party government of Fine Gael, Clann na Poblachta, Labour, Clann na Talmhan and independents was formed. John Costello of FG became the new Taoiseach with William Norton of Labour as his deputy and MacBride given the important post of Minister of External Affairs.[130]

What was now going to be of enormous interest was whether this new administration that included MacBride would take a more 'strident' attitude on partition. In particular he had repeated the offer to open the Dail for Northern Nationalists in a letter to Healy in January:

> What do you think of our proposal to give the right of audience to six County MPs and to nominate a number of leading Six County personalities in the Senate. I think it is the only constructive proposal that has been put forward and that it should be possible to reach unanimity in relation to it. What is the attitude of the APL in relation to it?[131]

In reply Healy declined to give a definite answer and merely commented that such a suggestion had previously been pushed for by the late Eamon Donnelly within FF without any success, but that they would consider it if an offer was made.[132] But, in an interview with the *Irish News* a few days after the election McSparran was more upbeat about the idea:

> It is I believe, the opinion of our party that probably a great deal could be done towards educating the public of the 26 Counties and the Irish overseas to the urgency and vital importance of the Partition issue by availing of this suggestion. If a majority of the elected representatives in the Dail extend this opportunity it will be availed of.[133]

The League also made it clear that it now expected more active assistance from the authorities in Dublin and, at its annual convention in March, McSparran made this plain:

> We have demanded and will demand that the problem is primarily one for the elected Government of the Irish nation which functions in the unoccupied portion of Irish territory. In our opinion that Government must face the issue. The present Irish Government has indicated that they will face the issue. They must demand that Britain also faces up to it. The Irish race and the Irish Government at home must put into force any sanction that lies in their power to ensure that this affair and outrage to the nationality, freedom and dignity of Ireland will end.[134]

It therefore, appears as if the APL had been encouraged by recent developments in the Free State. For instance, Conlon was to state that it was now very content with the way in which partition, due largely to their efforts had taken on a new importance in the South. The new government had indicated that it was prepared to 'tackle the situation manfully' and De Valera had now decided to embark upon his own worldwide anti-partition campaign.[135] However, beneath the rhetoric of the new government, such as Costello's promise that one of its chief goals was a determination 'to assert the right of the Irish Nation to complete territorial unity and absolute freedom',[136] as Rees shows this did not mean a new radical approach. MacBride was determined to proceed very cautiously and when he outlined the ten most important tasks facing the new administration in an interview with the *Irish Independent*, partition was not mentioned. He also suggested that, because of the diverse nature of the coalition, some parts of Clann's strategy 'would have to be left in abeyance'.[137]

With no immediate signs of anything changing, the APL quickly made it known that they were extremely disappointed. In June, at a major rally in Galway, there was bitter criticism at this lack of urgency and the recent trade agreement between London and Dublin brought a strong rebuke from Stewart:

> It could not be seriously suggested that the Irish people, who were enjoying freedom from British interference, should be anxious to feed John Bull while Britain denied to this country the right to self-determination ... surely the national outlook of people had not sunk so low as that they would sell their principles ...[138]

By August, in spite of further promises from Costello that the government still saw the task of removing partition as of great importance, Mulvey was describing the existing state of affairs as a disgrace. It was being left to those from the North to re-awaken the people of the Free State to their duty to secure a united Ireland and the League was now looking for more vigorous action.[139] However, the predicament that the APL now faced was that no matter how much it might wish that partition should cease to be a 'political football' in Southern politics there was no evidence that this was about to change. After his defeat in February, De Valera had embarked on an anti-partition tour that was to take him to North America, Australia, New Zealand and Britain. As Bowman highlights, the primary purpose of the trip was to re-establish his republican credentials at home and that there was 'little attempt to influence public opinion in the countries visited'.[140] A prime example of this is the account given by Hugh Delargy, who, in 1948 had as Chairman of the APL in Britain been involved with De Valera's visit that winter. Delargy described the meetings as:

> Enormous and enthusiastic ... always there were overflows. And the meetings were all flops. They were not political meetings at all. They were tribal rallies: tribesmen met to greet the Old Chieftain. The melodies of 1916 were played. A few IRA veterans with their Black and Tan medals, formed guards of honour. Sympathetic Englishmen who attended went away bewildered.[141]

For the APL, De Valera's tour was welcomed as 'spectacular'; and as Conlon was to state, 'his forceful, sane logical criticisms of Partition had acted as a cannonade against a hollow artificial barrier'.[142] But amongst the government in Dublin De Valera's campaign was greeted with 'some anxiety'. The party most concerned was Clann na Poblachta as it stood to lose most if De Valera regained the ground he had lost at the election.[143] Equally worrying for the APL was that instead of staying aloof from political squabbles in the South, De Valera's trip had seemed to brand them as pro-FF. In October Canon Maguire informed Healy that, 'Your folks seem well aware that Fine Gael won't touch you. Costello has already told you so and Anti-Partition workers in England because of your ... sending speakers to co-operate with him (De Valera) in England'.[144] This was rejected by Healy and he tried to reassure Maguire claiming that, 'I am certain that several Ministers of the Government are not personally hostile to us. I have talked with them ... and they appreciate the work we have been doing'.[145] It was thus, against this background that the Coalition decided to take a significant step, namely the repeal of the External Relations Act. Not only was this to have enormous implications for Northern Nationalists but, it also gives an indication of how little they were trusted or consulted over policy that might effect them by the authorities in Dublin.

The Act had been introduced by De Valera in the hope that external association with the Commonwealth 'would facilitate unification',[146] but for many in the South, like MacBride, it was seen as an anachronism that would have to be removed. However, as Lyons suggests, the decision to repeal it by the Coalition and leave the Commonwealth was due to more than just MacBride's prompting. What appears to have spurred them on was their concern that an Independent TD might introduce a Bill to annul the Act and threaten the stability of the government by forcing its members to decide whether they would support the measure or not. Furthermore, Costello was also known to consider it an 'untidy and inadequate' piece of legislation. He was acutely aware of the 'way in which the idea of a Republic had haunted and divided Irishmen since the Civil War' and was therefore determined to 'take the gun out of politics by settling the problem'.[147]

He finally announced the decision to repeal the Act whilst on a tour of Canada and not suprisingly the initial reaction of the APL to the news was mixed. Mulvey declared that while he was not prepared to give an opinion on the consequences of its repeal he felt sure that the 'Irish Government would not decide on doing so unless they were satisfied that it would lead to the unification of Ireland in a reasonably short time'.[148] But Murney was not as optimistic and, in two letters to the *Irish News*, outlined his opposition to the move. In the first of these, what appears to have alarmed him was the speed and the lack of disagreement amongst the Coalition when reaching their decision:

> Does it not seem rather a strange thing that a matter which was the subject of such widely different views a few months ago ... should now be resolved ... by the unanimous decision of the representatives of these same parties? "Political bargaining" is an unpleasant expression at the best of times, but might not one wonder if in this instance it would be fair to assume the existence of this unhappy principle ... I wonder would it be possible that ... further bargaining could compromise the position of the people? We are already cognisant of the fact that the Constitution already embraces the whole of Ireland in de jure sense at least. Will this position be bargained? That is the point.[149]

A few days later he raised further concerns:

I am not jubilant over the declaration of a 26 County Republic. It has been such for a number of years without special proclamation ... Every party has stated they would be prepared to offer every security and even to make concessions in order to effect a peaceful settlement ... We had men in Ireland that England forced to bargain on the Republican position ... Is there any evidence that there are men of the same political views in a bargaining position now? ... hence any Northman's anxiety ... I am not aware of any of the Anti-Partition officials being invited for any consultation on these questions that are of their very nature fundamental.[150]

By the end of the year it had become apparent that the APL wanted something positive to happen as a result of the repeal of the External Relations Act and Conlon made clear that:

to them in the North it was a matter of wounded pride, humiliation and shame that they had been left outside the Republic ... . APL knew that they had the sympathy of the whole of Ireland but they wanted more than that. They wanted some active co-operation and they wanted the people of the 26 Counties organised in the fight. They called on the Irish Government ... to use every iota of international influence to bring the searchlight of world opinion on Partition.[151]

As well throughout 1948 all the signs suggested that there was not going to be any significant moves coming from the Labour government in Britain and members of the Friends of Ireland continued to stress that any progress was going to be a long-term affair. For example, on a visit to Dublin Bing, repeated his belief that although the ending of partition could be assisted by the British government the main push would have to come from Ireland, both North and South. But other factors would also have to be involved, in particular living standards in the South would have to be improved in order to make a united Ireland a more appealing prospect for those in Northern Ireland.[152] Even on occasions when Northern Ireland affairs became an issue at Westminster, such as the decision by the Stormont authorities to ban a parade in Derry on 17 March, Herbert Morrison merely repeated the stock government reply that the 'Westminster Government felt it could not interfere on the question at issue'.[153] Elsewhere, attempts to raise the subject of Northern Ireland at the Labour Party's conference in May was turned down by Emmanuel Shinwell MP who ruled the subject 'out of order'.[154]

It is, therefore, not surprising to find at APL rallies that criticism of the

Labour government continued unabated. For Healy, they were now 'more Tory than the Tories in 1920' and although Conlon denied that the League was in any way anti-Labour he warned that some of its leaders were 'Tories at heart' and as a result the party was in danger of 'betraying its ideals'. McSparran referred to their decision not to intervene on the ban of the St Patrick Day parade as just another example of them turning their backs on the injustices inflicted on Northern nationalists. He cautioned that while the APL had no quarrel with ordinary British citizens he felt obliged to warn them that their government's actions over Ireland posed a major threat to their security. In particular in the 'atomic age' Britain could no longer claim to hold the North as a defensive bridgehead and if it did so it ran the risk of provoking the 'determined and perpetual hostility of the Irish race at home and abroad'.[155] Within the League in Britain frustration with Labour had also grown and calls began to be made for it to contest seats held by the party at the next general election. At the League's annual conference in Birmingham a debate was held on whether this should become policy. In the end a motion was passed calling for candidates to be put forward in constituencies where the Labour nominee refused to cooperate with the anti-partition movement.[156]

In Northern Ireland the early part of the year was to be dominated by the events surrounding a major anti-partition rally planned for Derry on 17 March. The executive of the League sent out invitations to all 'national organisations' to attend and by February the *Irish News* was reporting that arrangements were well underway, with up to two trains and 60 buses booked to take people from Tyrone and Fermanagh to the city. But on 1 March the parade was prohibited by the Northern Ireland government under the Special Powers Act. The APL whilst angered by the move also saw it as a boost to their campaign:

> The Minister of Home Affairs said a few days ago we "were on the run" ... It seems that they are on the run themselves ... History of Irish Nationalism shows that the more attempts are made to repress it the more does it gather momentum ... The Government has really rendered us a service in banning this meeting because the anti-partition movement will grow all the stronger.[157]

However, rather than attempting to flout the ban, the organising committee in the city called off all arrangements, believing this to be in 'the best interests of our people and our cause'.[158] As an alternative, the League organised a demonstration in Strabane, which, although boycotted by representatives from Derry, was designed to give other people a chance to protest at the decision. Up to 50 bands and up to 10,000 people attended and heard various speakers condemn the ban and the lack of interest shown by the authorities in London. In his speech McSparran pledged to use it as an example to show to the world that 'Ireland was not free and that so long as they in the Six Counties were denied their elementary rights the country could not be free'.[159]

By the time of its second annual convention in March the APL had been in existence for over two years and it still had no major breakthrough to show for its efforts. What it needed to do at this gathering was to show that it had been and would continue to be a worthwhile organisation to support and be part of. Before delegates from over 100 clubs Conlon attempted to do this in his report as Secretary. He pointed out that not only had it succeeded in 'bringing people together' in Northern Ireland but had made 'the partition of Ireland a live issue not only at home but in Britain and America'. This had been done by the successful launch of a series of leaflets and pamphlets highlighting some of the things inflicted on nationalists by Stormont.[160] These included examples of gerrymandering; discrimination against Catholic ex-servicemen in employment and housing; the widespread abuse of the Residence Permits System; the domination of local and central government by members of the Orange Order; and a booklet sent to every MP at Westminster answering an attempt by Stormont to justify the Special Powers legislation.[161] In addition, within the past year the League had opened up an office in Belfast where Sean O'Gallagher worked three days a week and employed a full-time assistant to help him. But the most important thing the League had achieved was that it had brought 'steadfast unity' to the anti-partition ranks and it was up to them to ensure that the disunity that had wrecked previous Nationalist organisations was avoided. The work of the APL was also praised by an editorial in the *Irish News* which commented:

> The annual meeting of the APL in Belfast ... gave a fitting answer to the people who alternate between a desire to dismiss the movement as a fiasco and a determination to prohibit free expression ... Representatives attended from ... all over the North. There were delegates from Dublin and from Britain, and their attendance emphasised the cohesion in the ranks of anti-partitionists ... The leaders of the movement for unity deserve credit for intensifying the enthusiasm among the Irish in every corner of the earth.[162]

Despite Conlon returning to this theme a month later in Castlewellan when he spoke of the success of the APL in forming branches in almost every parish in the North; in healing the 'tragic differences' which had divided nationalists for 20 years, and in channelling all their energy 'towards one end and one ideal-unity of our country',[163] there were signs that the League was struggling to achieve such goals. In June, Michael McGurk MP for Mid Tyrone died and the Executive of the League took the decision to call a convention to select a candidate. On the eve of this gathering a sombre article in the *Irish News* warned of the danger of disunity: not only could this lead to the seat being won by Unionists but it also could inflict a mortal blow on the current drive against partition. When the meeting got underway a dozen delegates walked out in protest at the composition of the convention. But this did not prevent D. McAleer, a local hotelier and auctioneer and member of the executive of the APL, being selected over J. Gormley and Edward McCullagh. However, in spite of calls by Rev A. McKernan, PP of Beragh, and of the executive for unity and for no other nationalist candidates to run, rumours began to circulate that at least two more were preparing to do so. To try to avoid a split in the vote at the last moment, just an hour before nominations closed, a meeting was held of 'Anti-Partitionists from all over the constituency'. With the prospect of a Unionist standing, an agreement was reached whereby the three existing nationalist nominees McAleer, P. Malone and A. Quinn would withdraw in favour of a compromise candidate, McCullagh. Although Healy was to announce that the 'APL were quite satisfied' the whole episode does not say much for its claim to have achieved 'steadfast unity'.[164]

But against the background of these events, the most significant development to have occurred was the decision of the Dublin government to leave the British Commonwealth. Although Costello had claimed when introducing the Republic of Ireland Bill in the Dail that it would not hinder progress towards unity, Rees suggests that everything points to the contrary. In the first instance, the Stormont authorities were determined to take advantage of the situation to seek additional constitutional guarantees from Westminster. Initially Attlee's cabinet went no further than to reiterate its policy 'that no change should be made in the constitutional status of Northern Ireland without its free agreement'. But after lengthy negotiations between the governments in Belfast and London, this began to change.[165] The reason for this change, Bowman, argues, can be found in the fact that:

Of greater interest to London was the wider security question of defending the North Atlantic, a dimension which Sir Norman Brook, Secretary to the Cabinet argued was "self evident". He suggested that the Ulster Unionists should be given a "rather more sympathetic hearing than they might be thought to deserve on their strict merits". Bearing in mind the lessons of the war, he believed that it would, henceforth, be impossible for any British party to retain a "detached attitude" on Partition: they would be compelled to take a positive line in support of Northern Ireland.[166]

As well as defence considerations, it was also clear that Labour was keen to avoid creating a situation whereby the Irish question would once again become a divisive issue in British politics. Accordingly, the Cabinet concluded that unless Northern Ireland was convinced 'of the support of the people of this country, there might be a renewal of Ulster violence and of other bodies intending to meet any threat of force by force'. The end result was therefore, an agreement between Belfast and London whereby a new guarantee would be given which established that 'In no event will Northern Ireland cease to be part of the United Kingdom without the consent of the Northern Ireland Parliament'.[167]

To strengthen his hands in his negotiations with Atlee, Sir Basil Brooke had taken the opportunity to call a snap election, 'We are going to the country on one question only: whether this country is determined ... to remain an integral part of the United Kingdom'.[168] This announcement did not catch the APL unawares as McSparran in October 1948 had dismissed the idea that an election, in the aftermath of the decision of the Free State to leave the commonwealth would give a fair indication of the wishes of the people of Northern Ireland. He argued that 'the result ... would be as true an indication of the will of the people ... as the recent general elections in Poland, Bulgaria ... and other occupied countries'.[169] Once the election had been announced this view was supported by an editorial in the *Irish News* but equally important was the belief that 'wherever possible National mind-ed people will fling back the challenge of Unionism'. This was backed up by the decision of the APL 'to put a strong team in the field' and to draw up plans to put up candidates in as many seats as possible.[170]

But the major development early in the campaign was a move that the APL had been calling for, namely, active assistance from Dublin. On 26 January Costello made it known that he was seeking to call a meeting of all political parties in the South to see how they could assist anti-partition candidates in the forthcoming election in Northern Ireland. This was agreed to and, after it was held in the Mansion House in Dublin, a statement was released by the party leaders calling on their followers to help by holding a public collection for funds to offset election expenses on the following Sunday.[171] Reactions in the province to what became known as the 'Chapel Gate Collection' were, not surprisingly, mixed. For the Unionists it was seen as a great boost to them and one told the *Irish Times* that it was 'worth 60,000 votes to us', and that it would shake 'apathetic Unionists ... out of their complacency'.[172] But the opinion of anti-partition forces seemed to be split on the issue. The *Irish Times* reported an unnamed individual as saying that the decision was 'misjudged, mistaken and misdirected. Those fellows in Dublin are playing party politics and that is not going to help us'.[173] But the *Irish News* stated that the APL was delighted and that McSparran saw its importance in the renewed confidence that it had given nationalists, and the signal it would send to the rest of the world.[174]

When nominations closed seventeen candidates had been nominated to stand under the anti-partition banner and many of these were in constituencies that had never been contested before. But this apparent show of strength masked continuing problems faced by the APL. Despite the fact that it was now allegedly active in Belfast, a convention to select possible candidates was called off by the Area Committee in the city without any reason being given.[175] Elsewhere at various conventions there were signs emerging that delegates wanted a return to the policy of abstention. On 24 January the *Belfast Telegraph* reported that unless this was agreed to, republicans in Tyrone would provide opposition. In East Tyrone, at the convention that re-selected Stewart, a motion calling for a boycott of Stormont was defeated by 53 votes to 28. Similarly in West Tyrone an attempt was made to force Roddie O'Connor to follow an abstentionist policy.[176] The biggest problem, however, looked to be in Mid Tyrone where the convention that again chose McCullagh was described by the *Belfast Telegraph* as being 'protracted and at times stormy'. A few days later, a meeting in Plumbridge selected P. Gormley to stand as an 'anti-partition republican'.[177]

Nonetheless, as polling day drew close all these internal squabbles were forgotten as anti-partitionists pledged to fight to ensure that they would 'continue to withstand the violence of persecution' in order to 'obtain justice for our nation'.[178] In a radio broadcast on the eve of polling McSparran declared that the election had given them their 'greatest impetus ... since Northern Ireland was established' and that the 'glare of publicity' had done more for their cause than '20 years' of propaganda. Finally, he anticipated that the campaign had resulted in showing the 'incontrovertible justice of the cause of Irish Unity' and that people would 'attach less importance to the results achieved' than 'the means taken to achieve them'.[179]

At first glance, the election results gave good reason for quiet satisfaction for the APL: a record vote of 101,445 was cast for their candidates and they managed to capture 27.2% of the votes cast.[180] However, the real winners were to be the Unionists who not only saw the size and share of the vote reach record levels but, more importantly, gained four extra seats from Independent Unionists and the Northern Ireland Labour Party. As a result, the hand of Sir Basil Brooke was undoubtedly strengthened in his ongoing negotiations with the British government.[181]

A few weeks after the declaration of a Republic on Easter Monday in Dublin the Ireland Bill was introduced at Westminster. To the alarm of Northern Nationalists, Clause 1(b) confirmed the new constitutional guarantee secured by Stormont

> that Northern Ireland remains part of His Majesty's Dominions and of the United Kingdom, and affirms that in no event will Northern Ireland, or any part thereof cease to be part of his Majesty's Dominions and of the United Kingdom without the consent of the Parliament of Northern Ireland.[182]

In spite of protests by MacBride to Ernest Bevin, the British Foreign Secretary over this provision, Bevin's reply merely confirmed that the government felt it had no option:

> many people in this country and many people in the present government, were in broad sympathy with the ideal of a united Ireland. But we could not ignore the history of the last 40 years. Northern Ireland had stood with us when the South was neutral. Without the help of the North, Hitler ... would ... have won the submarine war and the United Kingdom would have been defeated ... Until the majority of the North were persuaded ... that it was in their interests to join the South, the British people would oblige us to give them the guarantees that they could not be coerced.[183]

The response of the APL to these events was extremely hostile and its executive immediately passed a motion condemning the 'unfriendly action of the British Labour Government' in bringing a Bill before Westminster that would allow the 'maintenance of Partition as long as the six County

Tory Government so desire'. It also called on all branches of the League in Britain to use their influence to persuade Labour MPs, with a sizeable Irish vote in their constituency, that this could be lost if they supported the Bill.[184]

At the same time McSparran attempted to lift spirits by arguing that nationalists should not be 'disheartened' by the recent moves but, instead they should look to the positive aspects emerging. The most important of these was that at last every one could observe the 'true face' of the Labour government and that they could see that they were 'dealing with known enemies instead of alleged friends'. Further encouragement could also be taken from the fact that, thanks to the APL, Northern nationalists were now in a stronger position than ever, not only because they had united people at home but Irish emigrants throughout the world. He still believed that if 'the entire Irish people pulled their weight and used all their influence' then partition could be ended in a very short time.[185] Now was also the time argued the APL, for the Dublin government to 'make the most strongest protest' over the Ireland Bill and, launch an 'active' campaign worldwide against partition. The assistance of Northern representatives to assist this effort should also be guaranteed by inviting them to join the Mansion House Committee.[186] Initially the prospects must have looked encouraging as the above committee, established as 'an all party anti-partition group' at a meeting in the Mansion House on 27 January, met and agreed to hold a public rally in Dublin on 13 May to protest at the Ireland Bill with speakers to be invited from Northern Ireland. Over 100,000 people attended and heard Costello make it clear that their fellow citizens in Northern Ireland should not feel 'isolated and alone' and that they should remember 'that the Irish Nation was working for them and with them'. The invitation to attend was welcomed by Conlon, Lennon and McAteer who all spoke at the meeting. They declared that they had come 'to Dublin seeking a message of encouragement' and were glad to report that 'thank God they had found it'.[187]

But on their return home it became clear that the APL was expecting Costello to implement quickly his promise to 'thwart, hinder, obstruct and injure Britain in international affairs'. McSparran issued a challenge to the Dublin government to match the £100,000 that the Stormont authorities were now prepared to spend on propaganda. There was also a need now, he argued, for the people of the new Republic to make sacrifices in order to secure unity. He concluded that if the Irish government were 'serious' and 'intends to do what they promise they should seek some form of sanctions against Britain in order to make it unprofitable for them to maintain' partition.[188] Although the authorities did respond to some extent by establishing a Press Agency to co-ordinate anti-partition propaganda and agreeing to use the remainder of the 'Chapel Gate Collection' to fund a campaign,[189] the League believed that this was not enough. At an AOH demonstration on 15 August Stewart appealed to those 'people who were enjoying freedom in the free portion of their country' to 'at least make an effort in such a way that Britain would feel the effect'.[190]

The issue which many Nationalists saw as a test of the future intentions of the authorities in Dublin was whether there would be any progress on MacBride's offer to give them a right of audience in the Dail. After McAteer's election in February he had sent a telegram to the Minister of External Affairs informing him that the 'anti-partitionist electors of Mid Derry instruct me to claim my seat in the Dail immediately. Please prepare the way'.[191] He also informed the *Irish Times* that although Article 3 of the constitution 'limited jurisdiction' to the 26 counties this could be easily overcome by the fact that other parliaments offered 'distinguished' visitors a right of audience, and if this was offered to him there would be no need to change the constitution. It was also made clear that Northern representatives would not seek to interfere in the internal politics of the South and would restrict themselves to occasional visits to the Dail to express their views on partition.[192] This demand was then repeated at the annual convention of the League when around 250 delegates recommended that the Dublin government be asked to open up the Dail to 'six County representatives as soon as possible'.[193]

But no answer to their request came until 6 July when in reply to a question from Con Lehane TD, (CnaP), asking if the government had come to any decision on inviting Northern representatives to sit in the Dail, Costello replied that after 'full and careful consideration' on the matter it had been decided that due to the constitution and other difficulties they could not grant such a request.[194] By the end of the year the disappointment of the APL was summed up by McSparran when he referred to the 'very regrettable apathy', regarding the subject of partition in the South.[195]

As for activity in Britain, even before the Ireland Bill had been published, speakers from the APL on visits there kept up their verbal attacks on the Labour government. At a rally in Lanarkshire, McSparran claimed that it had done more to consolidate Stormont than any Tory administration and that as a result it was time that the Irish, especially those in Britain who had done so much to assist it to power, realised this and prepared to take action to show their displeasure. He did not feel that the League in Britain should oppose Labour candidates across the country at the next election but, they should target those constituencies that had a large Irish vote.[196] Once the Bill had been made public it was now finally clear that the APL could now give up on the Labour party and McAteer confessed that after years of being 'livened and encouraged by hope and confidence that British Labour ... would not do ... anything unfriendly towards Ireland ... They found the Socialist lion was every bit as British as its Tory counterpart'.[197]

The League in Britain was now coming under more and more pressure to actually contest seats against the Labour party. At its annual meeting on 29 May, a resolution calling for this policy to be adopted was debated. But it was decided to draw back from such a move and instead, due to the long links between the two organisations, it was agreed that such a step could not be justified until a 'thorough campaign of explanation was instituted'.[198] But the pressure from within its ranks to compete directly against Labour continued and on 26 June Mr Scott-Maunsell, secretary of the North-Eastern Area Council, pointed out that as the Labour Party had seemed to have forgotten about Ireland, only an organised protest against the passing of the Ireland Act would make it think again. If this resulted in the party losing the next election and people having to vote Tory, he still believed it would be better to have 'a declared enemy in power rather than a false friend'.[199] Finally, at a meeting on 30 October of League representatives in Britain, by 59 votes to 51, the decision was taken to nominate candidates in a number of constituencies: Bootle, Gorbals, Greenock, Coatbridge and to leave open the possibility of fighting other seats, 'if and when (they) consider it in the interests of the League to do so. The decision was too much for Delargy who decided he had no choice but to resign as Chairman of the organisation in Britain because:

> Firstly ... I cannot give the necessary time to the routine administration which the position ... demands ... Secondly, when I consented to become Chairman the organisation was for purely propaganda purposes. Now that it has become a political movement it would be improper for me, as a well known member of a political party to preside over its deliberations, since my being Chairman might prejudice its political decisions.[200]

The move was welcomed by the APL in Northern Ireland and, to try to reassure Irish voters that they could vote against Labour candidates, McSparran accused the party of following a secret agenda. He posed the question of why Labour was so hostile to the 'Irish Cause' and the only reason he could find was the same reason why it was hostile to Franco in Spain: namely, that many of its leaders were 'atheists' and it was time that the Irish and British Catholics realised this. Not only was the party hostile to Irish nationalism but its policies were a threat to the Catholic ethos. For example, they were 'secularising the schools and hospitals now, and they would do these things with greater rapidity if they were returned to power', so it was vital to show they were not 'dopes ... tumbling over themselves to vote for Labour'.[201]

These threats were obviously taken seriously by Labour government but in closing the Second Reading of the Ireland Bill Morrison warned that they were prepared to live with the consequences of their actions:

> There are elements outside who are seeking to make this question a bitter matter of politics in the United Kingdom, to squeeze and bring pressure to bear on Members of Parliament and Parliamentary candidates. This matter has ... to be settled in Ireland by Irishmen, and none of us, to whatever party we belong, ought to be parties to be squeezed and coerced on a matter which not ought to be a deciding factor in British politics ... I do not believe that Irish folk who have lived in Great Britain for many years will take the position that unless we seek to palm off another part of the United Kingdom and drive it somewhere else, they will let that influence their votes at Parliamentary elections. I hope that none of us will encourage them to do so or will pursue policies which will encourage them to do so, or this Irish issue might well become an embarrassing issue in British politics again.[202]

As Rees shows, the Ireland Bill did cause concern within the parliamentary party with 56 MPs opposing the inclusion of Clause 1(B) during the committee stage. But for many, their opposition was based not on support for a united Ireland but on their lack of confidence 'in the impartiality of electoral arrangements in force in Northern Ireland' and fears over 'leaving powers of veto in the hands of a parliament which did not accurately reflect the people's will'.[203] However, the possibility of a split emerging was discounted by the London correspondent of the *Irish News* who reported that the matter had ended with the rebels having been given a 'dressing down' by Attlee and Morrison and concluded that the reason was that the party was determined to remain united on important issues, whilst reserving the right to disagree on 'side issues such as the Ireland Bill'.[204] Further steps were taken to prevent the matter being raised further. At the party conference five local branches tabled motions calling for an end to partition but no time was allocated for them to be discussed. Finally when an attempt was made to raise events during the 1949 Stormont elections at Westminster Morrison refuted allegations that they had been conducted in an unfair manner.[205]

Throughout this period when the APL had been trying to interest people in Britain, similar efforts had been made to gain attention in America. Reference has already been made to the attempt to forge links with various Irish-American groups and on two occasions delegations had been sent from Northern Ireland. The first of these had taken place in 1947 when Maxwell and Dennis Ireland, who belonged to an anti-partition group called the Ulster Union Clubs, had visited a number of cities with the intention of presenting 'Ireland's case for the ending of partition'. As Maxwell argued on 3 May their hope was that Irish-Americans could be, if properly organised, of enormous benefit in persuading their government to stop lending money to Britain. In Chicago on 5 May at one of their rallies a resolution was passed calling on 'Truman and the United States Government' to approach Britain to persuade it to end partition 'in the interests of peace between nations and security in the North Atlantic'. Later, the Mayor of New York referred to the North as the 'last outpost of the British Empire' and warned that its existence could easily threaten the relationship between Britain and America. Although Maxwell had been forced to return early due to ill health, Ireland arrived home on 7 June to declare that the visit had been a 'terrific success' with lots of interest shown in what they had to say and 25,000 people having attended 14 public meetings.[206]

The second visit was made by Conlon and Lennon towards the end of 1949 along with a representative from the Irish government. On their arrival they made it clear that they hoped to see 'everyone and everybody who can help us achieve a free Ireland and make it awkward for enemies'. Their basic message was to be the same as that delivered two years ago in the hope that Irish-Americans would force their government to support the ending of partition. At their first meeting in New York, Conlon compared the plight of Northern nationalists to that faced by Jews in Nazi Germany and urged his audience to try to ensure that Britain received no financial assistance whilst it remained in Northern Ireland. A similar message was given in Philadelphia when speakers urged the American government to halt payment of Marshall Aid to Britain until a united Ireland had been achieved.[207]

Throughout the post-war period Rees argues that the authorities in London remained concerned that 'anti-partition bodies in the United States' could exploit the Irish vote and so threaten the relationship between Britain and America and, thus such visits must have been a worry. To try to prevent this, at the end of the war the Foreign Office had urged the Dominions Office not to raise Irish issues in case the 'increased attention' posed difficulties in its dealings with America. Even though Dublin had lost a great deal of sympathy due to its conduct during the war Britain was keen to keep a close eye on any developments and arranged for any significant moves by Irish Americans to be passed to their own information service in New York. In addition the British embassy in Dublin was asked to prepare a list of possible arguments that could be used by Irish nationalists to argue in favour of ending partition and a series of replies that British diplomats could use in America.[208] But it would appear that much of this anxiety was misplaced as the American government knew only too well that British support was vital in order to defend the North Atlantic and was therefore determined to stay out of the problem. A prime example of this surrounded the establishment of NATO, when as T.C. Achilles, the American diplomat, recalls:

> We did invite Ireland as an important stepping stone in anti-submarine warfare. We doubted that they would accept. They replied that they would be delighted to join provided we could get the British to give back the six Northern Counties. We replied in effect "It's been nice knowing you" and that was that.[209]

After having to endure such a difficult year it is no great surprise to find that the APL in Britain and Northern Ireland was facing increasing difficulties. At the local elections in Belfast there was a further erosion in Nationalist support with only one of their four candidates being returned.[210] On 19 October at a demonstration in Lurgan, Lennon, while attempting to highlight the success of the organisation, conceded that the condition of the League was far from satisfactory.[211] This is supported by the records of the County Armagh Executive of the APL which not only show a recurring worry over the lack of funds but begins to record a major drop in attendance of members. A meeting on 9 November had only 53% of its members present and on 14 December a special meeting to discuss policy had to be abandoned due to the fact that the turnout was so low. The trend seems to have continued in 1950 when the two meetings recorded on 20 June and 16

August the recorded attendance was 33% and 44% respectively.[212] As for the strength of the APL in Britain a letter to the *Irish News* from a former member, Captain H. Harrison, on 12 December paints a very poor picture:

> the Anti-Partition of Ireland League, as at present constituted in this country ... is of little service to the cause of Irish re-union ... The League in Britain is not representative, its numbers are pitifully small, its resources are minute and its political influence is virtually nil ... There is no effective leadership, no intelligible policy or activity ... (for) the task of moulding the forces of Irish opinion with a successful political instrument. Its voice is not heard or heeded outside the ranks of the converted.[213]

With the Ireland Act on the statute book it looked as if partition was now more firmly entrenched than it had been when the APL had been established. Not only were prominent members frustrated at this but they also warned of how future events could develop as a result. In Liverpool, Mulvey pointed out that unless the people of Britain were prepared to assist their peaceful efforts then they could face the prospect of violence in the future.[214] This theme was picked up by McAteer when he told a rally in Glasgow of the rising tide of anger in Ireland at the lack of progress that had been made and that this could easily lead to a fresh outbreak of disturbances in Ireland.[215] At an AOH demonstration, Lennon predicted violent methods breaking out and that Northern nationalists could not be blamed if it did. They had attempted to use constitutional means to bring about change but 'there was a limit' on their patience to endure 'the intolerable conditions' they had suffered for 25 years.[216]

However, there was still a determination to keep up their campaign no matter what happened. For Conlon, the Ireland Act instead of being a disaster, left them with a straightforward choice: to 'lie down and admit defeat or ... take off their coats and stand up and fight this injustice'. Due to the efforts of the APL, partition had become an issue around the world and if they could avoid acts of 'isolated patriotism' then 'direct and disciplined action' using peaceful means could succeed. It was important for nationalists to remember that the Ireland Act was just another piece of legislation that could be repealed at a later stage. Conlon urged people to remember the success of both India and the Jews of Palestine in forcing Britain to concede to their demands and he therefore argued that nationalists simply had to intensify their efforts.[217] A few days later he repeated his appeal for every peaceful means to be attempted before anyone resorted to violence and that the APL was still there to spearhead that effort. What was now needed however was 'to quicken the tempo' and for 'every boy and girl, every man and woman' to play a part in a campaign which would entail more than just 'attending meetings and waving flags' but actual 'sacrifices'.[218] Exactly what Conlon means by this is not made clear but if it suggests some kind of civil disobedience then such a move had already been raised by McAteer. In a speech in Dublin in January he had repeated ideas outlined in his pamphlet *Irish Action* when he called for an 'obstructionist and delaying campaign' against the Stormont authorities.[219]   Institutions like the Inland Revenue, the post office and customs service could be badly affected if people refused to deal with them. But such methods came in for criticism from an editorial in the *Irish Times* which instead gave the following advice:

> From every point of view the best thing that could happen in this country at present is that Nationalist politicians should forget about the border for a couple of years. The architects of the Republic have enough to do to build up a prosperous economy in the Twenty Six Counties. If and when, that economy becomes fact, the problem of partition may be tackled with some slight prospect of success. Mr McAteer's formula can only lead to disaster.[220]

Notes

1. *Sunday Independent* 17 July 1941, D2991/DS Scrapbook (2), Healy Papers.
2. R. Rees, 'The Northern Ireland Problem: A Study of the Northern Ireland Government in Context of its Relations with Dublin and Westminster 1945-1951', (UU. D.Phil 1986), p.265.
3. *Irish News* 23 May 1945.
4. *Irish News* 28 May 1945.
5. Profile of E. McAteer by Radio Foyle, February 1992, featuring interviews with Mr F. Curran, Mr J. Doherty and Mr S. McGonigle. Plus F. Curran, *Derry: Countdown to Disaster* (Dublin, 1986), pp.14-15, and T.M. McGurk, 'Agony of the Thirties', *Irish Times* 6 September 1980.
6. *Irish News* 26 May 1945.
7. *Irish News* 4 June 1945.
8. Ibid.
9. *Irish News* 11 June 1945.
10. Ibid.
11. *Irish News* 31 May 1945.
12. *Irish News* 30 May 1945.
13. Phoenix, ' Introduction and Calendar of the Cahir Healy Papers'. Plus Biographical Material, D2991/B/141, Healy Papers.
14. *Belfast Telegraph* 30 and 31 May 1945.
15. *Irish News* 11 June 1945.
16. *Irish News* 7 June 1945.

17. *Irish News* 9 June 1945.
18. *Irish News* 11 June 1945.
19. *Irish News* 6 June 1945.
20. Interview with Mr Harry Diamond 1 April 1993.
21. *Irish News* 1 June 1945.
22. *Irish News* 7 June 1945.
23. *Irish News* 11 June 1945.
24. *Irish News* 9 June 1945. Plus interview with H. Diamond.
25. *Irish News* 9 June 1945.
26. *Irish News* 12 June 1945.
27. *Irish News* 9 June 1945.
28. *Irish News* 7 June 1945.
29. *Irish News* 12 June 1945.
30. Ibid.
31. *Irish News* 4 June 1945.
32. *Irish News* 9 June 1945.
33. *Irish News* 25 June 1945.
34. *Irish News* 30 June 1945.
35. *Irish News* 19 June 1945.
36. *Irish News* 22 June 1945.
37. *Irish News* 11 July 1945.
38. *Irish News* 21 July 1945.
39. *Irish News* 27 July 1945.
40. *Irish News* 9 June 1945.
41. *Irish News* 1 August 1945.
42. *Irish News* 9 August 1945.
43. *Irish News* 17 July 1945.
44. *Irish News* 11 August 1945.
45. *Irish News* 22 August 1945.
46. B. Purdie, ' The Friends of Ireland: British Labour and Irish Nationalism 1945-1949', in *Contemporary Irish Studies*, T. Gallagher and J. O'Connell, (eds.), (Manchester, 1983), pp.85-86.
47. C. McNally to A. Mulvey, 3 January 1947, (PRONI), D1862/F/6, Anthony Mulvey Papers.
48. *Irish News* 21 September 1945.
49. *Irish News* 8 November 1945.
50. *Irish News* 14 November 1945.
51. *Irish News* 15 November 1945.
52. *Irish News* 22 November 1945.
53. Pamphlet, *The Irish Anti-Partition League: Constitution and Rules*, Collection of Material held by the McAteer Family and used with their permission.
54. Cutting from the *Derry Journal* 28 November 1945, D2991/A/Box 2, Healy Papers.
55. Ibid., 3 December 1945.
56. Ibid., 28 November 1945.
57. Ibid., 3 December 1945.
58. Ibid., Rev C. Byrne to Healy, 1 December 1945.
59. *Irish News* 5 and 7 December 1945.
60. Cutting from the *Derry Journal* 7 December 1945, D2991/A/Box 21, Local Press Clippings, Healy Papers.
61. *Irish News* 21 December 1945.
62. *Irish News* 22 December 1945.

63. *Irish News* 27 May 1949.
64. *Irish News* 22 January and 18 March 1946.
65. *Irish News* 13 December 1946.
66. *Irish News* 16 March 1946.
67. Rev T. Maguire to Mulvey, 21 January 1946, D1862/F/7, Mulvey Papers.
68. *Irish News* 26 March 1946.
69. M. Conlon to Mulvey, 7 February 1946, D1862/D/1, Mulvey Papers.
70. Maguire to Mulvey, 17 June 1946, D1862/F/7, Mulvey Papers.
71. Ibid., 8 July 1946.
72. Conlon to Mulvey, 24 July 1946, D1862/D/1, Mulvey Papers.
73. *Irish News* 29 April 1946.
74. *Irish News* 13 December 1946.
75. *Irish News* 30 January 1946.
76. *Irish News* 18 March 1946.
77. *Irish News* 27 February 1946.
78. *Irish News* 6 July 1946.
79. Rees, ' Northern Ireland Problem', pp.261-268.
80. H.G. McGhee to Mulvey, 16 November 1945, D1862/F/1, Mulvey Papers.
81. Ibid., 23 November 1946.
82. G. Bing to Mulvey, 14 February 1947, D1862/B/5, Mulvey Papers.
83. Rees, ' Northern Ireland Problem', pp.271-272.
84. Purdie, ' Friends of Ireland', pp.81-82.
85. *Irish News* 15 November 1945.
86. *Irish News* 1 December 1945.
87. *Irish News* 14 January 1946.
88. *Irish News* 12 October 1945.
89. *Irish News* 15 and 30 April 1946.
90. *Irish News* 30 April 1946.
91. *Irish News* 20 May 1946.
92. *Irish News* 3 June 1946.
93. Maguire to Mulvey, 11 August 1946, D1862/F/7, Mulvey Papers.
94. *Irish News* 3 December 1946.
95. *Irish News* 16 December 1946.
96. Ibid.
97. *Irish News* 11 November 1946.
98. Healy to Mulvey, 29 November 1946, D1862/F/3, Mulvey Papers.
99. *Irish News* 10 March 1947.
100. *Irish News* 14 January 1947.
101. *Irish News* 20 January 1947.
102. *Irish News* 7 February 1947.
103. *Irish News* 17 and 28 March 1947.
104. *Irish News* 31 March 1947.
105. *Irish News* 19 March 1947. Plus Purdie, ' The Friends of Ireland', pp.87-88.
106. Bing to Mulvey, 4 June 1947, D1862/B/5, Mulvey Papers.
107. *Irish News* 23 April 1947.
108. *Irish News* 13 June 1947.
109. Purdie, 'Friends of Ireland' , p.87.
110. *Irish News* 26 May 1947.
111. Rees, 'Northern Ireland Problem', p.285.
112. Pamphlet released by APL, *Trenchant Criticism of the British Labour Government*, D2991/E/32, Healy Papers.

58   *Holding the Ground*

113. *Irish News* 29 September 1947.
114. *Irish News* 13 and 14 October 1947.
115. *Irish News* 3 December 1947.
116. *Irish News* 19 December 1947.
117. *Irish News* 12 April 1947.
118. *Irish News* 17 February 1947.
119. *Irish News* 29 April 1947.
120. *Irish News* 2 September 1947.
121. *Irish News* 13 October 1947.
122. Bowman, *De Valera and the Ulster Question 1917-1973*, p.264.
123. Clann na Poblachta, *Outline of Provisional Policy*, D1862/D/1, Mulvey Papers.
124. F.S.L. Lyons, *Ireland Since the Famine*, (Glasgow, 1971) p.561.
125. *Irish News* 2 December 1947.
126. *Irish News* 10 December 1947.
127. *Irish News* 26 January 1948.
128. Ibid.
129. *Irish News* 14 February 1948.
130. Lyons, *Ireland Since the Famine*, p.561.
131. S. MacBride to Healy, 13 January 1948, D2991/B/60, Healy Papers.
132. Ibid., Healy to MacBride, 20 January 1948.
133. *Irish News* 13 February 1948.
134. *Irish News* 1 April 1948.
135. *Irish News* 7 April 1948.
136. *Irish News* 25 February 1948.
137. Rees, 'Northern Ireland Problem', p.298.
138. *Irish News* 21 June 1948.
139. *Irish News* 9 August 1948.
140. Bowman, *De Valera and the Irish Question*, p.274.
141. H. Delargy, 'The Man Who Outlived His Memory', *New Statesman*,
     5 September 1975, p.274.
142. *Irish News* 7 April 1948.
143. Rees, 'Northern Ireland Problem', pp.302-303.
144. Maguire to Healy, 6 October 1948, D2991/B145, Healy Papers.
145. Ibid., Healy to Maguire, 8 October 1948.
146. Rees, 'Northern Ireland Problem', pp.302-303.
147. Lyons, *Ireland Since the Famine*, pp.563-564.
148. *Irish News* 22 November 1948.
149. *Irish News* 24 November 1948.
150. *Irish News* 29 November 1948.
151. *Irish News* 13 December 1948.
152. *Irish News* 15 January 1948.
153. *Irish News* 12 March 1948.
154. *Irish News* 20 May 1948.
155. *Irish News* 23 February, 5 April and 27 September 1948.
156. *Irish News* 31 May 1948.
157. *Irish News* 1 March 1948.
158. *Irish News* 5 March 1948.
159. *Irish News* 18 March 1948.
160. *Irish News* 1 April 1948.
161. There are various APL pamphlets in the Mulvey Papers D1862/D/2; the Healy Papers
     D2991/E/32; P. McGill Papers, (PRONI), D1726/8; and J. Beattie Papers, (PRONI),
     D2784/22/3/3.

162. *Irish News* 1 April 1948.
163. *Irish News* 22 May 1948.
164. *Irish News* 6, 27 and 29 June and 17 August 1948.
165. Rees, 'Northern Ireland Problem', p.311.
166. Bowman, *De Valera and the Ulster Question*, pp.270-271.
167. Rees, 'Northern Ireland Problem', pp.319-320.
168. *Belfast Telegraph* 21 January 1949.
169. *Irish News* 27 October 1948.
170. *Irish News* 21 and 22 January 1949.
171. *Irish News* 26, 27 and 28 January 1949.
172. *Irish Times* 29 January 1949.
173. Ibid.
174. *Irish News* 29 January 1949.
175. *Irish News* 25 January 1949.
176. *Irish News* 26 and 27 January 1949.
177. *Belfast Telegraph* 28 January and *Irish News* 29 January 1949.
178. APL Election Manifesto, *Irish News* 8 February 1949.
179. *Irish News* 10 February 1949.
180. S. Elliott, *Northern Ireland Parliamentary Election Results 1921-1972*, (Chichester, 1973), p.97.
181. Rees, 'Northern Ireland Problem', p.334 ff.
182. *Ireland Bill*, D1862/D/1, Mulvey Papers.
183. Rees, 'Northern Ireland Problem', p.330.
184. *Irish News* 3 May 1949.
185. *Irish News* 27 May 1949.
186. *Irish News* 3 May 1949.
187. *Irish News* 14 May 1949.
188. *Irish News* 27 May 1949.
189. M. Farrell, *Northern Ireland: The Orange State*, (London, 1980), p.197.
190. *Irish News* 16 August 1949.
191. *Irish Times* 15 February 1949.
192. Ibid.
193. *Irish News* 31 March 1949.
194. *Irish News* 6 July 1949.
195. *Irish News* 9 November 1949.
196. *Irish News* 25 April 1949.
197. *Irish News* 9 May 1949.
198. *Irish News* 30 May 1949.
199. *Irish News* 27 June 1949.
200. *Irish News* 31 October 1949.
201. *Irish News* 14 November 1949.
202. H.C. Deb., v. 54, c.1966-1967.
203. Rees, 'Northern Ireland Problem', pp.331-332.
204. *Irish News* 28 May 1949.
205. *Irish News* 7 and 8 June 1949.
206. *Irish News* May and June 1947.
207. *Irish News* November and December 1949.
208. Rees, 'Northern Ireland Problem', pp.274-275.
209. Occasional Papers 1. 'Fingerprints on History: The NATO Memoirs of Theodore C. Achilles', p.28. Edited by L.S. Kaplin and S.R. Snyder. Lyman Lennitzer Center for NATO and European Community Studies, *Kent State University*, Kent, Ohio, 1992.

210. *Irish News* 20 May 1949.
211. *Irish News* 20 October 1949.
212. *Minute Book of the County Armagh Executive of the IAPL, 1948-1950*, (PRONI), D3184/1/1.
213. *Irish News* 12 December 1949.
214. *Irish News* 17 January 1949.
215. *Irish News* 9 May 1949.
216. *Irish News* 16 August 1949.
217. *Irish News* 7 June 1949.
218. *Irish News* 30 June 1949.
219. *Irish News* 10 January 1949. Plus E. McAteer, *Irish Action: New Thoughts on an Old Subject*, (Donegal, 1948).
220. *Irish Times* 11 January 1949.

2 1945-1949: Stormont, The Issues Defined

After the election in 1945 nationalists across Northern Ireland had requested that their public representatives, for the time being at least, should relax their policy of abstention and take their seats at Stormont. As a result, within a few days' of the new parliamentary session opening in July, all Nationalist MPs had taken the Oath of Allegiance that entitled them to participate in parliament. However, it was made clear that this decision did not mean any recognition of Stormont and the permanency of partition. As Conlon declared, 'I came into this House and took that Oath ... merely as an empty formula ... If I did not take the oath ... I would not have been allowed in here. I do not consider it to be an oath ... It is only so much nonsense'.[1]

What, then, were the aims and intentions of Nationalist MPs now that they found themselves at Stormont? Perhaps the best indication comes again from Conlon who stated:

> We use this House here today as a method of recording the fact that our efforts are being directed not to vilify our country but to expose those people who are actually vilifying it, not by words but by means and unjust actions .... as long as we have breath in our bodies we will continue to do it, and we will not rest until this ancient province of ours ... is part of the complete and united nation.[2]

Nationalists therefore believed that they had a twin task to achieve: firstly, to scrutinise the policies and activities of the Northern Ireland government in order to highlight the unjust actions that were being inflicted on the entire population, and secondly, to show that only an independent and united Ireland could offer a permanent solution. This chapter attempts to take the period 1945-1949 as an example of how Nationalist MPs used Stormont to try to raise the issues that were to continue to dominate the political debate in the province throughout the period of this book. In their efforts to do so it is important to highlight the main difficulty that was to confront the party, i.e. the fact that out of the 52 MPs elected to Stormont at each election, Nationalists never accounted for more than a fifth of the total number of MPs returned. Consequently not only was the party confined to permanent opposition but the size of the government's majority, in reality it never was to fall below 18 votes, meant that the impact of Nationalist MPs was always going to be very limited.

Electoral Matters

One of the main grievances held by Northern nationalists was the belief that since partition the electoral system, at both parliamentary and local government level, had been deliberately gerrymandered by Unionists in such a way as to deprive them of their fair share of public representation. They were therefore, most anxious to show how this policy was being operated. Their first chance came with the introduction of the Elections and Franchise Bill in January 1946.[3] The measure itself was an attempt to establish voting qualifications and arrangements for local government, Stormont and Westminster elections. In outlining the main provisions of the Bill, the Minister of Home Affairs, Edmund Warnock, gave a summary of how, since 1918, every adult in Northern Ireland and Great Britain had enjoyed the right to vote based on the principle that as taxpayers they had a right to have a say in how the government spent the money they had contributed. However, at local government level a different principle had always been used to determine the franchise. As the financial resources were provided by local ratepayers 'the principle was adopted that the persons who provided the moneys for the upkeep of services ... were the proper persons to elect the representatives who expended it'. Accordingly, it had therefore been accepted that 'every rated occupier enjoyed the local government vote'.[4]

He then went on to explain that in Britain as the war came to an end the feeling had grown that due to extraordinary circumstances: the enormous population shifts necessary to maximise the war effort, the destruction of large areas by bombing, and the millions engaged in the armed forces, it would be impossible to compile a new local government electoral register based on the old system. As a result the decision had been taken, rather reluctantly, that the only course of action was to use the parliamentary register. But, as Northern Ireland had largely escaped the disruption experienced in Britain, it was possible for the government to maintain a local government register based on the principle of rateable occupation.[5]

Yet according to Healy, the Bill was simply an 'outrage on democracy',[6] and along with his colleagues he attacked the Bill on two main grounds. The first was the condition that to qualify for a vote, 'a person must ... be a resident ... either as a owner or tenant ... of a dwelling house ...,"a dwelling house," does not include part of a house unless that part is separately rated'.[7] Secondly, the fact that the Bill provided for Company votes which meant that 'Limited Companies are entitled to appoint one nominee for every £10 of the valuation of their premises up to a maximum of six'.[8] For Maxwell it was completely unfair to claim that tenants did not contribute to the rates and he argued that by paying rent they indirectly contributed to the rates:

> we have a Bill which is now being introduced to disenfranchise people living in houses and paying rents ... In the city which I represent ... unfortunately there are a very large number of what are called tenement houses ... A few yards from my office there is a ... house in which there are 14 families living. Under this Bill none of those families will have a vote, although they are occupying a separate portion of this house ... because the portion of the house which they occupy is not separately rated.[9]

This point was also picked up by McSparran who claimed it was unjust to deny the vote to people, who, through no fault of their own had been forced into living in rented accommodation, as there was simply not enough houses for them. He estimated that, 'At the present time there are ... something like 100,000 houses required to accommodate the homeless people of the six Counties. If there are 100,000 houses required how many people are there who cannot have a home and who cannot have a vote?'.[10]

But for Healy the measure was simply another example of the policy of gerrymandering to ensure Unionist domination of local councils. This whole process had steadily undermined the confidence nationalists had in their local authorities carrying out their duties and responsibilities equitably. A good example of this, Healy argued, was the position in Fermanagh where he alleged that for almost 30 years Unionist-controlled councils had refused to build any houses for 'agricultural labourers'. Now 'the government are going to allow those councils to carry on, elected as they are, on a restricted franchise', which he argued 'under this Bill is going still to be further restricted'.[11]

Despite the passing of the Elections and Franchise Act, Nationalist MPs were keen to carry on with their attempts to prove their complaint that

Unionists 'could bear no opinion contrary to their own in local administration'.[12] The opportunities came when they introduced or supported motions
from other opposition MPs calling for reform or investigation of the whole
electoral system in Northern Ireland.[13] During these debates Nationalists
and other MPs like Diamond and Jack Beattie, MP for Pottinger, attempted
to show that through the abolition of proportional representation and the
gerrymandering of electoral boundaries, nationalist majorities could only
elect a minority of public representatives. In addition, evidence to prove that
the policy had the backing of the Unionist government was also brought forward. During a debate in June 1948 on a motion proposed by Diamond calling for 'one man, one vote' in all elections, Healy raised the speech made
by E.C. Ferguson, MP for Enniskillen, on 9 April at a meeting of the
Unionist Association of Fermanagh. With the Prime Minister present,
Ferguson had declared that 'the Nationalist majority of the county stood at
3,684' and that they must ultimately 'reduce and liquidate that majority'.[14]

These debates often rested upon Nationalists and Unionists producing
detailed statistical evidence which attempted to prove their respective case.
In a debate on a motion calling for a public inquiry into local government
electoral districts, Maxwell presented a detailed case of the history of gerrymandering in Derry City. He was supported by McAteer who pointed out
that in order not to disrupt the carefully drawn-up electoral boundaries in the
city, the Unionist-controlled Corporation had sited the Creggan Housing
Estate, 'up a mountain', in order to keep most of the Catholic majority in
one ward.[15]

Conlon brought forward the case of Armagh City which had been controlled by Nationalists up until 1934 when the council had been dissolved
by Stormont and where, for the next 12 years, a number of Commissioners
appointed by the government, had run the city. Then in April 1946 the City
Commissioner applied to the County Council, which was controlled by the
Unionists, to extend the city boundaries. At the subsequent inquiry, which
Conlon claimed had been rigged in favour of unionists, the decision had
been taken to redraw the boundary in such a way as to include unionist
strongholds at the expense of nationalist areas, in order to secure their control of the new city council.[16]

During the same debate Stewart produced figures to show the true
position in Tyrone. To begin with in the County Council area there were 70,
595 nationalists and 58,991 unionists, and yet this majority could only
obtain 11 seats compared to 16 for the minority. This pattern, Stewart,

maintained was also prevalent in both the rural and urban councils. For example, in Omagh Rural District Council 18,664 nationalists returned 18 members, while 11,678 unionists returned 21; in Omagh District Council 3, 573 nationalists got nine seats compared to 12 seats for 2,168 unionist voters; in Dungannon Rural District Council 12,168 nationalists returned six members whilst 11,674 unionist voters managed 13 members; and in Dungannon Urban District Council 2,068 nationalists returned seven members and 1,862 unionists gained 14 members.[17]

Healy outlined a similar story in Fermanagh where 30,000 nationalists could only return seven members to the County Council compared to 18 members for the unionist minority. This was also repeated in three local authorities in the county: in Enniskillen Urban District Council where a nationalist majority could only return seven members compared to 14 for the unionist minority; in Enniskillen Rural District Council where 8,577 nationalists returned nine members and 8,499 unionists returned 17; and in Irvinestown Rural District Council where 5,813 nationalists returned eight councillors but 5,944 unionists returned 11 members.[18]

Discrimination in Housing and Employment

Nationalists were so concerned with this whole question of alleged electoral malpractice because, they claimed that by controlling local government Unionists were thus in a position to ensure that things such as housing and employment, were allocated to their supporters. In many areas across Northern Ireland they, therefore, argued that Catholics were not being given the share of opportunities, that their numerical strength merited. With regards to housing, Healy claimed that certain local councils controlled by Unionists had a deliberate policy not to build houses in case they were allocated to Catholic families. He pointed to the situation in Fermanagh where he alleged that the rural councils of Enniskillen, Irvinestown and Lisnaskea had for some 25 years failed to build labourers' cottages. The reasons for this was simply political and he referred to a letter received by a Chairman of one of these councils from the Secretary of the West Tyrone Unionist Association. In the letter the suggestion was made that councils in Tyrone and Fermanagh should think very carefully before starting any scheme to build labourers' cottages 'because ... many of them were likely to go to people who did not support the Government'.[19]

This had taken on greater significance with the passing of the Elections and Franchise Act which reinforced the fact that each new council house represented a potential vote at local elections and so, for Nationalist representatives, it appeared that Unionists would continue to exert strict control over the allocation of housing. For Healy, Unionist intentions were quite clear and to illustrate this he quoted from a letter sent by the Unionist-controlled Armagh Rural District Council to the Home Office. Although the council admitted that there was a desperate need for housing in its area, they still asked the Home Secretary to either change the regulations or introduce legislation that would allow them to erect houses and to allocate them before receiving any applications, and so 'That, of course meant that they must be allowed to decide beforehand to whom they would give the cottages, irrespective of their need'.[20]

McAteer also attempted to draw attention to the position in Derry City and on 13 May 1947 he questioned the Minister of Health and Local Government over the distribution of temporary houses in the city's North Ward. In particular he was concerned that they were 'being reserved by the Corporation for non-Catholics, and whether he will instruct that body that houses be allocated on the basis of need and not on ... political expediency'.[21] Later in the year McAteer appealed to the Minister once more, this time for him to instruct local authorities to start publishing 'priority housing lists' to enable people to see how their application was progressing and so prevent accusations of malpractice. Again he made reference to the belief amongst nationalists in Derry that houses were being awarded on a sectarian basis to supporters of the government. This accusation was rejected by William Grant who stated that the system was being operated equitably by the people responsible for doing so in Derry City. As for any problems that did exist, Grant declared that these were the responsibility of Nationalist politicians in the city who were trying to prevent people moving into houses provided for them because they were fearful of losing votes in certain areas.[22]

But Nationalist concerns on this issue remained and were further heightened by a speech by the Prime Minister on 13 February 1947 at a meeting called to organise a fund to prevent nationalists buying land at public auction.[23] When he was questioned about the speech on 11 March Sir Basil Brooke replied:

> I think that any person or any body of persons are entitled to defend their own interests. In view of the fact the Protestant population in Eire has fallen by

41% and in view of the threats of the Honourable Members opposite, that any person who does not believe in a united Ireland should get out, I think the Protestant population are entitled to take whatever action they think fit, provided it is legal and legitimate ... to protect their own interests.[24]

Throughout this period Nationalist MPs did not produce any detailed statistical evidence to show widespread discrimination in the allocation of local government housing. As J.H. Whyte points out, this is largely due to the fact that it was not until the 1950s when public housing became more abundant that complaints about the way it was being shared out began to grow.[25] Instead, individual cases were raised in order to illustrate the general pattern. A typical case was the allocation of a cottage by Omagh Rural District Council to an unmarried man, rejecting the claim of a Catholic ex-serviceman with a family. Healy asked Grant if he was 'going to allow political jobbers to regulate the tenancy of cottages, giving them as prizes for membership of this (Orange Order) secret society'.[26] The standard government reply to such questions, as in this case, was that it had no control of housing which remained the sole concern of local authorities and that, the Ministry of Health and Local Government had no power to intervene unless there was clear evidence that the regulations laid down by parliament were being ignored or abused in some way.

With regards to employment, Nationalist complaints fell into three main categories: the behaviour of local authorities; the concentration of new industry in the east of the province and the neglect of areas west of the Bann; and malpractice by central government in the provision of jobs in the Civil Service. In the case of local councils, they still provided a range of services and therefore were an important source of employment. As with their complaints over housing, Nationalist MPs argued that their constituents were not getting their fair share. Once again however, there was a lack of statistical evidence to prove this and instead individual cases were raised. In particular the difficulties faced by Catholic ex-servicemen in the immediate post-war period were brought forward, especially after the government had urged local authorities to give them preference in job applications. During the debate on the King's Speech on 6 March 1946 McSparran questioned the sincerity of the government:

the Prime Minister assures us in regard to ex-Servicemen ... that whether a man is a Socialist, Tory or Liberal, if he put on the King's uniform that was good enough for the Government ... He omits from that group any person who is Anti-Partionist ... The vague statement that if a man is a Socialist, a Tory, or anything else, it is alright with the Government, means nothing. In actual fact the position is that it is not alright unless it suits their own purpose to do something for them. That is as far as the position is in regard to ... ex-Servicemen[27]

The promises of the Prime Minister were then contrasted by Healy with the statement by Senator Nelson at Garrison on 2 February 1946 when he had announced that, 'The Orangemen of Fermanagh and Tyrone should be ever watchful to see to it that their own people get precedence'.[28] According to Healy there was evidence that Catholic ex-servicemen with excellent records were being neglected for minor posts by the Fermanagh Education Committee and the Enniskillen Board of Governors. Instead, jobs had been filled by men who had never served in the armed forces and that the reasons for these decisions were that, in Healy's words, 'on all occasions the ex-Servicemen was of the wrong colour. That was all that was wrong.'[29]

In March 1949 Stewart raised the case of a Catholic ex-serviceman in Dungannon who had been overlooked by the local rural council for the post of Clerk of Works, in spite of his qualification and experience. The job had subsequently been given to a Protestant applicant, who not only was a non-serviceman with inferior qualifications, but who had worked in the office which had drawn up the questionnaire by which the applicants had been tested upon. For McSparran this was proof that local authorities were ignoring government advice and rejecting ex-servicemen because they were Catholics. It was therefore, time that the power local councils had over things such as job applications in 'gerrymandered' areas should be withdrawn, as they were failing to carry out their tasks impartially. But in reply to such queries, Grant made it clear that the government had no power to force local authorities to give preference to ex-service personnel, and all they could do was to try to encourage them to do so. With regard to this particular case he strongly refuted the allegations of discrimination and read out the report of the committee involved in filling the post, in order to show there was no evidence of wrong doing.[30]

On the question of the siting of new industry, according to Nationalists like Healy the problem was simple:

> there are not so many of the Government's supporters unemployed, because the Government takes good care that in industries set up out of public moneys a large proportion of the workers taken on are people who work for them and vote for them at election times and who are their supporters.[31]

Healy insisted that evidence to support this claim was not hard to find and he gave as an example the fact that of 147 new factories established in the province since the war, only one had been allocated to Fermanagh and this employed only around 200 people. The thinking behind this was obvious, Healy alleged: namely, that there was a policy to force people to emigrate to Britain and further afield to find employment. This was clearly the case in speeches by Unionist MPs when they had stressed the need to 'liquidate' the nationalist majority in Tyrone and Fermanagh.[32] Other MPs believed that the same principle applied to their areas, and men like McAteer and Conlon constantly asked questions of the government's efforts to bring industry to Derry City and South Armagh.[33]

Finally there was also the attempt to show that Catholics were seriously under-represented in posts filled by Stormont, especially in the judiciary and civil service. Healy produced evidence to show that of ten Resident Magistrates in the Province, only one was a Catholic and that of the six Clerks of the Crown and Peace Division not one came from the minority community. A similar problem existed in the Northern Ireland Civil Service where he estimated that 90-95% of all appointments were Protestants and that any Catholics who managed to pass the entrance exam were forced to look for posts outside the Province.[34]

Education

Since partition Northern nationalists had felt that 'Catholics were required to pay extra for the maintenance of their religious beliefs and practices'.[35] This view was to be strengthened by the political battles which were to be fought over two important pieces of post-war legislation: the 1946 Education Bill and the 1947 Health Services Bill.

The Education Bill introduced by the Minister of Education, Lieutenant Colonel Hall-Thompson, in Stormont in October set out to ensure that 'local education authorities ... contribute ... to the spiritual, moral, mental and physical development of the community by making available efficient education at each stage'.[36] This was to be achieved through 'three progressive stages – primary, secondary and further education'.[37] One of the most significant elements of this process was to be the introduction of an 'Eleven Plus' examination to enable children regardless of their 'economic and social background' to attend grammar schools'.[38]

However, for Nationalist MPs the major problem with the Bill was its provisions dealing with financial assistance to voluntary schools, which were mainly Catholic and remained outside the state system. Under earlier legislation such schools had been granted only 50% of their building and maintenance costs because of their refusal to accept public accountability through the so-called 'Four and Two Committees', whereby schools would have been managed by four appointees from the church and two by the local education authority. But now the government was willing to increase their support to voluntary schools to 65% due to the sharp rise in building costs and the fact that the changes proposed under the Bill would entail a heavy building programme in the future. Yet the Minister made clear that the government stood by its 'decision that full costs cannot be met from public funds unless the principle of public control is conceded'.[39]

This concession however did not placate Nationalist MPs and they argued that under the new Bill some children would still be penalised because of their religion. They had hoped it would have established a programme that would have improved the education system for all children, but instead it had 'degenerated' into another attack on the voluntary sector. During the debate on the Bill, McSparran highlighted the importance that Catholics placed on their schools and their conviction that the church and parents should have responsibility for the education of their children, rather than the state.[40] It was unfair to ask Catholics, McSparran asserted, who contributed their share of taxes and rates, to accept only 65% state assistance to help them in the running of their school system, when their consciences could not allow them to accept the system the government was trying to enforce.

On the question of 'public accountability' McSparran argued that up to 55-60% of the schools had chosen to remain outside the state system and therefore it was strange that:

> we are told that it is popular control and democratic to deny the majority of schools representing the majority of parents the same facilities and the same financial assistance as are given to the minority simply because the majority, it is said, have not popular control.[41]

Healy also attacked the government for refusing to provide voluntary schools with 100% assistance on the grounds that they remained outside 'democratic control'.[42] He maintained that the government had always accepted that the voluntary system had been well run and managed and that the standard of education they provided had always matched the state system. The high standards of voluntary school managers, he pointed out, was enshrined under Canon Law, which made it their duty to visit the schools once a week. He therefore asked 'Where can you find the regional education authority that can show service to the community comparable to that of clerical managers'.[43]

In any case, Healy submitted that Catholics were reluctant to hand over the running of their schools to local control. This was because the committees responsible were themselves the 'antithesis of democracy' as they were based on a local government franchise which withheld the vote from non-property holders and were in many cases based on gerrymandered electoral districts. As McAteer was to conclude:

> we regret that the unfortunate anti-catholic background to this government will not ... allow us to play our full and proper part ... The Minister should remember that the greatest essential towards even the partial working of this Bill is goodwill. Unless that good will is granted to the largest single denomination in this State, I am afraid that the principles of the Bill have only a very slim chance of reaching fruition.[44]

The Mater Hospital

Further controversy was to arise with the introduction of the Health Services Bill in September 1947 by the Minister of Health and Local Government. Grant declared that:

> The Bill sets out to provide for the people of Northern Ireland the benefits of a comprehensive health service. By the use of existing agencies and by the creation of some new agencies we hope to bring ... to every man, woman and child, the full range of medical science ... Every man, woman and child will be automatically covered ...[45]

Nationalist MPs, whilst largely welcoming the guiding principles of the Bill, were vehemently opposed to the provisions contained in it which dealt with the Mater Hospital. The Mater had been founded in 1883 to provide 'relief for the sick and suffering without distinction of creed',[46] but remained deeply committed to the maintenance of the Catholic ethos. Thus, to the trustees and supporters of the Mater, the Bill as it presently stood, threatened the relationship that the hospital had with the Catholic Church. The main obstacle was the proposal to centralise the control of all hospitals in Northern Ireland under a Hospitals Authority, with local management committees responsible for the day to day running of individual hospitals. Healy therefore pointed out that, 'The trustees of the Mater Hospital ... will not transfer their institution, whatever maybe the cost to them in hardship and inconvenience. They say they cannot do so in conscience'.[47]

The difficulty, according to Healy, was the fact that 'An assurance or guarantee against religious discrimination is inserted in the English and Scottish Acts ... but ... is omitted from our Bill where our experience shows it is vitally necessary'.[48] For example, Clause 61 of the English Act and Clause 60 of the Scottish Act established that:

> Where the character or the associations of any voluntary hospitals are such as to link it with a particular religious denomination, regard shall be had in the general administration of the hospital and in the making of the appointments to the Board of Management, to preserve the character and associations of the hospital.[49]

This claim was denied by Grant who pointed out that in two specific places in the Northern Ireland Bill, Clause 28 (7) and Clause 29 (7), an assurance had been given that the 'character and association' of every hospital would be guaranteed.[50] But this was not enough to satisfy Nationalist opinion and they referred to the fact that unlike the British Acts, the Northern Ireland Bill declared that any voluntary scheme unwilling to include itself within the state system, would not be entitled to any government assistance. As Wallace, concludes the government had decided that the Mater, by opting out, was 'deemed not to be a Hospital for the purposes of any of the provisions of this Act'. Furthermore, the Minister made it plain that on this issue there was no room for compromise, 'They are either coming in 100%, or they are staying out 100%. There is going to be no half way stage about this matter'.[51]

However, it was to be McSparran, leader of the Nationalist MPs at Stormont, who was to make the most detailed attack on the Bill. Not only was the question of the Mater of some importance to them but they were also troubled by some other aspects. Chief amongst these was whether it was really necessary that in order to provide an 'adequate and efficient health service', it had to be controlled by the state. In particular, he asked whether it was right that establishments like the Mater, which had been established and managed for religious and charitable purposes, should be taken over by the state without any form of compensation. He concluded that:

> For the first time this Bill introduces into the Government of Northern Ireland the principle of state control ... It provides for State control and for the nationalisation of hospitals without compensation and without consent. We will never consent to (that and) allow the endowments and the property held by trustees under charitable trust, given by donors now dead and gone ... (we) will never consent to that property being wrested in the Government. That is the position and (it) is justified by every principle of human or Divine law.[52]

Law and Order

As with the case over education and the Mater, Nationalist MPs believed that certain pieces of legislation had been enacted by Stormont down through the years, which had been designed specifically to control and repress the nationalist community in Northern Ireland. In the immediate post-war period, one of their main worries was the whole system of Residence Permits. This had been introduced under the Residence in Northern Ireland (Registration) Order 1942 by the British Government to try to control the number of people from the Free State who had moved north to find work in the wartime industries. Although the measure had been introduced at Westminster, it was left to be administered by the authorities in Northern Ireland. As the war came to an end, Nationalists began to voice their concerns that the system was being abused by the government in order to discriminate and prevent people from the south settling in the six Counties. In July 1945 in Stormont, Campbell raised the decision of the Minister of Home Affairs not to renew the permits of some 20,000 workers from the Free State.[53] The government's response to Campbell's query and a later one from Healy, was to explain through the Minister of Home Affairs, Edmund Warnock, that with the war now over, its main responsibility was to find work for its own citizens. This meant that citizens from Eire who had entered Northern Ireland as economic migrants would have to return home.[54]

But such a reply failed to convince Healy and he contrasted the attitude of the Northern Ireland government with the authorities in Dublin who allowed some 35,000 Northern people to live and work there without restrictions of any kind.[55] When this argument failed to work, Nationalist MPs then switched their attention to providing examples where the system was being abused. Typical of the cases raised would be the one outlined by Healy in October 1947, in which a local merchant in Lisnaskea had been prosecuted for employing two people from Eire without the necessary permits. Healy went on to explain that the merchant had needed six butchers for his business but had been informed by the Ministry of Labour that they could only provide him with one. In his response to Healy, Warnock pronounced that there were some 78 unemployed butchers in Northern Ireland and that the priority was to make sure they all found employment.[56]

Another area where Nationalist MPs attempted to highlight the problem was by describing how the system was preventing local farmers from recruiting the labour they required. For example, in March 1947 Healy inquired that whether in view of the poor weather conditions the government would extend Residence Permits in order to ensure enough farm labourers could be employed. The Minister of Finance, Major John Maynard Sinclair, assured him that the situation was being kept under constant review by the Ministry of Home Affairs, and if it was felt necessary permits would be extended on a short-term basis.[57]

However, the worst fears of Nationalists on this issue appeared to come true with the introduction in October 1947 of the Safeguarding of Employment Bill at Stormont. The specific task of the proposed legislation was to protect the employment interests of Northern Irish workers and, the Minister of Labour and National Insurance, Brian Maginess, announced that it contained:

> The proposal is that after the end of this year it shall be an offence, punishable by a fine, for anyone to take up employment under a contract of service or apprenticeship in Northern Ireland, and for anyone knowingly to employ such a person in such a way, unless that person holds an appropriate permit from my Ministry.[58]

In defending the Bill, Maginess stressed that it was based on sound economic principles and categorically denied that it had any 'political character'. Unemployment in Northern Ireland had remained stubbornly high at around 20,000 people since the war, and in spite of the best efforts to attract new industry, economic conditions beyond their control had prevented the government from reaching its own job creation targets. He rejected any suggestions that the Bill had any element of bigotry or discrimination contained in it and pointed out that governments elsewhere had introduced similar measures to tackle their own economic problems. In the Free State for example in 1932 and 1934, the Control of Manufacturing Act, had established that before a person could hold a manufacturing licence from the Ministry of Industry and Commerce, he needed to be a citizen of the Free State, or have been a resident there for at least five years. He concluded, therefore, that if it was considered proper for the authorities in the South to protect their employers, then there was nothing wrong in Stormont taking action to protect the employment prospects of people under its jurisdiction.[59]

Such arguments failed to impress any of the Nationalist MPs and as Conlon commented it was simply another 'piece of very wrong, very bigoted and very ugly legislation'.[60] It was seen by McSparran as yet another attack on the minority community in Northern Ireland in order to ensure that its numbers could never reach a point where it could challenge the Unionist ascendancy. He believed that:

> This Bill is introduced (here) to complete that work and to make as far as possible the position of people here untenable, to deprive them further of their ordinary rights to the franchise, and their right to work and to live in their own country. I say that is unprecedented. It is not practised against Northern Ireland by Southern Ireland and it is not practised against the people of Eire by Britain.[61]

Healy, in turn, questioned the real intentions of the government and asked them to produce evidence that any legitimate labour organisation in the province had requested such a form of legislation to protect their members. In addition he argued that in the past the authorities in Northern Ireland had only been too happy to welcome people from Eire. There was also the fact that, at present, there continued to be a labour shortage in many important sectors of the economy, such as in agriculture and tourism, where people from the North appeared reluctant to fill such vacancies. What alarmed him was that as a result of the Bill farmers would struggle to reach the productivity targets they had been set due to labour shortages. Finally, as with the rest of his parliamentary colleagues he was sceptical that the legislation would be administered fairly. This was due to the fact that it would be administered by local employment exchanges, whose staff in the past had shown little evidence of impartiality towards the nationalist community.[62] In spite of a spirited attempt by Nationalist MPs, with the assistance of others on the opposition benches, to delay the passage of the Bill by tabling various amendments at the Committee stage, the Safeguarding of Employment Bill negotiated all night sittings to become law.[63] Before it did so, McSparran launched one final attack on it and, in doing so, voiced the disappointment felt by Nationalists in the lack of concern felt by the Labour government at their plight. The new legislation was nothing more than a 'grotesque marriage between the right wing of the Labour Party and the Ulster Tories'.[64]

These same worries also touched on the whole question of law and order in Northern Ireland and Nationalist MPs were eager to show that Stormont had created and continued to operate a system that had singularly failed to be fair and impartial to all sections of society. As McAteer alleged, 'there has been no effort by the existing Government to bring about any reconciliation in the two points of view in this state'. Rather, down through the years they 'have simply fostered, carefully and deliberately all the old religious differences which have contributed to the unhappy history of Unionism here'.[65] This was clearly evident in the continuing use of legislation like the Civil Authorities (Special Powers) Act which gave the government power to intern and imprison its opponents without trial. In particular, Nationalists refuted government suggestions that the Special Powers Act was necessary to deal with the violent activities of the IRA. They contended that more often than not it had been used indiscriminately to harass and intimidate the nationalist community as a whole, especially constitutional politicians like themselves. Instead of the IRA being solely responsible, men like Stewart testified that the authorities in Northern Ireland themselves were part of the problem:

> The Attorney-General seems to have an obsession about the IRA. I am afraid the learned Attorney-General has not read the history of this country and of the IRA in 1914, 1915, 1916. After the great constitutional movement failed they took up arms and partly succeeded in establishing freedom in this country. The IRA in later years took up arms, not so effectively ... to get a complete overthrow of the Northern Government. Nevertheless they were imbued with the Irish national outlook and for the Attorney-General to describe them as murderers is simply an outrage on Irish Nationalists ... The seed of revolution in this country for the last 25 or 30 years was sown by the Unionists of Northern Ireland.[66]

Healy also issued a warning on this point during a debate on prison conditions connected with the hunger strike of David Fleming in Crumlin

Road jail, that although the government might succeed in breaking 'the body of poor ... Fleming ... you cannot break his spirit or the spirit of the ideal for which he stands'. Furthermore, he predicted that in spite of all the efforts of Stormont to combat the national ideal, these would prove futile as 'Residence Permits, gerrymandering of the Constitution are merely foolish attempts to keep out the tide with a wall of sand'.[67] As with other areas of contention, the government rejected such suggestions and, as Warnock declared, their priority remained the maintenance of law and order, and therefore they would 'not hesitate to use all its powers in the event of a recurrence of the troubles which have arisen in the past'. [68]

However, further controversy was to arise in the post-war period with the establishment of the APL. Its aim was to establish itself throughout the province in order to unite all shades of nationalist opinion in a renewed world-wide campaign against partition. It was not long before Nationalist MPs began to allege that the government was attempting to spy and inter-fere with what was a peaceful, constitutional organisation. These centred on claims that private mail was being opened and that telephone calls being recorded. During the debate on the King's Speech both Conlon and Healy alluded to such occurrences. For Conlon, who was also Secretary of the APL, this had entailed instances of his letters and correspondence being tampered with, and on one occasion whilst speaking to one of his fellow MPs in Derry, the call had been interrupted by the operator asking if the call was to be collected by the police for evidence.[69] McAteer also asserted that, 'This censorship is directed solely against Irish thinking people of these six Counties and I am waiting daily from some member of the Government a denial that this censorship any longer exists'.[70] The governments response was not to deny that such operations had been carried out, but rather as Warnock was to state, it had 'a duty', never mind the right, to monitor any organisation which campaigned for the destruction of Northern Ireland.[71]

Soon the argument had moved on to another contentious issue, name-ly the question of the holding of parades and marches. This was sparked by the decision of the government in March 1948 to ban a proposed demon-stration in Derry on St. Patrick's Day that had been organised by the APL. On 16 March McAteer asked Warnock that whether, in light of the decision to proscribe the parade in Derry the government, in order to ensure fair play, would consider it right to do the same with regard to an Orange Order parade on Easter Monday, in the predominantly nationalist town of Omagh. When Warnock answered that he could see no reason to do so McAteer declared that it was once more 'clear that there is one law for the Government and another for the Opposition. I think that is very clear from the answer'.[72]

But this particular row continued to rumble on into April when a motion proposed by Diamond calling for the repeal of legislation such as the Special Powers Act, the Trades Dispute and Trades Union Act, the Methods of Voting and Redistribution of Seats Act 1929, and the Franchise Act 1946, developed into a bitter debate on the events surrounding the proposed parade in Derry. Warnock denied that the government had not been fair in its treatment of the APL and pointed out that it had allowed many of its meetings to take place without interference. But on this occasion in order to prevent serious public disturbances the authorities had no option:

> I want to see the peace of this country is maintained, and no person in my position would have failed to do what I have done. I should have been wanting in my duty to the public if I had not banned this procession. Derry ... is one of the corners of the Province in which feeling runs very high and it is my view that it shows a reckless disregard of public order for any person to suggest that throughout the city of Derry and inside the Gates of Derry a Republican flag should be carried in procession.[73]

However, like other MPs, McSparran called into question the even-handedness of a system that prevented the nationalists of Derry, who numbered around 60% of the city's population, from marching. The decision by the Stormont authorities to ban the parade contrasted unfavourably with their actions in the past, when they had failed to consider a similar course of action following disturbances at Orange Order demonstrations. For example, in Belfast in 1935 an Orange march had degenerated into violence when speeches from the platform had inflamed the crowd. In the 'pogrom' that subsequently broke out, aimed at Catholic areas of the city, over 40 people had been shot and 500 houses attacked. As he remarked:

> When one recalls what has been said here by public speakers at various meetings that were not banned, it is the most absolute hypocrisy to get up here and say it is necessary for the preservation of peace and order that this meeting in Derry should be banned ...[74]

But he predicted by their actions the government had scored a massive 'own goal' because:

the banning of this meeting will have served its purpose and will have done far more good to our cause, if in the various parts of Britain and the world where Irishmen assemble on St. Patrick's Day ... they ... remember in the historic city of Derry ... Nationalists were denied the elementary rights of public speech and public meeting.[75]

If Nationalists harboured anxieties about the impartiality of the system of law and order within Northern Ireland then they also had grave concerns over the nature of the forces given the task of preserving it. In particular these centred around the existence and maintenance of the B Specials by the Stormont authorities. Not only did Nationalist MPs continue to argue that the force was a waste of money and resources but that it had serious flaws which could only be solved by its abolition. Their attitude towards it is probably best summed up by Healy when he expressed the view that it had been 'originally formed and maintained, on a sectarian and political basis', and that it was nothing more than a secret political society recruited' from the Orange Order.[76]

Agriculture and Rural Matters

After the loss of the Belfast Central seat following the resignation of Campbell in 1945, the Nationalist parliamentary party drew its MPs from largely rural constituencies, with the exception of the Foyle seat in Derry City. In such circumstances it is therefore not surprising to find that a great deal of emphasis and activity at Stormont dealt with matters concerning agricultural and rural issues. The main aim in the post-war period appeared to be to ensure that the agriculture industry in the province did not return to the slump it had experienced in the inter-war years.

The first area that needed to be addressed was for the government at Stormont to take active steps to halt the steady decline of population from rural areas. A start could be made in this process by providing alternative sources of employment such as the encouragement of schemes like afforestation, the growing of sugar beet and more extensive utilisation of resources such as turf. As a result MPs like Healy and Conlon began to call on the government to promote such activities as a way of persuading people, especially the young, to remain in the countryside.[77]

Nationalist MPs also believed that providing more jobs was simply not the answer and that to encourage more people to stay on the land, rural life had to be made more attractive. They felt very strongly that the present education system was failing to promote the skills and appeal of country life. During the debate on the Education Bill, as well as criticising its provisions for the voluntary school system, MPs like Conlon expressed their frustration that it had failed 'to stress the dignity of land and to encourage, not only those on it to remain on it', but to persuade 'young men and women with energy and brains to select agricultural activity for a profession in preference to already overcrowded urban professions'.[78]

Furthermore, there was an urgent need for the government to improve the infrastructure and basic facilities on offer in the rural areas of Northern Ireland. A good example was the need to speed up the whole process of electrification and in March 1948 the Electricity (Supply) Bill was introduced to tackle this problem. But for Nationalist MPs the measure simply did not go far enough, in that it still would be a long period of time before the majority of people in the countryside would enjoy the benefits of electricity.[79] Similarly, with the introduction of the Roads Bill in October 1948 the main criticism of the measure came from the fact that government resources were to be concentrated on trunk roads rather than on improving roads in rural areas.[80] More disappointment came from Nationalist MPs over their efforts to persuade the authorities to improve the amount and quality of rural housing. This applied to government attempts to try to remedy the problem, such as the Housing on Farms Bill introduced in December 1947, which Healy described as a 'white elephant'. This was based on the conclusion that the legislation proposed would do little to help the small farmer improve his own or the houses of his workers, as the money being made available would end up going to large farmers who had no real need for assistance.[81]

With regards to the agricultural industry, Nationalist MPs were determined to see that the government should take positive steps to protect farmers' incomes and to ensure that they got a fair price for their produce. When it appeared that this was not being done in the post-war period they urged that Stormont should protect farmers through subsidies and price supports. A good example of this was the controversy which followed the heavy fall in the price of flax after the war. Early in 1946 McSparran proposed the motion that 'this house wishes to express its dissatisfaction with the reasons advanced by the Government for refusing to grant the necessary subsidy to bring the price of flax to 30s. per stone'.[82] Later in the year McSparran presented a much broader motion attacking the government over its help for farmers hit by a disastrous harvest and outlining Nationalist suggestions to ease the crisis. He referred to the widespread fear of:

> the grave possibilities of the cattle, milk and egg industries suffering the fate of the flax industry ... that the Government take the following concrete steps ... To reduce the standard of grading ... that the farmers of Northern Ireland may be able to dispose of their saleable stock before the winter at economic prices; to demand from the appropriate Ministry of the Imperial Government ... increased allocation of feed stuffs as will enable farmers to maintain their (livestock) ... in a healthy and productive condition; and that failing a satisfactory response to such a demand, to appropriate by way of a subsidy or otherwise adequate funds to purchase such feeding stuffs ... if unprocurable to compensate farmers for the resultant loss.[83]

Then in March 1947 Nationalist MPs led a protest at the imposition of double summer time in Northern Ireland which they considered to be completely detrimental to the interest of farmers and rural dwellers. Both Healy and McSparran attempted to alert attention to the fact that it was being imposed at the behest of British authorities and that nearly every organisation representing farmers and residents of rural areas had called for single summer time.[84] In reply to government claims that Northern Ireland was being asked to make a small sacrifice in order to assist economic recovery in Britain, McSparran chided that it did not seem to 'make much odds what the farmers think ... it did not seem to make much odds what the farmers want their representatives to do; they must respond to the crack of the Whip'.[85]

Finally, in 1948, the Northern Ireland government attempted to try to tackle the difficulties facing the agricultural industry when the Minister of Agriculture, the Rev Robert Moore, introduced the Agriculture Bill. He stated that the cabinet had recognised that there was an urgent need to prevent the industry from returning to the problems it had faced in the inter-war period when various subsidies had been withdrawn and it had been left to fend for itself. At Westminster the British Government now realised that in the future, farmers would have to be given guaranteed prices and markets for their main products, and had taken steps to implement this. However, Moore argued that before this could happen the authorities in Northern Ireland would have to impose certain conditions to ensure that the industry was as efficient as it could possibly be. When legislation had been introduced in Britain to ensure that this would occur, it had been agreed that, as conditions in the province were so different, Stormont would be allowed to produce the necessary provisions to produce an efficient agricultural industry in the province, and that, explained Moore was what the Bill was trying to do.[86]

While willing to accept the goals behind the proposed legislation, Nationalist MPs were strenuously opposed to two important clauses in the Bill which they considered gave the government too much interference in how a farmer managed his affairs. These were Clause 15, which attempted to define 'good husbandry', and Clause 16 which gave the Ministry of Agriculture the power to issue classification notices on any farm which it considered to being run inefficiently. The opposition of the MPs was summed up by McCullagh who argued that the measures were 'too much nationalisation for my taste', and asked, 'Are we going to allow the inherent rights of our farmers to be taken away?'. [87]

The Economic Consequences of Partition

The attitude of Nationalist MPs towards the continuing existence of partition remained simple. As Healy declared they still clung to the idea that, 'A nation divided can never be at peace and there can never be economic stability. It is only when the whole of the people ... are pulling their weight' that 'you can obtain peace and ... material success'.[88] In addition, according to Conlon, they held out the hope that this message would reach 'the ordinary Protestant ... (who) is becoming aware of the absurdity and injustice of the situation, and ... at last beginning to inquire into the real facts and when he acquires them ... partition will disappear of its own accord'.[89] These 'real facts' not only included some of the areas already covered so far, but also the economic costs of partition. Nationalist MPs were therefore eager to show that Northern Ireland had failed as a viable economic unit and that its best interests lay not in the maintenance of the link with Britain, but in a united and independent Ireland.

In order to support this line of argument it was necessary to produce proof and this process began with Nationalists raising the financial arrangements which had been established under the Government of Ireland Act 1920. Healy argued that these had resulted in a situation where Northern Ireland had little control over its own finances. For example, he referred to a speech given by the then Minister of Finance in 1936, in which he had admitted, 'No less than 89% of our total revenue is collected by the Imperial

Authorities on a scale settled at Westminster on the needs of the Kingdom as a whole, and ... the 11% within our purview does not admit of much variation'.[90] To Healy, this seemed to suggest that 'You have no control over your own finances at all. You raise funds here but you have not the right to decide how they should be spent'.[91] Evidence of this came when Healy forced the Prime Minister to confess that, due to a decrease in Northern Ireland's Imperial Contribution, the government had been unable to finance badly needed housing schemes.[92] This was then contrasted with the Free State Government who had built over 30,000 houses in the last six years and where a new £75 million building scheme had just commenced.[93]

A further problem facing the Northern Ireland economy, Nationalists argued, was that all the important policy decisions taken on it continued to be made at Westminster. As Healy pointed out, this meant:

> We here have no policy to meet such a crisis if it arises. The Tory Party here are looking for guidance ... to a Socialist Party across the water, where the economic conditions are entirely different. We are an agricultural community and they are mainly an industrial one, and the Government may take it for granted that they would consider the interests of their own people in the first instance ...[94]

The best illustration of this, Conlon insisted, came from the fact that Stormont had been unable to take its own steps to either protect or encourage its most important industry, agriculture. In recent times the price of flax had been allowed to fall and that as a result farmers in areas like South Armagh were now being offered a top price of 'nine shillings per stone', not because their flax was of an inferior quality, but because the 'Linen Lords' of Belfast had been allowed to obtain cheap imports. There was also the fact that, at present farmers in the North had been lulled into a false sense of security; in return for accepting new laws and regulations, they were being offered guaranteed prices. But Conlon asked what would happen when Britain was able to obtain cheap food from continental Europe and he predicted that prices in the province would be allowed to drop and farmers told to fend for themselves. This was the complete opposite to the Free State where the authorities had established that certain agricultural produce would have a guaranteed price. However, in Northern Ireland the situation was that 'prices must rise and fall accordingly as England inflates or deflates the monetary balloon'.[95]

It was also vital for Nationalist MPs to demolish the argument that Unionists had always used that a united Ireland would bring economic collapse and ruin to the province. For MPs like Healy the opposite was very much the case and he argued that the province's economy was being exploited by Britain:

> With British capitalists the chief concern will always be the relative profit they can make out of anything. This involves in its turn, the question of whether they can get more units of work done here for a definite sum of wages than somewhere else. If not they will see no reason for giving your workers preference over their own.[96]

Lynn   makes no comment on this!

To counter the claim that the shipbuilding industry would somehow collapse if Northern Ireland ceased to be part of the United Kingdom, Healy raised the point that it had been 'a gang of British and Jewish financiers, calling themselves National Security Shipbuilders Limited, (who had) landed here some time towards the end of 1940', and preceded to give 'orders for dismantling the shipyard of Workman and Clarke'.[97] In addition as had been shown since the war, the remaining yard in Belfast had built ships largely for overseas buyers and there was no evidence that orders would dry up after unification.[98]

A similar story could also be applied in other areas of the economy where, through the lack of protection native industries had been destroyed by being undercut by British firms. Healy cited the example of Enniskillen where factories that had once been engaged in brewing, distilling, textiles and tobacco manufacturing, had all been forced to close due to unfair competition from the mainland.[99] There was, therefore, only one solution, and as McSparran concluded:

> From the point view of the Ulster man, of the Ulster farmer, and the Ulster working man, I say that if this barrier were removed between the 26 Counties and the six Counties, Ireland would become as Providence designed it to be, one economic unit, a community self-sufficient, and with commerce flowing between North and South. Ireland would be as she has been in the past – a prosperous and contented country.[100]

Conclusion: Stormont 1945-1949

Although Nationalist MPs had returned to Stormont after a period during which they had largely boycotted its proceedings, their reappearance did not herald any change in their fundamental political beliefs. As with those MPs who had followed Devlin into the Northern parliament almost 20 years earlier, they continued to believe that it was impossible to engage in any normal political activity in Northern Ireland and even though they remained the largest opposition group they refused to accept the title of official opposition. In spite of the fact that all had taken the Oath of Allegiance, men like Maxwell, Murney and Donnelly, found it hard to abandon their abstentionist principles, and, as time progressed made fewer and fewer appearances at Stormont. Those who remained determined to take their seats such as McAteer, McSparran and Conlon, stressed that the ultimate aim of Nationalists was still to seek for the unification and independence of Ireland. Thus, in the pursuit of this goal and in order to defend the interests of the nationalist community, they were prepared to use Stormont as a means to publicise the evils of partition.

Notes

1. Conlon, H.C. Deb. (NI), v. 30, c.2216.
2. Conlon, H.C. Deb. (NI), v. 31, c. 58.
3. H.C. Deb. (NI), v. 29, c. 1712-1757 and c. 1770-1826.
4. E. Warnock, H.C. Deb. (NI), v. 29, c. 1713.
5. Ibid., H.C. Deb. (NI), v. 29, c. 1713-1715.
6. Healy, H.C. Deb. (NI), v. 29, c. 1737.
7. Pamphlet, McAteer Collection.
8. *Ulster Year Book 1947*, (HMSO, 1947), p. 26
9. Maxwell, H.C. Deb. (NI), v. 29, c. 1801-1802.
10. McSparran, H.C. Deb. (NI), v. 29, c. 1780-1781.
11. Healy, H.C. Deb. (NI), v. 29, c. 1738-1739.
12. Healy, H.C. Deb. (NI), v. 30, c. 3054.
13. (a) Healy, H.C. Deb. (NI), v. 30, c. 3050-3085 and 3348-3384. Motion, 'That in the opinion of this House the gerrymandering of local government electoral areas, whereby minorities of electors are allowed to elect a majority of the public representatives is undemocratic and unfair, and a public inquiry should be held into the whole matter'.
    (b) Diamond, H.C. Deb. (NI), v. 30, c. 3781-3824. Motion, 'That in the opinion of this House the Government should initiate legislation to provide for PR as the method of election of Members of Parliament and public boards in Northern Ireland'.
    (c) Diamond, H.C. Deb. (NI), v. 32, c. 2216-2255. Motion 'That in the opinion of this House the Government should introduce legislation to provide for universal suffrage, irrespective of property qualifications, for all citizens at the age of 21, in State and local elections, on the basis of one man one vote, and to abolish university representation'.
14. Healy, H.C. Deb. (NI), v. 32, c. 2253.

15. Maxwell and McAteer, H.C. Deb. (NI), v. 30, c. 3059-3063 and 3082-3085.
16. Conlon, H.C. Deb. (NI), v. 30, c. 3349-3354.
17. Stewart, H.C. Deb. (NI), v. 30, c. 3357-3359.
18. Healy, H.C. Deb. (NI), v. 30, c. 3050-3059.
19. Healy, H.C. Deb. (NI), v. 29, c. 755.
20. Ibid.
21. McAteer, H.C. Deb. (NI), v. 31, c. 300.
22. W. Grant, Minister of Health and Local Government, H.C. Deb. (NI), v. 31, c. 1782-1783.
23. *Discrimination: A Study in Injustice to a Minority.* A pamphlet issued by the All-Party Anti Partition Conference, Mansion House, Dublin, p.9, McAteer Collection.
24. Sir Basil Brooke, H.C. Deb. (NI), v. 30, c. 4719-4720.
25. J. Whyte, 'How much discrimination was there under the Unionist Regime, 1921-1968', in *Contemporary Irish Studies*, edited by T. Gallagher and J. O'Connell, p.18.
26. Healy, H.C. Deb. (NI), v. 30, c. 1328-1329.
27. McSparran, H.C. Deb. (NI), v. 30, c. 77.
28. Healy, H.C. Deb. (NI), v. 30, c. 160.
29. Healy, H.C. Deb. (NI), v. 32, c. 105.
30. H.C. Deb. (NI), v. 32, c. 604-605 and 668-675.
31. Healy, H.C. Deb. (NI), v. 32, c. 1205.
32. Healy, H.C. Deb. (NI), v. 32, c. 100-106.
33. McAteer and Conlon, H.C. Deb. (NI), v. 32, c. 2628-2631 and 3429-3430.
34. Healy, H.C. Deb. (NI), v. 31, c. 324-325.
35. S. Wichert, *Northern Ireland Since 1945,* (New York, 1991), p.53.
36. R.J. Lawrence, *The Government of Northern Ireland*, (Oxford, 1965), pp.117-118.
37. Ibid., p. 117.
38. Wichert, *Northern Ireland Since the War,* p.45.
39. Lt Colonel Hall-Thompson, H.C. Deb. (NI), v. 30, c. 2012-2013.
40. McSparran, H.C. Deb. (NI), v. 30, c. 2163-2170.
41. McSparran, H.C. Deb. (NI), v. 30, c.2158.
42. Healy, H.C. Deb. (NI), v. 30, c. 2150-2159.
43. Healy, H.C. Deb. (NI), v. 30, c. 2150-2151.
44. McAteer, H.C. Deb. (NI), v. 30, c. 2322.
45. Grant, H.C. Deb. (NI), v. 31, c. 1453.
46. M. Wallace, *Northern Ireland: Fifty Years of Self-Government*, (Newton Abbot, 1971), p.112.
47. Healy, H.C. Deb. (NI), v. 31, c. 1511.
48. Healy, H.C. Deb. (NI), v. 31, c. 1514.
49. H.C. Deb. (NI) , v. 31, c. 1513.
50. Grant, H.C. Deb. (NI), v. 31, c. 1460.
51. Wallace, *Northern Ireland: Fifty Years of Self Government*, p.112.
52. McSparran, H.C. Deb. (NI), v. 31, c. 1707 and 1708.
53. Campbell, H.C. Deb. (NI), v. 29, c. 724.
54. J.E. Warnock, H.C. Deb. (NI), v. 29, c. 812.
55. Healy, H.C. Deb. (NI), v. 29, c. 811-812.
56. H.C. Deb. (NI), v. 30, c. 2307.
57. H.C. Deb. (NI), v. 30, c. 4709.
58. B. Maginess, H.C. Deb. (NI), v. 31, c. 1819.
59. Maginess, H.C. Deb. (NI), v. 31, c. 2112-2114.
60. Conlon, H.C. Deb. (NI), v. 31, c. 2065.
61. McSparran, H.C. Deb. (NI), v. 31, c. 2111.

62. Healy, H.C. Deb. (NI) , v. 31, c . 1951-1958.
63. H.C. Deb. (NI), v. 31, c. 2395-2410 and 2429-2648.
64. McSparran, H.C. Deb. (NI), v. 31, c. 2105-2106.
65. McAteer, H.C. Deb. (NI), v. 30, c. 1963.
66. Stewart, H.C. Deb. (NI), v. 30, c.4292-4293.
67. Healy, H.C. Deb. (NI), v. 30, c. 727.
68. Warnock, H.C. Deb. (NI), v. 29, c. 234.
69. Conlon and Healy, H.C. Deb. (NI), v. 31, c. 60-61 and 45-46.
70. McAteer, H.C. Deb. (NI), v. 31, c. 139.
71. Warnock, H.C. Deb. (NI), v. 31, c. 1163.
72. McAteer, H.C. Deb. (NI), v. 32, c. 712-713.
73. Warnock, H.C. Deb. (NI), v. 32, c. 488-489.
74. McSparran, H.C. Deb. (NI), v. 32, c. 495.
75. McSparran, H.C. Deb. (NI), v. 32, c. 501.
76. Healy, H.C. Deb. (NI), v. 32, c. 2882-2886.
77. Healy and Conlon, H.C. Deb. (NI), v. 29, c. 1548-1549 and 1761-1762.
78. Conlon, H.C. Deb. (NI), v. 30, c. 2197.
79. McGurk, H.C. Deb. (NI), v. 32, c. 795-797.
80. Healy, H.C. Deb. (NI), v. 32, c. 2771-2772.
81. Healy, H.C. Deb. (NI), v. 31, c. 3209-3213.
82. McSparran, H.C. Deb. (NI), v. 29, c. 2249.
83. McSparran, H.C. Deb. (NI), v. 30, c. 2391.
84. H.C. Deb. (NI), v. 30, c. 4850-4908.
85. McSparran, H.C. Deb. (NI), v. 30, c. 4877.
86. Rev R. Moore, H.C. Deb. (NI), v. 32, c. 3854-3868.
87. McCullagh, H.C. Deb. (NI), v. 32, c. 3919.
88. Healy, H.C. Deb. (NI), v. 30, c. 2037.
89. Conlon, H.C. Deb. (NI), v. 30, c. 2209.
90. Healy, H.C. Deb. (NI), v. 29, c. 1393.
91. Healy, H.C. Deb. (NI), v. 30, c. 374.
92. H.C. Deb. (NI), v. 29, c. 1081.
93. H.C. Deb. (NI), v. 30, c. 2213 and 1954.
94. Healy, H.C. Deb. (NI), v. 32, c.102.
95. Conlon, H.C. Deb. (NI), v. 30, c. 2211.
96. Healy, H.C. Deb. (NI), v. 29, c.1081.
97. Ibid.
98. Healy, H.C. Deb. (NI), v. 30, c. 2020.
99. Healy, H.C. Deb. (NI), v. 29, c. 1025.
100. McSparran, H.C. Deb. (NI), v. 30, c. 1983.

3 1950-1956:
Holding the Ground

With the passing of the Ireland Act in 1949, Northern Ireland's constitutional position within the United Kingdom had been reinforced and it was now clear that partition was now more firmly established than ever, especially as this had been done by a Labour government in which nationalists had placed some trust. The realisation that this was the case was bound to have a significant impact on Northern Nationalists, and in particular it begged the question of what was going to happen to their anti-partition campaign, initiated in the post-war period. This had been launched along with an attempt to create a united organisation, the APL, in which all shades of Nationalist opinion could work together towards their common goal of a united Ireland. The question now was whether it would be possible for this unity to be maintained or whether the divisions that had existed in the past would reappear.

The first test of nationalist opinion was to come with the announcement of a Westminster general election that was fixed for 23 February 1950 and, in particular, the twin seat of Fermanagh-Tyrone, which had, as a result of boundary changes, been split into the new constituencies of Mid Ulster and Fermanagh and South Tyrone.[1] Almost immediately the possibility of a split in the vote arose when Sinn Fein made it clear that it intended to put forward three candidates: Liam Burke in Mid Ulster, Hugh McAteer in Derry; and Jimmy Steele in West Belfast.[2] The danger of this occurring was also referred to by the *Irish News* a few days later when it pointed out that if SF entered the field in Fermanagh-South Tyrone the seat could be lost to the Unionists, due to the small nationalist majority.[3]

This problem was to be highlighted at the subsequent selection conventions that began in Mid Ulster. On 29 January in Omagh, around 160 delegates, met and decided by 83 votes to 78 that their nominee should go forward on an abstentionist ticket. However, this decision was to throw the selection of a candidate into some confusion, as Mulvey made it clear that he was not prepared to stand if that was the policy he was going to have to follow. But just before the task of choosing somebody else got underway 'the majority of the convention, priests and lay delegates made another appeal to ... Mulvey, and after some time, he agreed in the interest of unity to go forward ...'. The meeting then ended with 'all sides' agreeing that every effort should be made to prevent 'splitting the Nationalist vote and averting the danger of a Unionist being returned'. In order to try to prevent this from occurring it was resolved that Burke's supporters present at the meeting should consult with Mulvey in order to get SF to withdraw from the contest.[4]

On 31 January over 200 delegates gathered at a nationalist convention in Enniskillen to select someone to contest Fermanagh-South Tyrone. With Healy the nominee his selection was guaranteed but what was to provoke debate was whether or not he should take his seat, if elected. On his own behalf, Healy stressed that although he had 'no personal desire to go to Westminster', he did feel it necessary to go there to expose 'the iniquities of the British administration and to assert the right of the Irish people to determine their own destiny'.[5] However according to the *Impartial Reporter* abstentionists were 'adamant', 'determined' and 'prepared to split the Nationalist vote rather than yield'. On the other hand, the 'moderate section' argued that such a strategy was 'tantamount to disenfranchising the people', and that as a policy it had failed in the past. In the end it was agreed, as neither side was 'disposed to capitulate', to call another gathering after the election to decide the issue, if the seat was won.[6]

As campaigning got underway, this decision was stressed time and again, and in both constituencies different speakers emphasised the importance of ensuring that Unionists were not successful due to the nationalist vote being divided. At an election rally in Arney on behalf of Healy's campaign, the Rev J. Donnelly PP appealed for the question of attendance or abstention, to be left until after the election. In Enniskillen McSparran warned that any signs of disunity or apathy amongst them would not only hand the seats to Unionists but be used 'by our political opponents as another means of spreading false propaganda abroad'.[7] The possibility of this occurring in Mid Ulster receded somewhat when the *Dungannon Observer* reported that SF, following consultations with their supporters in the constituency, decided to withdraw 'when Mr Mulvey changed his policy from one of attendance to abstention'.[8]

However, it was not only the contests in Northern Ireland that anti-partitionists were interested in as the decision had already been taken to field candidates in four constituencies on the mainland. The Chairman of the APL in Britain was to declare that this was a useful way of 'protesting against the Ireland Bill'.[9] As well as urging support for these men, McSparran also appeared keen to settle the score with the Labour government. At a rally in Coatbridge he called on Irish voters in Britain to think very carefully about supporting Labour at this election. Not only had it been hostile towards Ireland but its 'attitude to Ireland's national faith' showed signs of 'contempt'. In particular he referred to its animosity towards Catholic regimes in Spain and Belgium, its haste in recognising Communist China and their response to the proposals put forward by the English bishops regarding Catholic schools. Accordingly, they had now a simple choice:

> I say to our people who are prepared to sell their birthright for a bowl of porridge: Have you any regard for your faith handed down to you by your forefathers and no thought for what may happen in the next five years if Labour survives. If Labour does, in the next five years, as in the last five we will be in a very little better position than the people of Poland, Czechoslovakia and Hungary.[10]

When the election results were declared, both Healy and Mulvey were victorious but their majorities showed how any split in the nationalist vote, or failure to maximise its full potential could have resulted in either seat being lost. What stands out, therefore, is the ability on the nationalist side to maintain an election machine capable of preventing this happening. (See Appendix 4: Election Results 1950-1956). Not so successful were the anti-partition candidates on the mainland, where, in spite of earlier pronouncements of mobilising five million Irish voters in over 70 constituencies, none of the four nominees failed to make a significant impact and in the end all lost their deposits. (See Appendix 4: Election Results 1950-1956).

After the election the issue of whether Healy was to take his seat at Westminster was finally resolved when on 13 April 150 delegates met in Enniskillen and agreed unanimously to concur with the decision that had been reached in Mid Ulster.[11]

It appeared as if the question was settled for the time being with abstention now the policy in both constituencies. However, as the *Belfast Telegraph* had reported at the time of the Omagh convention, the decision had 'not the support of leading Nationalists throughout the constituency and a large number of Catholic clergy are understood to be opposed'.[12]

It comes as no surprise to find that shortly after the election, Mulvey began to indicate that he was seeking to overturn the decision made in Omagh, by calling a second convention. In an interview with the *Irish News* he stated that he had been forced to take such a course of action as a result of the comments he had received throughout the election campaign, when many people had made it clear that they were reluctant to support a candidate following an abstentionist line.[13] Such a suggestion did not please the republican elements in Tyrone who reiterated their belief that Mulvey was obliged to abide by the decision reached on 29 January and that he had no mandate to seek to overturn it. In any case, they made it clear that no bona fide Republican would attend a second meeting and alleged that delegates would be carefully selected to ensure that he got the result he wanted.[14] These were claims that Mulvey was quick to deny and he pointed to the fact that at no stage had he pledged himself to an abstentionist policy and had only agreed to stand in the 'interests of unity' and to ensure that the seat was not lost.[15]

Finally, on 14 May the second convention was held in Omagh and in a lengthy speech Mulvey repeated his reasons for seeking to overturn the original decision. He believed that abstentionism had been tried in the past, had achieved little, and asked how it could now forward the cause of 'national reunification'. In addition he pointed to the fact that people throughout the constituency were steadfastly opposed to its adoption. This had become obvious during the recent election campaign when he had been forced to give a promise to large numbers of people to get them to vote, that he would seek to reverse a policy that had only been passed by five votes. Finally, in present circumstances it was vitally important to attend Westminster as:

> It was generally agreed that well-directed propaganda was invaluable in the National Reunification. He was convinced that apart from some world revolution yet unforeseen, Partition would never end without the consent of the British Government , and in spite of all they read about activities in America and elsewhere, the best place for such propaganda was in the lobbies at Westminster. [16]

Support for Mulvey came from Rev Byrne PP, who presided at the meeting, when he pronounced that Mulvey had not broken any promises and had only agreed to stand as the 'most suitable candidate to save the seat'. However, before any vote was taken up to 20 delegates and two priests left, in order, to register their opposition to the course of events. As a result the remaining 72 delegates unanimously passed a resolution calling on Mulvey to 'attend Westminster whenever he sees fit'.[17]

With this verdict it was not long before Healy, too, was to come under pressure to follow Mulvey's course of action and in June he received a request from the Belcoo branch of the APL suggesting he 'call another convention for the purpose of deciding your right to attend Westminster under the present circumstances'.[18] In his reply Healy indicates that although he was not a wholehearted supporter of abstention, he felt at present he was not in a position to change it, in case it provoked trouble:

> I am afraid to do so would be to stir up a lot of dissension. I agreed to abide by the result of the Convention ... which decided abstention during the lifetime of the present parliament. This cannot be long ... I am sure you will see the difficulty I should have to reopen the question at this stage after agreeing to abstain for the lifetime of the present parliament.[19]

The position was therefore somewhat bizarre: whilst Mulvey was willing to attend Westminter, Healy, albeit reluctantly, continued to abide by a decision he did not really agree with, in order to avoid opening a damaging split in his constituency which ultimately could lead to the seat being lost. Yet further evidence of the problems that the re-emergence of this question of attendance/abstention was beginning to cause, soon emerged elsewhere. In March Conlon, MP for South Armagh, died and the candidate chosen by local APL branches to replace him, Charles McGleenan, a member of the 'Old IRA', made it clear that under no circumstances would he 'take his seat at Stormont as his allegiance was to the Republic of Ireland only'.[20] A few weeks later at the League's annual convention in Belfast, a motion calling on all MPs to abstain from Stormont and Westminster was proposed, and defeated by 80 votes to 32. In his address as Chairman, McSparran admitted to some 'difference of view as to the paths to be taken', within the organisation. He urged the delegates, nonetheless, to remember that the most important thing was that there was 'no difference of opinion amongst members ... as to the end to be obtained'. Personally he held the view that abstention would not work:

> bearing in mind the hard facts and stark realities in the present situation for so many of their people living in the six counties. How many people were prepared to pursue abstention to its logical conclusion by refusing to send repre-

sentatives to County Councils and kindred bodies, and also refusing health services and subsidies. Very few people would be anxious to go so far as that.[21]

This was to be a point he would return to later in the year when he told an APL meeting in Bryansford that he 'could not see what could be achieved by such a policy. A negative policy was useless'.[22] Support also came from Healy, when at a rally in Tempo on 23 May he attacked those critics who urged their elected representatives 'to refuse to recognise the Governments', but who at the same time themselves 'were to be free to recognise them in every way they needed', such as in 'social and other services'.[23]

But it was not only this issue that caused disagreement amongst Northern Nationalists because connected with it was also the question of whether, as an alternative, they should seek to take their seats in the Dail. On 6 February the *Irish News* reported that Con Lehane, a CnaP TD, intended to introduce during the forthcoming parliamentary session a motion calling for legislation to be introduced 'whereby all parliamentary representatives in the North should have the right of audience in the Dail or Senate'.[24] This promise was taken up by MacBride on 17 February at an election rally in Dungannon when he spoke of his wish that Healy and Mulvey would be invited to take their seats in 'one or either of the Houses of Parliament of the Republic'. The response of Joe Stewart, who presided at the rally, was one of enormous enthusiasm and he proclaimed:

> We sincerely hope that the Government of which he is a member ... will implement the suggestion, and not alone make provision for Mr Healy and Mr Mulvey, but for us poor stalwarts in Stormont ... No Irishman worthy of his salt wants to enter an alien administration and we look forward ... that those who are responsible for the Government of the free portion of the country will see that this question is effectively settled and that the people we return as Irish Republicans in the six Counties will not have to take their seats in either a foreign assembly or an assembly controlled from Westminster[25]

This was then followed by the unanimous acceptance of a motion at the annual meeting of the APL calling for a delegation to be sent to Dublin to meet the Irish government to discuss the possibility of the entry of their representatives into Leinster House.[26] The meeting took place on 31 July when the deputation met the Taoiseach, Costello and his deputy, William

Norton. They were told that due to 'the absence of general agreement among members of the Dail', the government was not prepared to 'promote legislation to enable Northern Ireland representatives to attend the Dail'. In a short statement after the talks the deputation expressed their 'regret' and 'dissent' at the decision and repeated that they had come to Dublin to honour a resolution passed at their annual convention in May.[27]

It was not until a few days later that one of its members, Healy, gave a more detailed account of the meeting. He repeated that they had been told by Costello that nothing could be done 'unless there was virtual unanimity on the matter'. In addition he claimed that they had not been told 'whether the Government were unanimous' in their decision as Cabinet Ministers like MacBride, who were in favour of entry, had been in Dublin, but had not been present.[28] At the end of August the frustration at their rebuff was outlined by McSparran when he restated his conviction that entry to the Dail would be a major boost to the anti-partition campaign, as it would help attract world attention. Not only did he feel that the issue should be left to a free vote but he was deeply angered that a:

> reasonable request had been treated in far too cavalier a fashion and enough attention had not been paid to the requests by elected representatives, who have at least as good a mandate to speak on behalf of their constituents and the Nationalist people of the North as the government in the 26 Counties has to speak on behalf of people there.[29]

As for attitudes in Dublin, MacBride again made it clear that his party's view on the subject had not changed and that they still believed that 'reunification of our national territory ... (would) be materially furthered' by allowing Northern MPs into the Dail or Senate. On the other hand, Costello, in a parliamentary reply, reiterated that the government had no intentions whatsoever to take such a step.[30] But this attitude angered MPs like Connellan who dismissed claims that there were great legal differences to be overcome to allow them to take their seats and instead accused political parties in the South of 'sheltering behind one another' on the issue.[31]

However, it appears that not everyone believed that this was the right strategy and in November in a letter to Healy, Maguire attacked the idea, 'To bottle yourself up in the Dail, a puerile and sterile policy. To leave the battlefront – cowardice'.[32] But Healy's reply made it be known that he was no great enthusiast of the idea either:

We were asked to go to Dublin by the last Convention. That is why we went – the wishes of the people. I never had any hope in sitting there. We have no work to do in the Dail – we are needed outside badly. Yet a large section of our people think that something wonderful would develop if we were there. Numbers will believe anything a clever crank suggests – until they try it out and see the folly.[33]

Yet Healy's view did not prevent the by-election in South Armagh being largely fought on the issue of entry into the Dail. At an APL meeting in Newry an appeal was issued to Seamus McKearney, the Irish Labour candidate to withdraw. This was to 'ensure that the call from South Armagh for a 32 County Dail should be unanimous and a stimulus to the nation to resume the national advance from the point where unity was broken in 1921'. But this demand was rejected by Diamond, acting as McKearney's election agent, and instead he called for the contest to be decided on whether the people would advance with the 'National Republican Labour movement ... (to) unity and freedom or backwards into the political wilderness with those who preach a discredited and futile policy of abstention'.[34] The result was announced on 7 December and in spite of a low turnout McGleenan emerged with a comfortable victory. (See Appendix 4: Election Results 1950-1956).

In his acceptance speech McGleenan made it clear that he would now do his best to ensure that the policy of the APL regarding its determination to seek representation in the Dail would be carried out. His victory was warmly welcomed by McSparran who commented that it was proof that the people of South Armagh were behind the anti-partition movement, whether its policy was 'attendance at Stormont, abstention from Stormont or representation in the Dail'.[35] Further congratulations came from the Executive of the League which met on 19 December and which agreed to send a delegation to accompany McGleenan when he visited Dublin to take his seat in the Dail.[36] However, before this attempt was made the new MP visited Dublin and met with representatives of the Anti-Partition Association to discuss how best to rally support for McGleenan in his efforts to sit in the Dublin parliament. According to the *Irish News*, McGleenan's preference was for the calling of a conference of all elected representatives in Ireland to approve a scheme under which Nationalist MPs would be allowed into the Irish parliament. This would attempt to reach an agreement on the powers and duties that they would have until a united Ireland was finally achieved. All this activity led the correspondent of the *Irish News* to suggest that the subject was causing a great deal of interest in Dublin and that MacBride and

Dr Noel Browne, had pressed in cabinet for a positive response to this question. It was also rumoured that unless MacBride got his way on this issue, he was prepared to bring down the government.[37]

In spite of the increasing signs of differences of opinion amongst Northern Nationalists, the leadership of the APL continued to argue for people to remain united behind it, as the only body that could co-ordinate anti-partition activity throughout Ireland and the world. Early in January McAteer appealed 'to people who hold different opinions from us to realise the necessity of having a movement like the APL', and for them to 'concede that even if the APL does not contain itself the key to absolute freedom it does provide a national platform to give our people an opportunity to voice their protest against partition'.[38] To support this point different speakers called for people to remain patient and in May Healy pointed to the fact that in five years the League had done more than any other organisation had managed in 25 years.[39] At a rally in Dublin he argued that through publicity in America and elsewhere, people would be forced to take notice of partition.[40] The APL saw itself at the forefront of this effort by their contribution to and distribution of literature from the Mansion House Committee in Dublin, such as *Ireland's Right to Unity* and *One Vote Equals Two*.

Even the passing of the Ireland Act was seen not as a setback but rather a boost to their anti-partition campaign. At the League's annual convention McSparran suggested that it had finally proved that all political parties in Britain were equally hostile to Ireland. However, he reminded his audience that it was just another piece of legislation that could be repealed in the future, if they succeeded in uniting the Irish race at home and abroad, in order to force the British government to end its unjust division of Ireland.[41] But the problem appeared to be that it was proving difficult to maintain this effort. For instance in Britain, activity after the general election never approached the scale of previous years and at the annual meeting of the League in Britain motions were passed calling for greater emphasis to be placed on recruitment of members and propaganda, rather than attacks on other political parties.[42] Similarly, in the South attempts to interest people there began to falter and there was little response from the authorities to the appeals from Nationalists to take a more active role in their campaign. Not only were the appeals for entry to the Dail ignored but other suggestions met with a similar response, such as the one from Healy for nationalists in Northern Ireland to receive financial assistance from Dublin instead of being forced to emigrate.[43] Other ideas were also disregarded: McSparran gave his support for the establishment of a non-political body in the South to deal with partition, on which Northern representatives could sit, the Executive of the APL backed the idea for the need to form a National Government in order to avoid political infighting until unity was achieved, and McAteer endorsed the formation of a government department to manage the anti-partition campaign with its own cabinet Minister, who should preferably come from Northern Ireland.[44]

Even though by 1951 there appeared to be little progress being made, the APL continued to argue that only if nationalists remained united behind it could anything be achieved. At its annual convention in Belfast, McSparran referred to the successful work it had carried out across the world and compared the position today with what they had found in 1945 when the League had been established. He remained confident that they could achieve their goal of a united Ireland, but in order to do so it was vital that they should 'avoid disharmony'.[45] Later in the year, however, Senator O'Hare spoke of the danger of widespread apathy and warned that if constitutional means were to succeed they would continue to need the assistance of the entire Irish race.[46] But there was little evidence of this occurring and, as a result calls continued to be made for greater help and assistance from the Republic. Although the Mansion House Committee had produced another in its series of anti-partition pamphlets, this time called *The Orange Card*, the demand was for more to be done. As in the recent past however, these requests went unanswered. One example being in February when the executive of the League asked the Minister of Posts and Telegraphs to allow them to broadcast a half-hour programme a week on Radio Eireann on the subject of partition.[47] Thus, the APL executive felt it necessary to pass a resolution heavily criticising the lack of attention given to partition in the South.[48] Further proof of this came with the general election in May that followed the collapse of the inter-party government. Healy received a letter from E.D. O'Gowan, asking for assistance, in his effort to stand as an anti-partition candidate in Cavan. In it, O'Gowan comments on the '... almost universal silence, on the subject of the Border's abolition during this election ...'.[49]

The only encouraging sign that was welcomed by the APL came from the organising of an all Ireland Local Government Conference in Dublin by the APA in December that attracted a large number of councillors from the North. It was organised according to the programme with the intention:

to strengthen and enlarge the scope of National policy in regard to Partition by giving men and women who have been fighting for their people as local government representatives, an opportunity to give their first hand evidence ... on problems confronting the representatives of nearly half a million loyal citizens of the Republic ...[50]

If things looked bleak in the South, it was nothing compared to the growing apathy faced by the APL in Northern Ireland that threatened its survival as an effective province-wide organisation. In June the Belfast Area Council of the League took its first and only entry into the election process when it nominated a candidate to contest the by-election for the Smithfield Ward on Belfast Corporation. However, in spite of the backing of the League's executive on 17 July, and appeals for the 'people to forget political differences and work for the common good', their nominee J. McGivern, lost his deposit in a contest dominated by a clash between the two main Labour heavyweights in the city, Diamond and Beattie. (See Appendix 4: Election Results 1950-1956).

As for activity by the League across Northern Ireland, the *Irish News* does not report the same number of meetings, rallies and other activities by local branches that it had done in previous years. The only area that seems to have been an exception was Derry City where, according to James Doherty, a prominent member of the APL at the time, the growing sense of frustration had produced a feeling that public protests had to be made in order to highlight the injustices felt by the nationalist majority in the city.[51] As mentioned earlier McAteer had advocated in his pamphlet, *Irish Action*, the need for peaceful acts of civil disobedience and in April he had been taken to court for refusing to pay his rates.[52] However, the most dramatic step taken by the APL was the decision to hold a small meeting within the city walls on 17 March, in order to challenge the traditional ban on nationalist demonstrations in the city centre, which had last been evoked in 1949.[53] About a dozen members of the League including McAteer, James Hegarty, Jack Harvey, Alderman McCarroll and Councillor Coyle, paraded down Shipquay Street with the Tricolour. The *Irish News* was to report that when the group entered Shipquay Street the RUC attempted to seize the flag, and in the struggle that followed, Doherty and a number of his colleagues were arrested, then released after several hours.[54]

But, as both James Doherty and Frank Curran made clear, the problem was that after a few days' publicity in the Irish press, the events in Derry were forgotten about.[55] There was now no organisation within Northern

Ireland capable of building on such protests as attention was focused on the internal debate going on within Nationalist ranks, as how best to advance their cause. This can be seen in the continuing attempts by McGleenan to gain entry to the Dail. At a rally in Dundalk he argued, that under the Irish constitution, he was entitled to take his seat and support came from Senator Lennon who told the same crowd that McGleenan had won the backing of the people of South Armagh for his demand to be allowed to sit in the Dail.[56] Then at its monthly meeting on 19 February the executive of the APL announced that a delegation would accompany McGleenan on his trip to Dublin on 1 March when he would seek to fulfil his electoral mandate.[57] However, Healy was extremely pessimistic that Lehane's motion on the subject, which was to be debated on the same day would be passed. He told Judge M.J. Troy of New York, 'We believe that FF will oppose our getting seats in the Dail. Fine Gael won't like us to be there ... only Clann ... are on our side ... when the ... motion comes before the Dail it is likely to be defeated'.[58] This prediction was to prove correct and, the *Irish News* reported on 2 March that the deputation of Healy, Connellan, Senator Lennon, McCullagh, Senator McNally and McGleenan heard their request to be admitted rejected by the Speaker. Earlier they had been present when Costello had told the Dail that Lehane's motion would not be heard until after the Easter recess.[59]

The disappointment felt by many within the APL was expressed by McSparran at its annual convention when he restated his belief that entry would have been a useful propaganda tool for their campaign. In spite of this setback, delegates unanimously passed a motion congratulating McGleenan in his attempts and calling on all TDs to support these moves.[60] But the question has to be asked whether all this effort was worthwhile since there was never any indication that it was a move that either of the two major parties in the South was prepared to make. This was again made clear when De Valera, the new Taoiseach after the May general election, told the Dail that he stood by his comments that the presence of Northern MPs would not assist the campaign against the Border. He concluded that it was impractical, 'since the Six Counties were not under the effective control of the Dail ... it would (not) be of much advantage. It would be tantamount to giving them representation without responsibility ...'.[61]

In spite of this statement, MacBride introduced on 19 July a motion calling for 'the elected representatives of the Six occupied counties ... (to) be given the right of audience in the Dail or Seanad'. When the debate got underway, De Valera repeated the reasons for his opposition to it and his determination to ensure that his parliamentary party voted against it. Whilst Costello was prepared to grant a free vote on the matter to his party, he outlined his hostility to the measure and his agreement with De Valera's assessment, 'that far from advancing the interests of ... the ending of Partition, it would very gravely jeopardise it'. In addition he shared the Taioseach's fears that it would bring the divisions amongst Northern Nationalists to the South and help, 'to cause further friction among our people ... particularly Deputies in this House'. Furthermore, he believed that it would be impossible for them not to become involved in domestic issues. This meant that 'the proper place' for Nationalist MPs was at Stormont where they could '... use that forum as a sounding board to disseminate our views and their views against the injustices of Partition and against the injustices ... inflicted upon them by that parliament of which they are members'. Not surprisingly, therefore, when the vote came to be taken MacBride's motion was comfortably defeated by 82 votes to 42.[62]

With their attempts to gain entry to the Dail blocked, the debate amongst Nationalists returned to the question of what their attitude should be towards taking their seats at Stormont and Westminster. Early in February McAteer strongly defended their presence at Stormont and expressed his disappointment to read of 'the wholesale and destructive criticism of those people who had gone unwillingly and at great personal sacrifice', to the Northern parliament. He argued that it was vital to show that the 'Nationalist people in the six Counties are still alive', and derided the alternative of abstentionism as 'sticking your head in the sand and doing nothing'.[63] Then in March Mulvey travelled to London to take his seat at Westminster and he informed the *Irish News* that, not only would he put forward the case of Irish unity, but that he would expose 'the growing religious intolerance and (loss) of civil liberty in Northern Ireland'.[64] His arrival was warmly welcomed by J. Fogarty, President of the Welsh APL, speaking at a meeting of the League in Enniskillen, and he urged them to send their other MP to Westminster 'to help their friends across the water ... to interest and enlist the sympathies of the British people in the cause of a united Ireland.'[65]

However, it would appear that not everyone agreed with such sentiments and Brian McBride, one of the nominees rejected by the Mid Ulster convention back in January 1950, accused Mulvey of breaking the 'faith' placed in him by the delegates who had voted in favour of abstention. He

firmly refuted Mulvey's claim that the 30,000 who had voted for such a policy had somehow changed their mind.[66] To try to reconcile the different
views McSparran, at the League's annual meeting, touched on the growing
dispute over whether MPs should remain at Stormont. In the interest of
unity he called on delegates to accept that 'neither attendance at Stormont
or the Dail' was going to hasten the abolition of the border, and asked them
to 'continue our movement with the same perseverance'.[67]

Meanwhile, pressure continued to mount on Healy to join his colleague at Westminster especially to assist the anti-partition campaign by
taking part in a debate in the House of Commons scheduled for June. In an
open letter to Healy, Maguire urged him to attend in order 'to prove the
organised discrimination and liquidation of the Catholic population of these
six Counties'. Not to do so would be to 'fail ... miserably and unjustly the
Catholic ... people of Ireland and the world'.[68] But, in his reply Healy, made
clear that although he was prepared to assist sympathetic MPs, he could not
attend in person as such a move would threaten Nationalist control of the
seat:

> Much as I regret differing from so vigorous an opponent of Partition as your-
> self, I feel I must ... observe the pledge I gave for the present. We have unity
> in the constituency. It would be a pity to stir up strife at this juncture. We
> may have a general election before the year is out, when the people ... shall
> have an opportunity of deciding ... upon representatives and the policy they
> want.[69]

In spite of Healy's absence on 1 June, G. Thomas, Labour MP for
Cardiff West, introduced a motion calling for a thorough review of the
working of the Government of Ireland Act 1920. In particular, he called
upon it to be 'amended (so) that the people of Northern Ireland are guaranteed by the Parliament of the United Kingdom, the same democratic rights,
impartial police, the absence of religious discrimination and franchise', that
the people in the rest of Great Britain now enjoyed. The ensuing debate
allowed Mulvey, and the remnants of the Friends of Ireland group, to highlight some of the alleged examples of discrimination and malpractice suffered by nationalists in Northern Ireland. But the mood overall of the debate
was summed up by the attitude of Labour and Conservative spokesmen who
implored people in the province to forget past differences and to begin to
work together. In the end Healy's judgement not to attend the debate looked
to have been fully justified when, after appeals from the Home Secretary,

Ede, and his Tory counterpart, the motion was withdrawn without being put to a vote.[70]

His caution was also vindicated when his prediction of an early general election was proved correct with the fall of the Labour government at the end of September with polling day fixed for 25 October. Soon the *Irish News* was suggesting that the mood in favour of abstention was declining in both Nationalist held seats. According to its correspondent, the feeling was that nothing could be achieved from boycotting Westminster and that it was more important to have both MPs present to 'contradict the false statements by Unionist members in regard to the political set up in the six Counties'.[71] Further evidence for the policy of abstention to be relaxed came with the call from the APL executive for the forthcoming conventions to select those 'prepared to attend Westminster on such occasions as they consider their attendance would be in the national interest'.[72] Yet there were elements within Mid Ulster in particular, who did not agree with such a view and at a republican gathering in South Derry, Brian Agnew was selected to contest the seat on an abstentionist ticket. It was also made quite clear that Agnew would not be withdrawn under any circumstances, even if it meant a split in the nationalist vote.[73]

The first selection convention to be held was for Mid Ulster where Mulvey had earlier made clear that due to ill-health he was unwilling to accept nomination again. On 7 October 180 delegates representing 30 of the 33 parishes in the constituency met and selected Michael O'Neill, a farmer and county councillor from Dromore, as their candidate. As to whether he would attend or abstain, if elected, it was agreed that the matter would be decided after the election was over, when a 'constituency committee' would meet and make a decision. In his address to the meeting O'Neill made no mention of the question and instead issued a request for nationalist unity and for everyone to use their vote, as it 'was the only weapon they could use in the present circumstances'.[74]

A couple of days later, the selection convention for Fermanagh and South Tyrone was held in Enniskillen and, with Healy's name the only one before it, he was unanimously re-selected. Again no decision was taken on whether he would take his seat and as Fr. Nolan PP of Fivemiletown commented, 'they could later decree their policy, but their paramount duty was to show their unity and strength and win the election'. This point was picked up by Healy in his speech when he stressed that the election, like every one since 1920, was an opportunity for the 'voice of the people (to tell) ... Governments in Westminster, Belfast, Dublin, America and everywhere else that they wanted to be included in a free land'.[75]

As in the past, the election looked as if it acted to draw the various shades of nationalist opinion together with the aim of ensuring that the seats were not lost. No further word was heard regarding Agnew's campaign in Mid Ulster and then a statement was released by the South Armagh Board of the APL, which contained the following appeal, 'While we vehemently dislike having any connection with Westminster or Stormont, we realise a vote not recorded is as good as a vote for the Unionists. Hence, 'If you have not ... protested through the ballot box against the Partition of Ireland, do so now'.[76]

When the results were announced both Healy and O'Neill had succeeded not only in retaining the seats but in slightly increasing the size of their majorities. (See Appendix 4: Election Results 1950-1956).

With Healy and O'Neill safely returned, moves began to be made to determine whether or not they would take their seats. Just before polling the Secretary of the Mid Ulster convention, F.H. MacBride, had written to Healy suggesting that a constituency committee, similar to the one they had established, should be set up in Fermanagh and South Tyrone. He then hoped that at some stage in the future the two could come together to draw up plans to hold a joint convention to decide on a policy.[77] Then on 5 November the *Irish News* reported that a joint meeting would be held in the near future to draw up plans to hold a meeting to decide upon whether the two MPs would take their seats.[78]

This took place early in the new year and it announced that a joint convention would be held in Omagh on 10 February.[79] Around 300 delegates attended and heard the case for remaining outside parliament put forward by Captain F. Devlin (ex-Eire Army). He maintained that 'parliamentary representation' had been a failure and that the retention of an abstentionist policy would make for useful propaganda in Ireland and further afield. The case for attendance was outlined by Frank Traynor and Fr. Nolan, PP of Fivemiletown, both of whom stressed the importance of both MPs taking their seats. They quoted from a letter sent from Tadgh Feehan, organiser of the APL in Britain, to the League's executive in Belfast, stating his belief that the presence of O'Neill and Healy was essential to their efforts on the mainland. After what the *Irish News* described as a 'lengthy discussion', the decision was taken by 189 votes to 142, for both MPs taking their seats.[80]

A few days after the meeting in Omagh, Healy and O'Neill travelled to

London to take their seats and they told the *Irish News* that they would not seek to affiliate themselves with any party or grouping at Westminster. In addition they 'would not take part in any debate unless the question of the Partition of Ireland could be discussed'.[81] When they finally arrived they issued a statement outlining their intentions:

> We are Anti-Partitionists who have been sent over to do what we can do to enlighten public opinion on the wrongs which the division of our country has caused. We hope to make friends with all members who are willing to help us. In British domestic affairs we have no desire to meddle ...[82]

In view of the events of recent months it is not surprising to find that for the time being the mood within the APL was very much against abstentionism. At the annual convention in March, McSparran issued a fierce attack on abstention, describing it as a policy that would bring only 'apathy and obscurity'. Furthermore, with their attempts to enter the Dail blocked, the only place 'where they could make their voices be heard was at Stormont and Westminster when ... their interests were involved'. It was perfectly clear that they 'could not help Irish Unity by sitting and doing nothing'.[83]

But there continued to be voices of dissension, especially in South Armagh, where the local board of the League repeated its intention to continue its work to secure a seat in the Dail. In addition, they believed that the vast majority of people in the area supported their view of the need for complete abstention from both parliaments.[84] On the other hand, Healy continued to stress the need for attendance and, at a meeting in November, claimed that due to their presence at Westminster a 'great deal could be done to bring pressure upon British MPs, especially in constituencies where the majorities are ... small, if they could get the Irish emigrants alive to the Partition issue'. He was to receive the backing of his audience for his stance when they unanimously passed a resolution advising him to carry on taking his seat at Stormont and Westminster.[85]

In spite of the problems that this ongoing debate continued to cause, there was still a determination to maintain the League's anti-partition campaign. Particular emphasis was placed on the need to secure greater assistance from the Republic. In August, at a demonstration in Clonmel McSparran invited the 'people of the 26 Counties to shake off their present apathy concerning the six Counties', and to put pressure on their politicians to become more active on the question of the border. The neglect of the issue in the South had, for many in Northern Ireland, been summed up by the refusal of the Irish government to allow them entry into the Dail. He warned that this had created the impression that they were frightened to admit Northern MPs, as they 'knew the very sight of our faces and the sound of our voices remind them that the problem for which men have fought for centuries is still unresolved'.[86] In order, therefore, to raise the awareness of partition in the South, the APL was happy to cooperate with the APA in Dublin to hold joint Easter Week celebrations in 1953, culminating in a major parade on Easter Monday in O'Connell Street.[87]

With Healy and O'Neill back at Westminster, the campaign in Britain looked as if it had received a boost and in September Feehan informed Healy, 'You are in great demand and I am constantly writing areas that at present you cannot speak for them'.[88] At a rally in Dromore, O'Neill spoke of the impact made at Westminster by the distribution of photographs showing the actions of the police at the disturbance in Derry on St. Patrick's Day 1952.[89] In June Healy was present at a meeting organised by the APL in Manchester and congratulated them on the 'vigorous state of the League there'.[90] But, in spite of these pronouncements there is little evidence to suggest that partition was on the verge of becoming a major issue in Britain. The problem remained the fact that the impact O'Neill and Healy could make at Westminster was negligible due to the tradition that matters concerning the internal affairs of Northern Ireland were not dealt with there. This was seen when Healy's attempt to raise the events in Derry on 17 March failed when the ruling was given that they concerned matters under the remit of the Stormont authorities.[91]

Within Northern Ireland the APL continued to try to promote itself as a body that spoke for the nationalist community in Northern Ireland. A prime example of this was to come with its call for a complete boycott of all events planned to celebrate the visit and coronation of Queen Elizabeth II. In April, they appealed to 'all school teachers not to associate themselves or children under their care with the forthcoming British coronation celebrations organised by Unionist groups in the area'.[92] Then on 1 July 1953 a proclamation was released which stated:

> Whereas we ... the elected representatives of the greater part of the portion of
> Ireland over which the British Crown and Government claim sovereignty and
> jurisdiction ... hereby repudiate all claims now made or to be made in the
> future by or on behalf of the British Crown, and Government to jurisdiction
> over any portion of the land of Ireland, or of her territorial seas.[93]

In addition the League also saw itself as the organisation that could successfully co-ordinate anti-partition propaganda, but by this stage there was little evidence of action on this front. The only real sign of any work came with a series of meetings to coincide with the visit to the province in April of Rev Lodge Curran, who had helped to organise various events in America. By October the Newry branch was calling for the adoption of a more vigorous approach, as they felt that the 'present policy was not broad enough in scope to hold the interest of all who favoured the abolition of the border'.[94] But, as in recent years, the message from the League's chairman, McSparran, at its annual convention was unchanged. With no significant developments, all he could do was to draw attention to the fact that it was the APL which was responsible for making partition an issue that was now known about around the world. It had also been responsible for overcoming the apathy it had found in 1945 and reviving 'the national spirit of the people'. He believed that the considerable progress being made in Britain and America would cease if they allowed the League to die at home. Finally, only the League could protect the minority community from having further injustices inflicted upon it by Stormont and act as an alternative to a policy of violence which would involve 'intolerable sacrifices for their people'.[95]

Only in Derry did the local branch of the League continue to try to engage in activities which attempted to arouse the interest and participation of local people. At Corporation meetings members maintained their policy of disrupting business when possible and in May, the election for Mayor was abandoned when McAteer seized the chair to protest at his defeat for the post.[96] There was also the attempt to hold a major parade in the city centre on St. Patrick's Day 1952. According to James Doherty, this was planned as an act of defiance against the 'unjust and oppressive' actions of the Stormont authorities in prohibiting the majority population from marching in their own city. Unlike the previous year, a large crowd participated and as they dispersed violence erupted on a scale, which men like James Doherty and Curran, later described as matching the events of 5 October 1968.[97]

Owing to the fact that it was impossible for the APL to influence events in the North, they continued to press ahead with their efforts to try to ensure that partition became a major political issue in the Republic. This can be seen, as already mentioned, with their involvement with the APA to hold a joint demonstration at Easter to coincide with the launch of De Valera's 'An

Tostal' celebrations.[98] This was held on Easter Monday in Dublin when, according to the *Irish News* up to 30 bands and 5,000 people marched in front of a crowd of 30,000 spectators. The occasion was used by McSparran to request that the Irish people play a much bigger part in their efforts to achieve a united Ireland. He also argued that the Irish government should take a more positive approach by taking steps such as allowing Northern MPs to use the Dail to raise the issue of partition, or establishing a committee representing all political parties which would work to solve the problem once and for all.[99]

However, the reality was that the issue was not on the immediate political agenda in the South and in February, a despondent MacBride informed Healy:

> Partition here is in the "Doldrums", neither Dev or Aiken even mentioned it in introducing their Estimates – which is the usual occasion for the declaration of policy in regard to it. We have had only one meeting of the Mansion House Committee in the last 12 months and were told by Dev that he was ... disposed to wind it up soon.[100]

The problem was recognised by Healy when he denounced 'southern apathy on Partition', which had been shown up by the fact that a recent appeal for funds by the League had resulted in subscriptions from only four TDs.[101] Disappointment was also expressed by Paddy McGill, who had recently been appointed Secretary of the League, when he criticised De Valera's An Tostal Celebrations. In particular, its failure 'to give our people here proof that we are part of the nation. The acceptance of our exclusion from the "national" celebrations is most disturbing ... I believe it is affecting our morale in the towns and villages'.[102]

Certainly all this did not help the APL, and although at its convention, McGill and McSparran stressed the important work it was carrying out, behind the scenes it appears as if it was in serious decline. The best illustration of this came when McGill suggested to Healy 'whether it would not be a good thing to try and keep clubs active and interested by a weekly news letter'.[103] Healy's reply hinted at the poor state of the League, '*Clubs*: Many of them exist upon paper and meet perhaps once a quarter. Your letter would go to one man and lie in his pocket'.[104]

Final proof that attempts had failed to draw the various shades of nationalist opinion together through the APL, came with the calling of a Stormont election on 8 September. As campaigning got underway it became clear that in three Nationalist held seats there would be contests between candidates who favoured attendance, and those who supported abstention. These were: Paddy Gormley against Agnew in Mid Derry, McAteer versus Maxwell in Foyle, and McCullagh against Liam Kelly in Mid Tyrone. In other areas there also appeared to be growing support for candidates pledged to boycott the new parliament. For instance, in South Armagh McGleenan was once again nominated and in East Tyrone a contest between the sitting MP, Stewart, and a Republican nominee, D. Mallon, was only avoided when negotiations to find an agreed candidate failed and Stewart secured the nomination on a toss of a coin.[105]

The depth of the split in Nationalist opinion can be seen in the bitterness of the struggles in these three constituencies. In Foyle, although McAteer was to describe his dispute with Maxwell as a 'family squabble', in reality it had a more serious tone and centred on the differences in approach of both men. For many in Derry, Maxwell represented the old style of politics, largely abstaining from parliament and tending to work on his own. On the other hand, McAteer represented a new approach which was not afraid to confront the Unionist establishment in the city. He had been at the forefront in the St. Patrick Day Parades of 1951 and 1952 and had worked closely with his colleagues to expose malpractice in the Corporation. This also involved public shows of defiance, such as his involvement in the protest of Nationalist members at the visit of the Northern Ireland Governor in February. As James Doherty later observed, McAteer was a "team player" whilst Maxwell was an "individualist".

The rivalry between the two men was not helped by the selection process established to choose a candidate. At the first meeting a tie resulted and the Chairman, Monsignor J. O'Doherty, refused to bow to tradition and use his casting vote for the sitting MP. A few weeks later a second convention was held and a number of delegates switched sides to support McAteer, and in the end he emerged victorious by a few votes.[106] However, this outcome did not please everyone and the *Irish News* reported that Maxwell had been approached by a number of delegations, to stand in order to protest at the 'method of selection adopted at the Convention ... (which) represented no more than 30% of the electors of the Foyle Division'. He then announced that, owing to these representations, he had agreed to stand as an Independent Nationalist and that he was happy to leave the choice up to the people of Foyle.[107]

Whilst Maxwell decided against holding any public meetings, the

McAteer camp held a series of election rallies at which they attempted to point out the differences between the two men. On 18 October, James Doherty, who was McAteer's election agent, declared it was up to the electorate to decide 'whether they wanted matters to be in the hands of an individual or team'. He also informed them that if Maxwell won then the present 'anti-partition' members of the corporation would consider resigning, as they would feel 'people were sick of the vigorous policy carried out by McAteer and his colleagues'.[108] In addition, McAteer was quick to refute allegations being spread that he had been forced out of Mid Derry. His decision to run in Foyle was based solely on the fact that Maxwell had failed to pursue a more active approach and declared, 'If I thought Mr Maxwell, even at this eleventh hour, were going to pursue a determined policy I would stand down and follow him to the bitter end as I have done in the past'. As for the controversy produced by his selection, he pointed out that at the outset both men had agreed to abide by whatever decision was finally reached.[109]

In Mid Derry, Gormley had decided to stand as an Independent Nationalist after having been approached to do so by business and farming interests. He was also keen to stress that the feeling in the constituency, especially amongst local government representatives, was that the APL was now a discredited and worthless organisation which had failed to look after the day to day needs of people.[110] His opponent, Agnew, had been selected at a Republican meeting in Dungiven and pledged to run as an abstentionist. As campaigning got underway his candidature received the public backing of Sean MacBride who spoke on his behalf at an election rally in Claudy. He described Agnew as standing for a 'concrete and definite policy' and would support him in his attempts to sit in the Dail.[111]

The intervention by MacBride angered Healy who sought to assist Gormley in defeating his abstentionist opponent by speaking on his behalf and trying to arrange others to do so as well. However, when it came to attracting speakers from the South to help, Healy was to encounter a few problems. On 17 October Senator P. Baxter, in reply to such an invitation, refused on the grounds:

> I don't agree at all with abstention but if the best we can do for the North is to go in there and take a partisan line on the internal situation then we had better remain out. You know I always disagreed with six County Nationalists coming down to ... the Republic as being harmful ... and (there) couldn't be any good coming of my going up there to support Gormley, even though I agree with his going to Stormont.[112]

This refusal angered Healy, who pointed out that Agnew had already received support from Southern politicians and that all he wanted to do was to try to 'balance matters so that the issue could be treated afterwards in a personal and not a party sense, as it will now'. In addition, he made clear his view that most of, 'if not all of our trouble is an imported commodity coming from across the Border'.[113] It was left to Healy himself to organise speakers from Northern Ireland to support Gormley and men like Lennon, McGill, O'Hare and Stewart did so. He also attacked MacBride's participation in a press statement by pointing out that, when a delegation had visited Dublin to further their claims to be allowed into the Dail, he had not bothered to attend the meeting 'to support the point of view which he now asserts is so vital'. As for abstention, at various public meetings Healy maintained that it had been a policy that had been tried in the past, had failed as it had got them 'nowhere', and as a result they had been 'obliged to go to parliament'. It was essential that they used parliament as a 'sounding board for their grievances' and referred to the fact that it was 'inconsistent to ignore parliament and to operate the laws passed here in their courts and local councils'. With regard to access to the Dail, he pointed to the fact that he had been part of the delegation which had been refused and, as a result, he asked whether they were 'to remain mute outside all assemblies as some were now suggesting.' Finally, he criticised the disunity being sown amongst nationalists in Northern Ireland and begged to know why people were attempting to 'disrupt' the APL in its purpose of 'embracing everyone', and why 'Mr Agnew entered the field and plunged them into a needless election'.[114]

The contest between McCullagh and Kelly in Mid Tyrone, although it received less publicity than the other two, still highlighted the same differences of opinion and future strategy. At the selection convention in Carrickmore where McCullagh was chosen, the delegates also recommended that the question of whether he should take his seat at Stormont should be left to the elected Nationalist MPs to decide.[115] However, just over a week later, Republicans also gathered in Carrickmore and selected Kelly, an 'ex-political prisoner', to fight the constituency on an abstentionist ticket.[116] In order to try to prevent 'further discord in our midst' McCullagh announced that he would not hold any public meetings to aid his campaign.[117] But this was not matched by Kelly who arranged a series of public meetings at which he made clear where he stood. He disputed Britain's right to govern Northern Ireland and attacked Stormont's right to exist and urged that people should not give it any credibility by associating with it. A few days later he repeated that under no circumstances would he take the Oath of Allegiance to sit in Stormont and that the people of Mid Tyrone had a choice which 'lies between the allegiance you have given in the past to the one undivided Republic declared in 1916, or a grovelling declaration of loyalty to a foreign Queen. Any self-respecting Irishman should have no difficulty in making the choice'.[118]

When the results were announced the issues raised were far from resolved. Although McAteer and Gormley had succeeded in defeating their opponents, in other areas there continued to be support for a return to abstention, with McGleenan returned unopposed in South Armagh and Kelly scraping through over McCullough in Mid Tyrone. (See Appendix 4: Election Results 1950-1956).

The aftermath of such a bruising contest saw an attempt to try to heal divisions and draw nationalists together again. The first indication of this came with the passing of a resolution at the monthly meeting of the APL executive, proposed by Healy and Gormley, whose presence had been welcomed by Stewart, who, according to the *Irish News*, commented that 'they were delighted to know that Mid Derry would be co-operating with them in the common task of the reunification of their country'. Their motion called on all elected Nationalist MPs to recognise the fact that 'as our people have given us a mandate to seek admission to Dail Eireann', that they 'should present ourselves as a body' to try to ensure this was granted by the Irish government.[119] This call had been made by the executive at its meeting in September when it had asked all candidates at the forthcoming selection conventions to ask 'electors for a formal mandate to continue their efforts' to achieve representation in the Dail.[120] An example of this was the gathering in Fermanagh which not only chose Healy as a candidate, but requested that he 'consult with his colleagues at Stormont as to the making of a further approach' to the authorities in Dublin on this subject.[121] Further support for this call of action came from O'Neill who, in a letter to Healy, pointed out some of the advantages:

> it would resolve a difficult problem here by completely cutting the ground from under the abstentionist's feet. Our main object is to preserve the Fermanagh and Tyrone seats at all costs. As you know in the present circumstances we are a bit apprehensive and I doubt if we could command sufficient united effort in the future.[122]

At the beginning of November, a delegation consisting of Healy, Stewart, McGleenan and Gormley visited Dublin to put their case before De Valera and Frank Aiken, the Minister for External Affairs. But as in the past the message they received was the same: a firm but polite 'no', and after a three hour meeting Aiken declared 'That the Taoiseach explained that the Government cannot depart from the policy already announced'.[123]

Around this time, events in Northern Ireland were dominated by the arrest of Kelly on charges of having made seditious speeches during his election campaign. After a trial in which he had refused to recognise the court, he was found guilty and bound 'over to keep the peace for five years', an offer he refused to accept and so he was imprisoned for a year.[124] These events seemed to provoke renewed interest in the South and in the Dail, Costello warned that Kelly's imprisonment could provoke unrest in Northern Ireland. Whilst, MacBride recommended that the government should allow his family to attend the Dublin parliament, in order to show their support for his stand.[125] Then a few weeks earlier the APA, at its Ard Feis, had passed a resolution calling on all Nationalist MPs to boycott Stormont until he was released.[126]

In Northern Ireland a gathering of up to 600 delegates from all over Tyrone met in Pomeroy to establish a new political party, with Kelly as its Chairman. The new organisation was to be called Fianna Uladh (FU) and amongst its stated objectives was '(1) to secure integration as a complete free and independent Republic ...', and '(2) that they recognise and accept the Constitution of the Republic enacted by the people on the 1 July 1937'. The meeting made clear its intention to form 'an organisation of Republicans in occupied Ireland into a disciplined political movement and to use every legitimate means possible to bring about the unification of the territory of the Republic of Ireland'.[127]

This acceptance of the 1937 constitution and recognition of Dail Eireann, which Sinn Fein and the IRA still refused to give, seemed to attract support in the South for FU and Clann na Poblachta tabled a motion criticising the imprisonment of Kelly. More worrying for men like Healy was the fear that this new movement could begin to interest anti-partition groups in the Republic, which had previously worked closely with the APL. In particular, he was angered by the passing of a motion at the APA's annual meeting calling on Nationalist MPs to stay away from Stormont and must have made these feelings known. In a letter to Healy from Eoin O'Mahony, Secretary of APA, the claim was made that the executive had worked hard to prevent a resolution being approved which had 'called on you and your colleagues to abstain with no time limit'.[128] A week later, he informed Healy that Kelly's case 'may lead to some awakening of conscience in the South ... that's why we are interested. We want to keep all good Irishmen and Nationalists together'.[129]

But this did nothing to placate Healy and he referred O'Mahony to sections of the speech made by the Chairman of the APA, P.T. O'Reilly, in which he had made it clear that, 'we (the APA) are in no way responsible for the decisions made by the League in the Six Counties'. He also wanted it made known that the reason for:

> the original decision of independence of the APA was the fact that the six County League is a political party handling the Nationalist Republican point of view there, but now another Nationalist Republican Party is in formation our original decision of independence is justified.[130]

This row with the APA simmered on into 1954 when Healy received an invitation from O'Mahony asking for assistance to organise a joint parade in Dublin on Easter Monday, similar to the one they had arranged in 1953.[131] This brought an angry riposte from Healy:

> It will be difficult to work up any enthusiasm for your day this year, after the resolutions you passed at your Convention which meant a repudiation of Northern Representatives especially from ... Fermanagh and Tyrone ... Even the Chairman in his address made it clear that your Association was not desirous of being too much identified with us in the future, now that you had ... Fianna Uladh to rely upon.[132]

A further attempt by O'Reilly to placate Healy, by stressing it was vital to hold a parade to arouse interest on the question of the Border due to the approach of a general election in the South,[133] met with an even more bitter attack on the APA. Healy concluded 'I cannot understand Eoin or you being taken by surprise ... Do you think we enjoyed being spat upon'.[134] This assessment appears to have been shared by others and in April McGill told Healy 'I had a pathetic note from ... O'Mahony beseeching me to go to Dublin for them. I am sorry to have to pass ... but we have been shoddily treated by that element of recent months'.[135]

However, in spite of these problems the APL was determined to try to continue with its campaign. At the annual convention in April which, according to the *Irish News* still attracted several hundred delegates, McSparran predicted that if people could remain united behind the League a great deal could be achieved. Although he recognised it would be a long struggle, he believed 'If we maintain our unity and ignore those critics ... we will be able to do much good for the people, and in the end achieve or make possible' the resolution of the 'one cause of dissension and enmity amongst the people here in the six Counties and between Ireland and Britain'.[136] As a result, the campaign on the British mainland was maintained with Healy and O'Neill engaged to speak at public meetings to try to get their message across. For example, in London in January Healy had again asked Irish exiles to organise themselves so that they could act as 'Ireland's missionaries in London and help in spreading the light that Ireland would never accept Partition'.[137] In order to sustain this effort the Mansion House Committee in Dublin had produced a film dealing with discrimination against Catholic families in the allocation of housing in the Tyrone village of Fintona. The film received its first showing in London in April before a group of journalists and it was announced that it would be distributed by the APL throughout Britain for screenings before interested MPs and trade unionists.[138]

However, these efforts in Britain continued to be hampered by the fact that it remained virtually impossible to raise issues at Westminster which were still considered to be the sole responsibility of Stormont. As O'Neill was to comment 'Whether it was from shame or embarrassment it was difficult to draw any comment from British leaders on the Partition issue'.[139] The difficulties were further highlighted by Healy's attempts to raise the Flags and Emblems Act which had become law in Northern Ireland in 1953 and which had given the police the power to prohibit any parade or event where the Irish Tricolour was to be flown. In a reply the Speaker's Office, at Westminster, had informed him:

that your question which stands on the Order Paper ... deals with a Bill now before the Northern Ireland Parliament ... Mr Speaker ... is ... of the opinion that the answer given on the 25 February by the Home Secretary to Mr O'Neill "has made it perfectly clear that this matter refers to the internal law and order of Northern Ireland, with which we have nothing to do".[140]

Furthermore, the British government continued to stress that the constitutional position of Northern Ireland was secure within the United Kingdom and this was made clear by Sir Anthony Eden on a visit to Belfast in April.[141] It comes as no surprise to find that McAteer, now League chairman, admitting that there had been a 'falling off in the formal organisation'. But whilst they had 'no definite ironbound policy to end Partition', he pleaded for people to give the League a chance to prove its worth and not to castigate it for failing to solve the 'problem of freedom for the Irish (which) had been with them for several centuries and ... had not been solved'. There was still a need for a body like the APL in which people who held different political views, could continue to come together to work to make partition a live issue.[142]

Whether the League was now capable of carrying out this task was open to question and, for Canon Maguire, the answer was a resounding no. In correspondence with Healy he denounced its recent efforts to arouse interest in the border question, 'It won't come through your APL, not enough vigour – too many there feathering his own nest'.[143] Earlier he had suggested the need for an alternative strategy, such as an 'awareness campaign', which would entail events and activities 'to focus the peoples' attention on the injustice of Partition'. As part of this process he proposed that Nationalist MPs should 'give up the idea of self respect in (their) Stormont tactics' and instead consider a more 'rowdy' line in their parliamentary work.[144]

But, Healy continued to defend the League and pointed out that, its executive 'consists of a majority of those outside Parliament ... It is a question of getting the most active ... we fill it as well as we can'. He also believed there was no alternative to the APL and that Maguire's 'awareness campaign' would amount to nothing more than 'talking to the converted'. With regards to parliamentary tactics, he pointed to the behaviour of Gormley and himself during the debate on the Flags and Emblems Bill which had ended with Gormley producing the Tricolour in the chamber and being suspended for his troubles. But he warned that 'If we get suspended too often the act will lose its novelty and indicate that we are just up to make disorder for its own sake'.[145]

Maguire kept up his demands for more activity, especially in parliament, and wondered why it was not possible 'to see the Opposition benches filled every day that business is on, and ... a vigorously active party outside ... Can we get no General Convention to go into all this in secret session?' This would then avoid the 'squandering of political energy on skirmishing with attendance and abstention'.[146] In his reply Healy was forced to admit that it was increasingly difficult to get a full turnout of his fellow

MPs as ' They believe in theoretical attendance' and pointed to the fact that only five had turned up for the committee stage of the Flags and Emblems Bill. Finally, in disagreeing with the suggestion of a 'general convention' to decide upon an agreed policy, Healy illustrated not only the problems this could cause but how deep the divisions amongst nationalists now were, 'it would only end up in some group walking out and showing our disunion upon the very issue that does not matter'.[147]

Although Maguire was calling for a more active participation at Stormont, others questioned whether they should be there at all. As a result, Gormley had to defend their presence by insisting that even though they had taken their seats, this did not mean they were 'compromising on the national issue'. They went 'to study the Unionist Party as a body and as individuals' and to 'gain some knowledge of their intentions'. Attendance at either Stormont or Westminster was a matter of tactics and not of policy'.[148] But there still remained others who completely disagreed with this especially in South Armagh and, at the annual meeting of the local APL, its secretary B. Magee declared that even though their request to enter the Dail had been rejected twice, they were determined to try again.[149]

Renewed interest in this idea surfaced again following the failure of De Valera to achieve an absolute majority in the election held in May and the formation of another coalition government under Costello. Within a few weeks of this the remaining Clann na Poblachta TDs, announced that they intended to nominate Kelly for a seat in the forthcoming Senate elections in order to 'allow him to represent the people of Mid Tyrone' and to 'show solidarity with the people of Northern Ireland in their struggle for a united Ireland'.[150] When confirmation of Kelly's election came the executive of FU warmly welcomed the move, 'We are glad to realise that the people of the 26 Counties have endorsed Liam Kelly's stand'. They also saw it as support for 'his policy of abstention from a foreign controlled parliament'.[151] However, the development alarmed O'Neill and Healy and they outlined their anxiety to Costello. They now renewed their demand to be given representation in the Dail and warned of the dangers if this was not granted:

> The recognition by An Dail of their separated kinsmen over the border would give them new hope ... Thus the views of the six Counties minority would be expressed in the National Assembly and the sympathy of that body conveyed to the people who need encouragement ... The position has somewhat changed of late, since the elected Representatives of Unoccupied Ireland have elected to the Senate one who has not been following a purely constitutional course

hitherto. If the Dail takes no further steps it may well be assumed in the North that the physical force policy is the only one which meets with approval down here.

Furthermore, they gave notice of the growing feeling amongst nationalists that attendance at Westminster, 'gives some show of authority for the occupation of their country' and the growing desire 'to withdraw our representatives from Westminster provided they can be admitted to Dail Eireann'. However there was a real danger that:

> If Abstentionist and Nationalists contest the seats we shall inevitably lose them to the Tories. That would be hailed in Britain and abroad as a new departure from our old policy and indicate satisfaction with matters as they are. This is, we fear, the likelihood ... at the next election unless our members to Westminster find seats in the Dublin Assembly.[152]

The test of the Irish government's intentions came late in October when MacBride and McQuillan again brought forward proposals calling for the introduction of legislation 'to provide that all elected parliamentary representatives of the people of the six Occupied Counties of Ireland be given the right of audience in the Dail or Seanad'. Once more, however, as the debate got underway it quickly became obvious that the main political parties were against any such move. Costello declared:

> I was, as I said at the start sympathetic at first towards allowing the right of audience in the Seanad ... I thought it might give comfort to our people in the North, that it might allay or even dissipate the feeling that exists that they are being neglected; but after the fullest consideration ... I arrived at the clear and definite conclusion that it might cause division down here, and would, if anything hamper, hinder and embarrass us in our efforts to end the unnatural boundary that exists in our country.

The Taoiseach's opposition was backed by De Valera and he concurred that it would not 'in the slightest help to solve the partition problem'. When the vote came to be taken, the motion suffered a heavier defeat than the proposal in 1951 by 100 votes to 21.[153]

Its rejection was followed by a final appeal from McAteer, in his role as chairman of the APL, which was carried in the *Irish News* and which requested a 'courtesy audience' in the Dail to enable him 'to put the Northern viewpoint on the question of the right of audience for six County representatives'. But Costello made it clear in a parliamentary reply that, in his opinion, the matter had been closed following the result of the recent debate and hence he rejected McAteer's appeal. McAteer's subsequent reply merely highlighted the frustration that had been building for years over the amount of help and assistance given to Northern Nationalists by the authorities in Dublin. It was now 'Evidently (clear) that the two main parties in the Dail are determined that no reproachful voice from the North will disturb their Kathleen Mavourneen policy on Partition'.[154]

In the background for a number of years there had been growing evidence that patience in constitutional methods was running out in certain quarters and Tim Pat Coogan charts the gradual build-up of preparations by the IRA to renew its military campaign against Northern Ireland.[155] Evidence of this stretched back to June 1951 when the IRA had raided Ebrington Barracks in Derry and had seized a huge haul of arms and ammunition.[156] This view was strengthened by another successful raid in June 1954 on Gough Barracks in Armagh which not only proved a major publicity coup but also, as Farrell suggests, raised morale within the organisation and boosted recruitment. Then in October, came the failed attack on the barracks in Omagh in which eight men were captured and later given lengthy prison sentences. Undoubtedly, as Farrell points out, 'the Omagh raid proved almost as invaluable as the Armagh one because the eight prisoners became heroes and martyrs to much of the Nationalist population'.[157]

Tension in Northern Ireland had also been considerably increased by the serious outbreak of rioting in Pomeroy in August when police had clashed with protesters holding a rally to mark the release of Kelly from prison.[158] At these developments Healy had taken time to warn the Stormont authorities, 'Ours is a constitutional movement, but I warn you that you will ... drive the people to other methods in the near future if you persist in this shameful and malignant course'.[159] But earlier, in response to the growing signs of a rise in support for non-constitutional methods to remove the border, he had made it clear that Nationalists were completely opposed to such a course of action. In a letter to the *Ulster Herald* he established that they shared the views of:

> Mr De Valera who in this matter speaks for Ireland, (and who) says that the present approach to partition must be a constitutional one. He sees no good in a rising of young men in one corner of the country ... We cannot have two opposing forces in operation at the same time ... (whilst) force may be advisable at certain points in a nation's history, but its timing must be determined by reasonable men.[160]

Of more immediate concern for Nationalists by the beginning of 1955 was the threat hanging over their hold of the two Westminster seats, which Healy and O'Neill had already made clear in a letter to Costello in July. Early in the new year SF had met in Northern Ireland to establish an election committee to begin preparations for the forthcoming United Kingdom general election, and to announce that candidates for all 12 Northern Ireland constituencies had been chosen.[161] There was now a real possibility of abstentionist candidates standing against Healy and O'Neill. But at the League's annual convention McAteer argued that this was a challenge they should meet head on, regardless of the risks involved, 'Let us if necessary lose the seats but at the same time we will have gathered the feelings of the people in those constituencies'.[162]

Yet behind this bravado there was concern that in any contests it would be SF who would come out on top and this can be seen in the search for suitable Nationalist candidates. In April McGill wrote to Healy:

> How about a candidate? We will need a strong man to run with Michael if we are to poll highly ... It is not fair to ask Michael to carry the burden unless he has a first class man with him. You are the only one who will get all the votes we need. You know this as well as any of us. I leave the implications to yourself but I am sure you will not refuse a service that is needed now more than ever.[163]

Despite this plea Healy felt obliged to refuse, as he had already announced on his last nomination that he would not be seeking another term in the future, 'I have said so many times that I cannot go back on that for any reason. I have not grown any younger in the interval'.[164]

When the announcement of the election came on 15 April, the *Irish News* was predicting that any split in the nationalist vote would undoubtedly result in the loss of the three seats currently held by non-unionists.[165] The risk of this occurring was referred to by an unnamed Nationalist spokesman who spoke to the *Irish News* and alleged that, in the past, the involvement of republican candidates had only resulted in seats being lost. It was then left to "Northern Nationalists" to come along and to begin picking up the pieces by rebuilding election machinery to regain the seats. In addition it was a disgraceful situation that candidates were being forced on local people from a 'small group in Dublin' without any consultations. Finally, he warned that a split in the vote would allow the Unionists to gain the seats and that such a result would be 'hailed by Partitionists and their British masters as a mandate for the immediate consolidation of Partition'.[166]

The first selection convention was held for Fermanagh and South Tyrone on 3 May in Enniskillen when 185 delegates met to decide on the two names before them: Frank Traynor and Philip Clarke, the SF nominee who had been imprisoned following his involvement in the raid on Omagh Barracks. In proposing Traynor, Healy insisted that a number of important issues had to be decided at this election. The first of these was whether they would allow 'outsiders' to dictate to local people over their choice of candidate. Secondly, they had to ask themselves the question of whether they were prepared to give support to a group which advocated the use of a 'physical force policy'. As to the intervention of SF in an election in Northern Ireland, he pointed to the fact that it had no mandate or popular support in the South. It was also important to remember that SF did not recognise Dail Eireann, which meant if Clarke were elected, and if in the future the Dail was opened to Northern representatives, they would be left with an MP who refused to take his seat even there. This would result in their constituency having a representative who refused to use any parliament as a sounding board to publicise the case for Irish unity or the examples of discrimination practised against nationalists by the Stormont authorities. He concluded by denouncing abstention as a worthless policy which had been tried in the past with disastrous results. For instance, he pointed to 1935 when 'the people who came down here from Dublin to force abstentionists upon them' and 'when the election was over, cleared out and they had not heard a hilt or hare of them since'. Over the last 20 years a great deal of money and effort had been put into building up a successful registration machine in the constituency which could now be ruined if SF triumphed. This would quickly fall into disrepair and the nationalist majority in the constituency would disappear for good.

The case for Clarke and SF was put by F. Drumm who appealed to the delegates to support Clarke as a reward for the sacrifice he and his fellow prisoners had made and to recognise that 'the spirit of young Ireland is abroad again'. When the vote was called Clarke emerged as a comfortable victor by 114 votes to 78. As the meeting closed Monsignor Gannon, who presided, called for everyone to assist Clarke, as it was clear that although they had differences on how to achieve their common goal of a united Ireland, this would be secured if they all worked together. The customary call was also made for unity to ensure that the seat was not lost and a request was made for the APL to 'put their machine and strength behind the selected candidate', not necessarily, to show they approved of SF, 'but to show

Republican unity against the enemies of Irish unity'.[167]   This brought no immediate public reaction from Healy but his disappointment at the result was shared with Desmond Greaves. In a letter he concluded 'I rather think the young people are so dissatisfied with Partition they are prepared to try any policy by way of a change'.[168]

The following week 167 delegates gathered in Omagh for the Mid Ulster selection convention and the decision was taken not to nominate anyone. This move was agreed upon, after a letter was read to the meeting from SF headquarters in Dublin requesting that their nominee, Thomas Mitchell, be given a clear run against any Unionist opponent. A delegate then proposed that the gathering should endorse Mitchell as their candidate. However, the former MP for Mid Tyrone, E.V. McCullagh, stated that if that occurred, he would seek to put forward somebody else. In order to avoid any dispute the convention secretary, Frank MacBride, suggested that they should agree not to nominate anybody and this proposal was carried unanimously.[169]

As campaigning got underway, the mood of the contest in the two constituencies is probably best summed up by a piece in the *Belfast Telegraph* by John Cole which dealt with matters in Fermanagh and South Tyrone. He drew particular attention to the fact that, although many nationalists with 'saner heads' were concerned about 'the threats of violence that have characterised SF campaigning in the Province', many were still being 'drawn to them by a mixture of sentiment for old battles and emotion about the young men in prison'. Furthermore, 'constitutional nationalists' were now being asked difficult questions 'which highlighted the frustration of many'. For example, 'What have you achieved?'; 'How many houses or jobs have you got for the people you represent?'; and 'What did you get done about the Flags Bill?'.[170]

When the results were announced, Mitchell and Clarke had managed to retain both seats although, their majorities were considerably less than they had been for Healy and O'Neill in 1951. (See Appendix 4: Election Results 1950-1956).

This performance was denounced by Healy and he alleged that instead of uniting the nationalists, SF had caused further division and this could be seen in the drop in the vote in both constituencies. The result, he believed, had caused enormous damage to the anti-partition cause:

It is difficult for any national-minded person to look upon the result with satisfaction. The census shows that we are 34% of the population but the total poll of SF is only 23.6% ... SF claimed they were coming up to unite the people; the figures show they have left them divided. Unionists are rejoicing ... They have handed over West Belfast to the Unionists ... in Mid Ulster they polled 29,737 against ... O'Neill's 33,097 in1951 ... in Fermanagh and South Tyrone ... polled 30,529 ... my own poll in 1951 was 32,717 ... in these centres alone they failed to poll 5,548 Nationalists ... Only for the public appeals like that of Canon Maguire ... to come out as Catholics, their numbers would have been smaller. The Nationalists left the field to them and they have made a sorry mess of it.[171]

The election victories of Clarke and Mitchell however, were soon in doubt as both men were serving prison sentences, and thus it appeared that they were not legally entitled to be MPs. In Clarke's case, the defeated Unionist candidate filed an election petition seeking to disqualify him and at Westminster steps were taken to have the result in Mid Ulster declared void. The investigation ended with Mitchell's victory being overturned and the ordering of a by-election. This was held in August between the same two men, with no signs of a Nationalist candidate being nominated. Much to the delight of SF, Mitchell was again victorious and this time his majority was increased to almost a thousand votes.[172] Following this, Beattie joined his colleague in petitioning the courts to have both men disqualified. Then in September and October came the decisions that as both men were 'convicted felons', they 'had been ineligible to be elected' and their seats were awarded to their Unionist opponents.[173]

The successful re-emergence of SF had seriously undermined the efforts by Nationalists to carry on with their own anti-partition campaign and they were forced to admit that there were growing signs of frustration at their lack of progress. Early in 1955, Healy had admitted to Rev Lodge Curran, 'I cannot say truthfully that we have progressed much towards freedom ... Our people are dissatisfied.'[174] Yet in public, the leadership of the APL continued to argue that their organisation offered the best chance of making any advancement on partition. At its last recorded annual convention in March, McSparran pleaded for people to be a little more patient and to allow the propaganda machine created by them a little more time to do its work. He remained convinced that Britain could be persuaded to leave Ireland once and for all by peaceful means. As a result he did not 'believe physical force is a policy that would produce fruit at the present time'. That the strategy of the League was working was picked up by McGill, who pointed to the successful distribution by the League of material such as the pamphlets produced by the Mansion House Committee. This had even been admitted by Lord Brookeborough who, on a recent visit to Australia and New Zealand had stated, "Up to my visit the people had not heard nothing but the Anti-Partition cause". Finally, McAteer urged everyone to unite behind the League and emphasised that it was not in the business of competing with other 'National organisations', but instead was working for the same goal of a united Ireland. When this was achieved the League would be more than happy to wind itself up. He finished by calling on the delegates to use the year ahead as a time of 'consolidation' before they made their 'final effort' against partition'.[175]

But the involvement of SF in political activity Northern Ireland had appeared to put an end to such ideas and Nationalists seemed to be unsure what to do next. After the Westminster election in May, James Slevin, a prominent Nationalist figure in Fermanagh and South Tyrone, had written to Healy. He not only expressed his disappointment at the result and Clarke's success but called for urgent action to be taken to prevent SF consolidating their position. One suggestion was to ask Healy if 'debates could not be arranged to argue the pros and cons of the Sinn Fein case'.[176] Whilst Healy agreed with the need to get 'our people' to meet to see if they could 'fashion some means of keeping the sane policy alive', he urged caution, 'With celebrations in the air ... I feel it best to let sleeping dogs lie – for a spell'.[177] Then, just before the by-election in Mid Ulster, the Bishop of Clogher informed Healy of his absolute opposition to the policies of SF and the IRA and his support for purely constitutional methods. The following offer was then made, 'These are my views and you are at liberty to make use of them if you think right'.[178] Healy, whilst thanking the Bishop was reluctant to bring him into a 'political quarrel' but would tell his colleagues of the proposal and that 'if a suitable opportunity offers ... make them known more widely'.[179]

If Nationalists were unsure of their next step, there were now those who believed that the time for constitutional methods to solve the border question had run out. Late in November, the police barracks in Roslea came under fire in an attack later attributed to Saor Uladh (SU), the military wing of Kelly's political party FU.[180] The growing threat of violence was then acknowledged by Costello in the Dail when he declared that the people in the South shared the 'feelings of resentment and frustration among the Nationalists of the Six Counties', and that it was not surprising 'that some of our people should despair of securing a rational settlement by non-violent means'. But he warned that only the Irish government, with the support of the Dail, could sanction the use of force and urged caution at this time as its adoption now 'would involve us in a civil war with those of our countrymen who are opposed to reunion'.[181]

Meanwhile, just as though it looked as if the saga in Mid Ulster had ended, came the news in December that an investigation had started at Westminster into the eligibility of Beattie. These centred on claims that at the time of his election he had held 'office under the Crown' as a member of a national insurance tribunal.[182] This raised the prospect of a second by-election and early in January 1956 SF held a selection convention in Omagh at which delegates from 23 branches in the constituency met and unanimously re-selected Mitchell.[183] The question now was going to be whether the Nationalists would stand aside yet again to allow Mitchell a free run. On 14 January Nationalists gathered in Omagh and at a meeting which the *News Letter* claimed was 'small and unrepresentative', consisting mainly of past and present MPs, Senators and a handful of their trusted followers', the decision was taken that they should enter the contest.[184] According to James Doherty, although Nationalists were reluctant to be seen as splitting the vote, they felt obliged to take on a group who advocated physical violence, in spite of the opposition of men like De Valera and Costello to such a move.[185] A statement was released after the meeting which made public their reasons for doing so:

> That as a united anti-partition vote in the previous elections in Mid Ulster has been represented as support for the Sinn Fein policy of defiance of the Irish Government, even to the extent of physical force against that government, it has been decided to put forward an Anti-Partition candidate ... on the simple issue of recognition by the people of the authority of the Irish Government to rule this country.[186]

However, it was to be the *News Letter* to ask whether 'Nationalists ... have been aroused by strong representation from Dublin where Fianna Fail and Fine Gael believe that they have been let down by the faint heart of Nationalists' in the constituencies of Mid Ulster and Fermanagh and South Tyrone.[187] Whether or not this was true is unclear, but there is evidence to suggest that some pressure was exerted on Nationalists from Dublin to take part. In a letter to Judge Troy in America, after the by-election was over, Healy bitterly commented, 'The APL in Mid Ulster would not have come into the open against Mitchell if it had not been encouraged by the Dublin Government. They said they would come down and support a campaign but they never turned up'.[188]

Now that the decision had been taken to enter the contest a selection convention was called for 22 January. The *Irish News* reported that around 250 delegates gathered and selected O'Neill as their candidate. In his acceptance speech he outlined his reasons for standing, 'My policy will be to maintain the Mid Ulster tradition of resistance to British claims to rule any part of Ireland', and to reassert its loyalty to the Irish government 'as the supreme authority in this country'. McAteer, who presided at the meeting, also defended their decision and pointed out they were keen to avoid 'hostility and ... will avoid any personal criticism of the candidate ... selected by the other side'. But, he claimed, as 'a group in the constituency', they had a 'better right to be heard than any group outside the constituency'.[189]

From the accounts in the *Irish News* it would appear that the decision was warmly received and the meeting held without any rancour. However. a different story emerges in the *News Letter* which gives some indication of the difficulties Nationalists were to face. From the floor came numerous complaints 'that the attendance was not fully representative of the constituency'. A delegate from South Derry declared that he was the only person present from that 'wide area' and support for his claims against the make up of the convention came from Strabane. As a result, a number of delegates made their protest and left the hall.[190]

With a contest between Nationalists and SF inevitable, interest now focused on the intention of the Unionists. On 17 January the *News Letter* reported that opinion in Mid Ulster was divided on the subject: some felt that they should take no part in another by-election, whilst others believed that they must take advantage of any split in the vote. Finally, the constituency's Unionist Association met and decided not to nominate any candidate on the grounds that 'having been twice at the polls in recent months they had sufficiently demonstrated the Loyalist strength of Mid Ulster'.[191] But this decision was to prove highly unpopular and over the next few weeks the *News Letter* carried reports of branches of the Orange Order and the Apprentice Boys openly criticising the move. It came as no surprise when George Forrest, an auctioneer and publican from Stewartstown, announced that he was preparing to stand as an independent Unionist. He told the *News Letter* that his actions had been 'prompted by the fact that the official Unionist Party have decided not to contest the seat. I have been approached by a large number of Loyalists ... to allow my name to go forward'.[192]

On 7 February, the report on Beattie by a Select Committee was presented to the House of Commons and it accepted the findings that, due to the fact Beattie had held paid government posts at the time of his election, he 'was incapable of being elected or returned as an MP'.[193] Subsequently, the by-election was fixed for 8 May and as campaigning got underway the *Irish News* reported that Nationalists were quietly confident of success. In particular they pointed to the fact that thousands of voters had refused to vote for Mitchell on 'conscience grounds'.[194] But in private they were less bullish and McGill told Healy, 'Michael is off to South Derry today. I hope he fares well but it is difficult territory and he will need the maximum assistance there'.[195] Similar views were expressed by Healy when he asked McSparran to assist O'Neill's campaign by speaking at some of his rallies, 'If we are to win, it will be necessary for everyone who can help to do so'.[196]

But the real difficulties facing O'Neill quickly became evident as his rallies were often plagued by crowds of hecklers, or from complete indifference from the electorate. On 30 April rival meetings were arranged for Plumbridge at the same time and when Gormley attempted to speak on O'Neill's behalf, the *Irish News* reported that 'practically everyone left' to go to hear the SF speakers. In Castlederg O'Neill and James Doherty had to endure a gauntlet of abuse and interruptions when they attempted to address a crowd.[197] The following weekend O'Connor and McGill had to abandon a meeting in Moortown when their loudspeaker van came under attack from a mob, which threw stones and attempted to overturn the vehicle. At a rally in Magherafelt McAteer alleged that threats had been 'mouthed to some of their speakers'. As a result, O'Neill was forced to cancel all his public meetings arranged for that weekend in response to what he described as, 'organised interruptions', a claim categorically denied by SF.[198]

These events had shown that in spite of the pleas made by McAteer back in January for a clean contest, the struggle between Mitchell and O'Neill had turned very nasty. This can also be seen in one of O'Neill's election pamphlets when he had denounced SF and all it stood for:

The issue is a very simple one. Sinn Fein, a small largely anonymous splinter group located in Dublin, having ... failed to get any support for their policy or candidates in the 26 Counties, put forward candidates in the six County elections, selected ... by nobody but themselves, relying on Nationalist solidarity in the face of the common enemy. The consequent victory ... was hailed as a Sinn Fein triumph. Strenuous efforts were made on every occasion to keep Nationalist candidates out of the field. This time those efforts have failed ... Sinn Fein claim that they alone ... represent the Irish people. They regard Dail Eireann as a "Partition" assembly ... They assert the right to wage war in the name of the Irish people ... Are you as responsible electors prepared to endorse these opinions from a self-constituted group elected by nobody, representing nobody and responsible to nobody but themselves ...

Reference was also made to the recent statements made by Costello and De Valera opposing the use of violence without the permission of the 'great body of public opinion'. This was backed up with the declaration of the Archbishops and Bishops on 29 January when they had declared, 'No private citizen or group or organisation has the right to bear arms or to use them against another state, its soldiers or its citizens'. Further, 'it is a mortal sin for a Catholic to become or remain a member of an organisation or society which abrogates to itself the right to bear arms'. O'Neill then ended with a plea to the electors of Mid Ulster not to be deceived 'by those who would use young men in jail for their own ends'.[199]

With the split in the vote Forrest emerged as a comfortable winner, but the real shock came with the extent of O'Neill's defeat as he finished in last place, thousands of votes behind Mitchell. (See Appendix 4: Election Results 1950-1956).

In spite of the outcome, in an address after the result was declared O'Neill emphasised that his decision to take part in the by-election remained a correct one as it had been essential to show that 'all National-minded people were not misrepresented as being in favour of a policy of physical force contrary to the advice of the leaders of the Irish people'. The blame for his performance was laid at the door of his Unionist opponent and he was convinced that without their 'deceitful tactics ... in putting up an unofficial candidate by backdoor methods', he would have defeated Mitchell.[200] The outcome in Mid Ulster passed without comment in the *Irish News* and it is left to an editorial in the *News Letter* to conclude on the reasons for O'Neill's poor showing:

> The Nationalist candidate has accused the Unionist Party of deceitful tactics, but the charge cannot be sustained ... for if he (O'Neill) and the Sinn Fein candidate had been left to fight the ... probability is that the Nationalists would have lost. Physical force and sentiment ... have greater pulling power with the Nationalist electorate. Besides ... (it) may well have felt that the Nationalist

candidate who came forward only at the third time of asking had left things too late ... Nationalists made a great mistake in giving the Sinn Fein candidate a clear run at the general election and subsequent by-election, and they are now paying for their timidity. It is regrettable that the Sinn Fein candidate should have scored so heavily at the expense of another, who declared himself opposed to any policy of physical force, but sentiment probably weighs more with the electorate than a desire for violence.[201]

The setback Nationalists had received was considerable and this was a fact they recognised themselves. Just a few days after the result, Lennon wrote to Healy and informed him that although they had been right to enter the contest, the outcome had been a complete 'debacle'. He described the help they had received from within the constituency as a 'disgrace' and which was 'fully reflected in the result, the consequences of which could be disastrous'.[202]

This was a conclusion that Healy was also to share and, in September, he notified Judge Troy that 'Our organisation has got a setback here'.[203] An example of this came with a letter to Healy from Traynor, a member of the APL executive, calling on the Chairman and Secretary to resign before the next convention in the hope that it 'would help to placate the public and (to) at least clear the APL of something for which they as a body were not responsible ... (for) participation in the Mid Ulster by-election'. He then went on to caution that unless 'drastic' action was taken immediately 'I don't think we shall ever recapture even a small part of our former popularity'.[204] Healy's response perfectly summed up his mood and the current state of Nationalist politics:

> The Chairman and all the officers will resign before the next convention. Meanwhile nobody wants these posts ... I don't see any good coming out of calling a convention now to wash our dirty linen and have scenes. The public seemingly are not much interested as to when we meet, nor indeed as to any National organisation at all.[205]

Now that matters had finally come to an end in Mid Ulster, the IRA carried on with its preparations to renew its campaign against Northern Ireland. In late November 'Operation Harvest', aimed at 'destroying communications, military installations and public property on such a scale as to paralyse the six county area', was launched with a series of bomb attacks along the border.[206] The threat of violence that Nationalists had warned of since the start of their anti-partition campaign had finally materialised. They deeply regretted its occurrence but firmly believed that the blame, lay not with their failures, but with the Northern Ireland government. As McAteer was to comment:

> The Stormont Government is a victim of its own folly and can take responsibility for the present tragic situation. They have been warned before, by myself and others, that their continual repression of and contempt for, the basic rights of the Nationalist minority would shatter everyone's faith in normal political action.[207]

Notes

1. *Irish News* 11 January 1950.
2. *Irish News* 17 January 1950.
3. *Irish News* 23 January 1950.
4. *Irish News* 30 January 1950.
5. *Irish News* 1 February 1950.
6. *Impartial Reporter* 9 February 1950, D2991/DS/Scrapbook (1), Healy Papers.
7. *Irish News* 7 and 17 February 1950.
8. *Dungannon Observer* 18 February 1950, D2991/D/Box 21, Healy Papers.
9. *Irish News* 2 February 1950.
10. *Irish News* 16 January 1950.
11. *Irish News* 14 April 1950.
12. *Belfast Telegraph* 30 January 1950.
13. *Irish News* 28 April 1950.
14. *Irish News* 1 May 1950.
15. Ibid.
16. *Irish Press* 15 May 1950, D1862/D/3, Mulvey Papers.
17. *Irish News* 15 May 1950.
18. M. O'Dolan to Healy, 26 June 1950, D2991/Box 3, Healy Papers.
19. Ibid., Healy to O'Dolan, 29 June 1950.
20. *Irish News* 24 April 1950.
21. *Irish News* 13 May 1950.
22. *Irish News* 12 June 1950.
23. Newspaper clipping, 23 May 1950, D1862/D/3, Mulvey Papers.
24. *Irish News* 6 February 1950.
25. *Irish Independent* 18 February 1950, D2991/DS, Healy Papers.
26. *Irish News* 13 May 1950.
27. *Irish News* 1 August 1950.
28. *Irish News* 7 August 1950.
29. *Irish News* 28 August 1950.
30. *Irish News* 17 August and 26 October 1950.
31. *Irish News* 13 November 1950.
32. Maguire to Healy, 3 November 1950, D2991/B/145, Healy Papers.
33. Ibid., Healy to Maguire, 5 November 1950.
34. *Irish News* 4 and 5 December 1950.

35. *Irish News* 8 December 1950.
36. *Irish News* 19 December 1950.
37. *Irish News* 22 December 1950.
38. *Irish News* 10 January 1950.
39. *Irish News* 23 May 1950.
40. *Irish News* 8 March 1950.
41. *Irish News* 13 May 1950.
42. *Irish News* 15 May 1950.
43. *Irish News* 8 March 1950.
44. *Irish News* 18 July, 3 October and 7 October 1950.
45. *Irish News* 29 March 1950.
46. *Irish News* 13 July 1951.
47. *Irish News* 20 February 1951.
48. *Irish News* 22 May 1951.
49. Brigadier E.D. O'Gowan to Healy, 22 May 1951, D2991/B/53, Healy Papers.
50. Programme of the All Ireland Local Government Conference, 10-12 December 1951 Mansion House Dublin, (PRONI), D3257/2, M. O'Neill Papers.
51. Interview with Mr James Doherty 16 August 1994.
52. *Irish News* 6 April 1951.
53. Interview with J. Doherty.
54. Ibid. and *Irish News* 19 March 1951.
55. Ibid. and Interview with Mr Frank Curran 2 March 1953.
56. *Irish News* 9 February 1951.
57. *Irish News* 20 February 1951.
58. Healy to Judge Troy, 15 February 1951, D2991/B/116, Healy Papers.
59. *Irish News* 2 March 1951.
60. *Irish News* 29 March 1951.
61. *Irish News* 6 July 1951.
62. D.E. Deb., v. 126, c. 1995-2270.
63. *Irish News* 7 February 1951.
64. *Irish News* 2 March 1951.
65. *Irish News* 3 April 1951.
66. *Irish News* 5 March 1951.
67. *Irish News* 29 March 1951.
68. Maguire to Healy, May 1951, D2991/B/145, Healy Papers.
69. Ibid., Healy to Maguire, May 1951.
70. H.C. Deb., v. 470, c. 564-653.
71. *Irish News* 26 September 1951.
72. *Irish News* 27 September 1951.
73. *Irish News* 26 September 1951.
74. *Irish News* 8 October 1951.
75. *Irish News* 11 October 1951.
76. *Irish News* 25 October 1951.
77. F.H. MacBride to Healy, 25 October 1951, D2991/B/39, Healy Papers.
78. *Irish News* 5 November 1951.
79. *Irish News* 19 January 1952.
80. *Irish News* 11 February 1952.
81. *Irish News* 19 February 1952.
82. *Irish Independent* and *Irish Press* 22 February 1952, D2991/DS, Healy Papers.
83. *Irish News* 27 March 1952.
84. *Irish News* 14 June 1952.

85. *Irish News* 14 November 1952.
86. *Irish News* 25 August 1952.
87. *Irish News* 18 and 22 December 1952.
88. Feehan to Healy, 18 September 1952, D2991/B/81, Healy Papers.
89. *Irish News* 24 April 1952.
90. *Irish News* 19 June 1952.
91. H.C. Deb., v. 497, c. 118-120.
92. *Irish News* 22 April 1953.
93. *APL Proclamation*, 1 July 1953, Irish Pamphlets: Anti-Unionist, Box 2, Political Collection, Linen Hall Library, Belfast.
94. *Irish News* 17 October 1952.
95. *Irish News* 27 March 1952.
96. *Irish News* 30 May 1952.
97. *Irish News* 18 March. Plus interviews with J. Doherty, Curran and Anonymous Sources in Derry.
98. *Irish News* 22 January, 3 February, 18 February and 25 March 1953.
99. *Irish News* 7 April 1953.
100. MacBride to Healy, 26 February 1953, D2991/B/60, Healy Papers.
101. *Irish News* 12 May 1953.
102. P. McGill to Healy 22 January 1953, D2991/B/24, Healy Papers.
103. Ibid., Undated.
104. Ibid., Healy to McGill, 9 February 1953.
105. *Irish News* 18 September, 21 September and 12 October 1953.
106. Curran, *Derry: Countdown to Disaster,* pp.12-13. Plus interviews with J. Doherty and Curran.
107. *Irish News* 9 and 10 October and *Belfast Telegraph* 10 October 1953.
108. *Irish News* 19 October 1953.
109. Ibid.
110. *Irish News* 17 October 1953. Plus interview with Mr Paddy Gormley 7 October 1992.
111. *Irish News* and *Belfast Telegraph* 19 October 1953.
112. Senator P. Baxter to Healy 17 October 1953, D2991/B/65, Healy Papers.
113. Ibid., Healy to Baxter 19 October 1953.
114. *Irish News* 19, 20 and 21 October 1953.
115. *Irish News* 30 September 1953.
116. *Irish News* 9 October 1953.
117. *Irish News* 14 October 1953.
118. *Irish News* 19 and 20 October 1953.
119. *Irish News* 28 October 1953.
120. *Irish News* 23 September 1953.
121. *Fermanagh Herald* 3 October 1953, D2991/DS, Healy Papers.
122. O'Neill to Healy, 4 August 1953, D2991/B/30, Healy Papers.
123. *Irish News* 6 November 1953.
124. Farrell, *The Orange State*, p.206.
125. *Irish News* 10 December 1953.
126. *Irish News* 30 November 1953.
127. Press Clippings, D2991/Box 3, Healy Papers.
128. E. O'Mahony to Healy, 5 December 1953, D2991/B/49. Healy Papers.
129. Ibid., 12 December 1953.
130. Ibid., Press Clipping, 29 November 1953.
131. Ibid., 10 March 1954.
132. Ibid., 11 March 1954.

133. Ibid., O'Reilly to Healy, 21 March 1954.
134. Ibid., Healy to O'Reilly, 22 March 1954.
135. McGill to Healy, 15 April 1954, D2991/B/24, Healy Papers.
136. *Irish News* 1 April 1954.
137. *Irish News* 19 January 1954.
138. *Irish News* 8 April 1954.
139. *Irish News* 19 April 1954.
140. D. Gordon, Second Clerk Assistant (Westminster) to Healy, 8 March 1954, D2991/B/Box 3, Healy Papers.
141. *Irish News* 3 April 1954
142. *Irish News* 1 April 1954.
143. Maguire to Healy, 3 April 1954, D2991/B/145, Healy Papers.
144. Ibid., 10 and 23 February 1954.
145. Ibid., Healy to Maguire, 13 February and 3 April 1954.
146. Ibid., Maguire to Healy, 17 February 1954.
147. Ibid., Healy to Maguire, 19 February 1954.
148. *Irish News* 17 March 1954.
149. *Irish News* 26 May 1954.
150. *Irish News* 16 June 1954.
151. *Irish News* 16 July 1954.
152. Appeal to An Taoiseach July 1954, D2991/B/51, Healy Papers.
153. D.E Deb., v. 147, c. 161- 248.
154. *Irish News* 15 and 18 November 1954.
155. T.P. Coogan, *Prelude to the Border Campaign, The IRA*, pp.327-376, (London, 1987).
156. Ibid., p.336.
157. Farrell, *The Orange State*, p.205.
158. *Irish News* 20 August 1954.
159. *Irish News* 13 October 1954.
160. Healy to the *Mid Ulster Herald*, October 1953, D2991/B/13, Healy Papers.
161. *Irish News* 14 January 1955.
162. *Irish News* 31 March 1955.
163. McGill to Healy, 5 April 1955, D2991/B/24, Healy Papers.
164. Ibid., Healy to McGill, 6 April 1955.
165. *Irish News* 18 April 1955.
166. *Irish News* 27 April 1955.
167. *Irish News* 4 May 1955.
168. D. Greaves to Healy, 5 May 1955, D2991/B/72, Healy Papers.
169. *Irish News* 9 May 1955.
170. *Belfast Telegraph* 26 May 1955.
171. Healy's Comments on the 1955 Election, D2991/E/38, Healy Papers.
172. F.W.S. Craig, *British Parliamentary Election Results 1950-1970*, (London, 1977), p.665.
173. Farrell, *The Orange State*, p.210.
174. Healy to Rev Lodge Curran, Undated 1955, D2991/B/108, Healy Papers.
175. *Irish News* 31 March 1955.
176. J. Slevin to Healy, 1 June 1955, D2991/B/32, Healy Papers.
177. Ibid., Healy to Slevin 6 June 1955.
178. Bishop of Clogher to Healy, 4 August 1955, D2991/B143, Healy Papers.
179. Ibid., Healy to the Bishop of Clogher, 5 August 1955.
180. *Irish News* 28 November 1955. Plus Coogan, *The IRA*, pp.360-361.
181. *Irish News* 1 December 1955.

182. Farrell, *The Orange State*, p.210.
183. *Irish News* 9 January 1956.
184. *News Letter* 17 January 1956.
185. Interview with J. Doherty.
186. *Irish News* 16 January 1956.
187. *News Letter* 17 January 1956.
188. Healy to Judge Troy, 29 September 1956, D2991/B/116, Healy Papers.
189. *Irish News* 23 January 1956.
190. *News Letter* 23 January 1956.
191. *News Letter* 17 and 21 January 1956.
192. *News Letter* 23 February 1956.
193. *News Letter* 8 February 1956.
194. *Irish News* 24 April 1956.
195. McGill to Healy, 31 January 1956, D2991/B/41, Healy Papers.
196. Healy to McSparran, 23 April 1956, D2991/B/27, Healy Papers.
197. *Irish News* 1 May 1956.
198. *Irish News* 7 May 1956.
199. Election Address, D2991/B/30, Healy Papers.
200. *Irish News* 10 May 1956.
201. *News Letter* 10 May 1956.
202. Lennon to Healy, 11 May 1956, D2991/B/15, Healy Papers.
203. Healy to Judge Troy, 29 September 1956, D2991/B/116, Healy Papers.
204. Traynor to Healy, 21 October 1956, D2991/B/34, Healy Papers.
205. Ibid., Healy to Traynor, 26 October 1956.
206. Coogan, *The IRA*, p.370.
207. *Irish News* 17 December 1956.

4 1956-1963:
The Illusion of Success

The electoral debacle in Mid Ulster and the start of the IRA campaign, not surprisingly, had led to a measure of confusion in Nationalist circles. Although Healy recognised the fact that 'Our national public up here feel they have been neglected ... (and) just look for revenge for the slights they have been subjected and any sort of raid seems to be of satisfaction',[1] it was also made perfectly clear by McSparran that nothing had 'altered his view or ... the views of other members of the Party, that the solution of partition would not be achieved by physical force'.[2] The question that now had to be answered was how the Nationalist Party was going to respond to the failure of its own anti-partition campaign and whether, this was going to entail a significant review of how they should seek to achieve their goal of a united Ireland, or work within the existing structures of Northern Ireland.

The first challenge to be faced was a Stormont election fixed for 20 March 1958. It appeared that the prospects for the Party had been improved significantly with the introduction, in 1957, by the Northern Ireland government of the Parliamentary Elections Procedure Act. This had established that at future Stormont elections candidates would not only have to sign a declaration promising to 'take their seats if elected and recognise the authority of the Stormont Government', but that this would have to be taken in front of a Justice of the Peace or Coroner of Oaths. According to a report in the *Irish News* the measure had been designed to 'prevent members of illegal organisations being returned and to prevent abstention'.[3] However, this did not rule out the possibility that SF would seek some way to avenge its defeat in Mid Ulster and the possibility that this could occur had already been indicated. A call had been made at a SF meeting in October 1956 for a call to be made for a complete boycott of future Stormont elections by its supporters and to hold some kind of an alternative poll either by people abstaining or spoiling their ballot papers.[4]

Nowhere was this threat more apparent than in the three Nationalist controlled seats in Tyrone, where small majorities meant that any such move

135

could result in the seats being lost. It was necessary to warn the electorate of this danger and O'Connor pointed to the intervention of Unionist candidates as an 'attempt to misrepresent Tyrone as no longer (being) a predominantly Nationalist county'.[5] To ensure that their vote was maximised it was going to be essential that the Nationalists stuck to their traditional message of stressing their determination to end partition and to highlight the injustices inflicted on the minority by the Unionists. A good example of this was the election broadcast presented by Lennon and McAteer on 12 March. Lennon bitterly attacked Northern Ireland as a 'Puppet state which exists ... as a result of anarchy, treachery and disloyalty', and that partition had been 'followed by a continuous record of ... injustice, intolerance and discrimination'. Whilst he ruled out the use of violence to achieve unity he repeated that his Party still believed that 'a re-united country would be a far better, happier and more prosperous place in which to live than a divided country could ever be'. McAteer, on the other hand concentrated on using Derry as an example of the way in which Unionist policy was geared to keep the 'Catholic minority in submission'. As a result he contended that it was no great surprise to find 'that our people have lost faith in democratic institutions', and that he and others had long 'predicted that frustration and cynicism of our political life here would inevitably lead to violence'. Yet, as Lennon concluded, until re-unification was achieved Nationalists were determined to 'expose Unionist injustice and to safeguard as far as possible, the welfare of the people in this area'. However, if this was going to be done it was essential that a strong presence was maintained at Stormont and so it was vital 'that every Nationalist vote is made to count in every constituency'.[6]

This message applied to contests right across the province. The South Down Election Committee urged all anti-unionist parties to co-operate and that in 'traditional-Nationalist constituencies' the main objective should be 'the healing of old sores'.[7] In Mourne, James O'Reilly, who had been selected to replace McSparran, who had decided to retire from political life, pointed out that 'our political opponents are encouraged' by the present divisions amongst those who called for a united Ireland. But it was important for people to remember that although 'we may differ as to the method of achievement, we all firmly agree on the main issue ... to see all our people united as God intended them to be'.[8]

In two constituencies, Foyle and Mid Tyrone, the election was to produce the first stirrings of a debate on what direction Nationalists should take to secure this aim and whether this should entail sticking to their present approach and principles, or whether they should attempt to broaden their electoral support and appeal. In Foyle, McAteer found himself opposed by Stephen McGonigle, a Labour candidate, and although both men were to stress their commitment to securing a united Ireland, they differed on how it could be achieved. On accepting the nomination, McAteer made clear he would fight on the basis of 'representation without compromise'.[9] The principles underlying this had been seen a few weeks earlier, when along with his colleagues on Londonderry Corporation, McAteer had opposed a resolution condemning the closure of the Royal Naval Air Station at Eglinton with the loss off around 400 jobs. As James Doherty commented at the time 'any Irishman who said he was sorry to see "occupying forces" leave would be a renegade Irishman'.[10] A similar response was McAteer's message, at various election rallies, when he refuted allegations that Nationalists had ignored social issues and pointed out that 'Where no question of national principle is involved, I have worked as hard as any man can work for employment, housing and the welfare of our people'. Furthermore, he warned the electorate not to be 'misled by the promise of a wonderful paradise. There is going to be no paradise for us until we have control of our affairs'.[11]

But on 8 March the *Irish News* reported that opposition to the stance taken by Nationalist Councillors at the closure of the military installation at Eglinton had grown in Derry. It then went onto speculate that McGonigle, secretary of the local branch of the Irish Transport and General Workers Union, was thinking about contesting the Foyle seat as a result.[12] Once he had decided to do so and had begun campaigning, McGonigle concentrated on accusing the Nationalists of becoming a 'single issue party' which ignored the important social problems such as unemployment. All that McAteer could do was to tell 'them about their ills, but he did not prescribe a remedy'. McGonigle promised that he would 'press strongly for measures to redress this evil' of unemployment from the authorities at Stormont. In addition, he would also seek to promote the cause of unity by 'promoting understanding and tolerance amongst all sections of our people as ... this is the only basis on which the real solution of this position can be attained'. It was not enough simply to keep on denouncing the border, he argued, and that even if Unionists agreed and partition 'disappeared overnight', they would still be faced with 'problems far more pressing than those now existing'.[13]

In Mid Tyrone the picture was complicated by the failure of nationalists in the constituency to come up with an agreed candidate and as a result
two men sought election: F. McConnell and Tom Gormley. The *Belfast
Telegraph* speculated that the contest had more to do with a personal rivalry
which had originated as a result of a clash in a local government contest.[14]
Yet there was an important difference and McConnell made clear that he
stood as a Nationalist who was determined to 'hold the fort', and 'keep alive
our national expectations and to strive to unite our people again for the common purpose that is dear to the hearts of all of us'.[15] For Gormley the decision to stand as a "Farmers" candidate did not entirely hide his other main
goal, which, according to his brother Paddy Gormley, MP for Mid Derry,
was to create 'a basis for a new policy broad enough to embrace all sections,
Nationalists, Sinn Fein and Labour'. In an interview with the *Irish News*
Paddy Gormley spoke of the need for this 'new approach' and the need for
a more 'realistic policy' on the facts of the 'situation as they found them
today'. He stated that:

> We want to get away from the conflict of Green and Orange and attempt to
> unite people on the material aspect. If there is to be representation at
> Stormont it should be on the material issues and really supplemental to our
> representation at local government level. We should try to promote the econ-
> omic solidarity of our people by every means in our power. The basic idea is
> co-operation and getting away from politics based on religious division.[16]

When the results were announced, Nationalists, like Healy, expressed
their pleasure at the results and the fact that their 'candidates did well in the
circumstances. We went out with seven; we return with eight'. McAteer
also made clear his delight not only at his own victory but at the defeat of
various Labour and Unionists opponents in other constituencies. In addition
he described the results as being a clear indication that people wanted the
revival of traditional, Nationalist unity and in a telegram to Eddie
Richardson, the victor in South Armagh, appealed that 'With your victory,
let our ranks be closed to meet the common enemy'.[17] (See Appendix 5:
Election Results 1957-1963).

With the election now over, attention began to focus on what role the
Nationalist MPs would take at Stormont and the *Belfast Telegraph* reported that there was a possibility of a change in tactics. In particular, the paper
speculated that there could be a move away from the old style policy of
attendance where there had been no attempt to organise or co-ordinate activity, and where it had been left up to individual MPs whether or not they

should take their seats and join in debates. The paper stated that there were MPs who believed that the increase in support for Nationalist candidates was a clear mandate for a 'more vigorous parliamentary representation',[18] and, according to Curran rumours began to circulate that this would involve the Nationalist Party becoming the Official Opposition at Stormont.[19]

The probability of change occurring had also been increased by the return of four NILP MPs in Belfast seats and they had quickly made it known that if the Nationalists did not want this role they were quite prepared to accept it. The impact that these Labour MPs might have on proceedings also greatly interested Frank Hanna and Diamond, the MPs for Central and Falls respectively, and both wrote to Healy. For Hanna it presented 'us with an interesting situation', and Diamond talked of the need to reconsider their position at Stormont in the face 'of all the enthusiasm, violence and sheer emotion'.[20] A few days later, Diamond's Republican Labour Party released a statement calling on all Nationalist MPs to assist the effort to form an effective and vigorous opposition to the Unionist government. This would allow for a more 'critical appraisal of the failure of the Northern Government to provide work and houses for all the people without discrimination of any kind'.[21]

The likelihood of the Nationalist Party becoming the Official Opposition at Stormont in conjunction with MPs of other political groupings was considered at a meeting on 31 March. At this, other Catholic MPs like Hanna, Diamond and Charles Stewart, an Independent member for Queens University, were invited to attend and according to the *Belfast Telegraph* on that afternoon it was decided to become the Official Opposition.[22] However, Diamond, whom the paper mentioned as the Chief Whip of this new body, was only too aware that the move suggested was not welcomed by all of the Nationalist parliamentary party. This was confirmed by Paddy Gormley who spoke of the intense debate the proposed step provoked and in particular the steadfast opposition from McAteer.[23] For Curran, McAteer's hostility was based firmly on his knowledge 'that in the prevailing mood of Derry Catholics it would be politically unacceptable for the Foyle MP to expouse such a policy'.[24]

It would appear that McAteer's views had a major impact on the debate. The next day a meeting of Nationalist MPs and Senators took place at Stormont and an extraordinary turn of events took place. In a complete reversal of the previous day's announcement a statement was released which announced that 'Our Party does not intend to take any steps to be recognised as the Official Opposition. As a Party our view has never been otherwise'.[25] A few years later Stewart, who had just been chosen to replace McSparran as Chairman of the parliamentary party, claimed that the decision had been reached unanimously. A different story, however, is recounted by Paddy Gormley and Curran, as well as reports in the *Belfast Telegraph* on 1 April. They suggest that McAteer backed by men like O'Connor and McGill, had threatened to resign and become an Independent Nationalist, rather than accept a move which he saw as a betrayal of principle, and recognition of the permanency of partition.[26] The possibility of a split seemed to have had its desired effect and the agreement reached on 31 March never materialised. As a result there was to be no 'associated Opposition, no Whip and no official leader of the Opposition'. The way was now open for the NILP to press ahead with its attempt to claim the title and on 4 April the Speaker, Sir Norman Stronge, announced that in the future they would be recognised as such.[27]

Another reason why certain Nationalists were reluctant to take on the role can be found in the reaction of leading Party figures to the election results and their interpretation of them. On 27 March McGill had written to Healy expressing the view that, 'All round the ... results are very heartening considering the gloomy forecasts ... we got strong support from several quarters hitherto apathetic; prominent individuals who had been on the other side a few years ago, came out and did their best for us'. One of the lessons he believed had to be learnt from the election was that attempts to bind various groups into a single body or organisation was futile and he advocated that 'we must organise on our own lines and let others who do not agree with us on policy do whatever they like'. It was perfectly clear attempts to 'organise everyone on the basis of a fatuous unity is only an annoyance'. In McGill's opinion, 'Labour are of no interest to us, they are a pro-partition group and as bad as the Unionists. Any form of Labour would only be a burden on us'. He concluded by arguing that the most important step to take was to ensure that Nationalist MPs and Senators had control of their own affairs and to 'make sure that there is no recurrence of the irritating and niggling moves from some of our associates on the former (APL) Executive'.[28]

This determination to ensure that the parliamentary party in the future would follow its own course was developed further by the end of 1958, when steps began to be taken to wind up the League. Frank Traynor, who was to act as spokesman for the remnants of the APL's Executive, requested from McGill a 'final meeting to wind up the affairs of the League in a proper manner'.[29] This inquiry was met with some suspicion by McGill and he informed Healy that the real reason was 'to make trouble', and 'to have a big pow-wow with all the dissidents gathered and hold a grand inquest to their glorification'. The fact that they had 'survived the recent election has given heart to the peevish ones', and they must take immediate action to ensure there would never be another 'Executive to harry and hinder the MPs and to assume the direction of affairs again'. Instead of a formal meeting McGill suggested that an audited statement be published and if necessary a 'formal winding up resolution' could be 'adopted and the money disposed of'.[30]

This offer obviously failed to satisfy Traynor and his associates and, in November, Healy received a letter signed by him, in his position as temporary secretary, along with McGleenan, as Chairman and two members of the executive Michael O'Neill and F. Hanratty, announcing that they had met on 17 November. They had unanimously decided to call, 'a full meeting of Executive members to consider the continuance or winding up of League activities in a proper manner', for 1 December in St Mary's Hall, Belfast. In addition, Healy was asked to bring with him all 'written or printed records,' accounts and documents or other papers ... in your possession and are the property of the IAPL'.[31] According to McGill, he had already informed O'Neill that 'there could be no question of the League being continued ... and that we could not recognise tomorrow's meeting', as it had been called without authority by 'discontented groups which had invited only those it thought well to ask'. Furthermore, he had again emphasised that the 'malcontents' were seen by the parliamentary party as trying to 'keep in being an Executive that in effect would be a sort of a directorate, insulting and commanding the Parliamentary Group and at the same time taking credit for Stormont exposures'.[32]

In the end, both sides must have come to some kind of an agreement and a meeting was arranged for 2 December to properly dispose of the League's assets and funds. However, McGill made it known to Healy that he had written to McAteer to advise him that as League Chairman, he should take a strict line. It was up to him to ensure:

> that Tuesday's meeting must be brief and deal only with the disposal of funds ... others would ask nothing better than that we had a whole discussion on Policy; having done their best to put the Attendance Group down (and failed), they would now like a share in discussing public issues ... Our men ... must see to it that they must be answered strongly on, what I suggest should be the

following lines: the balance is really a Special Fund, which has had to be robbed to pay the League's overdraft. Armagh did not pay one penny towards the Special Fund. The Fund should now be placed with the trustees to disburse for propaganda purposes ... at their discretion ... Gallagher, McGleenan and Co are all out to get some of the money. We must avoid this.[33]

Undoubtedly, 1958 had been a difficult year for the Nationalist Party but much to its relief, and satisfaction, it had survived the election relatively unscathed. Apart from the loss of Mid Tyrone they had managed to retain their other seats and see their total vote and per cent share of total votes increase from 27,796 and 10.8% in 1953 to 36,013 and 15.3% in 1958.[34] As the editorial in the *Irish News* concluded the 'prophets of gloom who foresaw the disappearance of the Nationalist Party are also disappointed. One seat Mid Tyrone, was the victim of disunity ... Elsewhere the Anti-Partitionists stood up to the battle well'.[35] Yet, this apparent position of strength does not hide the reality that the Party had serious problems to face and overcome. The most significant of these was the fact that with the collapse of the APL, the MPs and Senators had no effective, province-wide organisation behind them, either to assist their work or to seek advice on policy or strategy. This was a point Healy was later to concede to K. Smith, a member of the APL in Britain, when he pointed out 'we have practically abandoned any political organisation since the Mid Ulster constituency election some eight years ago'. As a result they had been forced 'to rely upon non-political bodies like the Nationalist Registration of Voters Committees for support'.[36] To a certain extent, as has been shown by the events surrounding the end of the APL, this was something that the parliamentary party had sought to enable them to dictate their own affairs. However, as Curran highlights, by doing so Nationalist MPs 'could almost be classified as Bishops in their own constituencies', running their areas as they liked and only coming together at Stormont to follow a broad anti-partition line.[37] A good example of this had occurred in 1958, when O'Connor bitterly objected to Healy receiving the credit in local papers for securing the release of an internee from the MP's own West Tyrone constituency. In a reply Healy apologised, 'I cannot say how sorry I am', and that he had taken steps to ensure that reports would appear which 'credit you alone with bringing influence to bear'.[38]

The lack of any proper party structure or organisation amongst Northern Nationalists had been a frequent occurrence since partition but, although a hindrance, had never been an issue that had provoked widespread public protest. As Ian McAllister concludes:

> Conventional conceptual definitions of the modern political party see its main function as providing an organisational framework that can, when set in motion, nominate candidates ... supply them with a coherent policy and hopefully win elections ... In Northern Ireland only one question- that of the constitution has dominated politics – this political activity has been rooted in tendency rather than ideology or political programme. This has consequently overshadowed both candidate and policy (and hence made organisation irrelevant) so long as a candidate declares his position on the constitutional issue. As the Catholics in Ulster were in a minority, the Nationalist Party could never hope to win elections, so political organisation became for them an irrelevancy. By contrast, organisation was essential to the Unionist Party in ensuring a uniform approach by candidates to the constitutional question and maintaining a cohesive Parliamentary majority.[39]

In addition to the point which McAllister makes, remained the attitude, as expressed by Rev Tomelty, President of Garron Tower, at a Social Study Conference at the school in August 1958, of the views that still existed within the Catholic community. For many the 'attitude on the part of the majority has produced in us a feeling of frustration, in that we are excluded from taking any effective part in the affairs of the community at large', and that the 'inclination is to isolate ourselves partly in self-defence'.[40] If this was therefore the case then there was no need for any kind of a political organisation. Rather, as E. Rumpf and A. Hepburn, suggest, all that was required was for the local Catholic Registration Committees to ensure that Catholics remained on the electoral register. As long as this was done they would be able to hold onto the seats where their numbers guaranteed a non-Unionist victor. Thus these committees had become 'a flexible instrument which could be put at the disposal of any anti-partition candidate of any persuasion according to the circumstances'.[41]

At the same time however the signs began to appear that not all of the Catholic community were entirely happy with the current position and that the time had come for them to move out of their "bunker mentality". The Social Study Conference in August 1958 had seen two speakers, Miss M.A. McNeill and Mr G.B. Newe, advocate the need for Northern Catholics to re-examine their attitude to the Northern Ireland state. For example, McNeill urged her co-religionists to accept the constitutional position as it now existed. Whilst Newe regretted that for far too long Catholics had used their 'vote to give expression to or to support views which all too often are rooted in emotionalism rather than shaped by reason'. As a result they had allowed a 'two nation concept to develop here in Northern Ireland' and 'where wide sections of the community did not co-operate with one another in many fields in which co-operation was possible without the sacrifice of sincerely held religious or political convictions'.[42]

By 1959 others began to pick up on this theme and at a Christus Rex Congress in Kilkeel, Mr D. Kennedy, a science teacher at St Malachy's College, Belfast, presented a paper entitled *Whither Northern Nationalism.* In this he referred to the significant developments that had occurred in recent times of which he believed the nationalist community had to take account. Amongst these were the first 'signs of a thaw in the political set up' in Northern Ireland with the recent electoral success of the NILP. There had been greater provision for nationalist and Catholic viewpoints by the BBC in Belfast which 'have dispelled many illusions about our faith in Protestant homes'. A further example of this change, he suggested, was the decision to fly the flag outside Belfast City Hall as a mark of sympathy at the death of Pope Pius XII. In the face of these events it was essential that the sterility of 'anti-partition' as a policy be reviewed in order to provide young people with some alternative to 'armed revolt'. It was, therefore, vital that:

> The new Nationalism must be prepared to accept the idea of the de facto Government and to cooperate with it in everything that was for the good of the community. But such co-operation must be from strength and not weakness. There must be a party in Northern Ireland willing to work with their Protestant fellow countrymen, a party believing in their national traditions, and with faith in their national future; a party openly committed to the cause of a united Ireland.[43]

This was followed, a few weeks later, by a series of letters to the *Irish News* by James Scott, a lecturer at Queens University. He too called for Catholics to become more involved in Northern Ireland society in order to improve conditions for all its people regardless of their religious or political persuasion. Now was also the time for the Nationalist Party to reconsider their present political position. In particular, he argued that the only alternative to the use of violence to achieve unity was by persuading the unionist majority in the North that their best interests lay with a united Ireland. As this was going to be a long-term process:

It seems to me obvious that the first step in such a programme is for the Nationalist Party to accept fully and honestly the present constitutional position ... and to make the basis of its policy the establishment of a constitutional opposition with a well thought out programme regarding matters such as employment, agriculture, social services and the removal of sectarian mistrust.[44]

Initially, it did not appear as if such views struck a public chord; instead, as an editorial in the *Irish News*, attacking the speeches of Newe and McNeill, commented it looked as if 'A false picture has been drawn of the Catholic community' with regards its reluctance to become involved or co-operate more fully with the government. It argued that 'Good neighbourliness will come if kindness, generosity and freedom from bigotry prevail on all sides, and not on one side alone'.[45] The attitude of the Nationalist Party to this debate was something similar and was probably best summed up by Stewart during a debate at Stormont. He submitted that Nationalists had gone as far as they could and had always tried to hold out the hand of friendship but had received little in return. There was therefore a limit to how far they could go:

The Nationalist Party had accepted the constitutional position to the extent they attended the House ... Co-operation could not be all on the one side. How could they have co-operation with public bodies who hold caucus meetings to make appointments of their choice irrespective, of the claims or qualifications of other candidates ?[46]

Before this whole topic developed any further, Northern Ireland braced itself for another election campaign this time, for the Westminster parliament in September 1959. In many ways it could not have come at a worst time for the Nationalists, as it once again exposed the party's lack of any kind of a structure or organisation. This became apparent as the question began to be asked whether or not it would field any candidates. At an early stage the *Irish News* felt safe to predict that they would not be doing so, as there were few signs of any meetings being arranged to summon selection conventions.[47] The decision not to do so was due largely to the fact that as far back as February, SF had made it clear that they once again intended to contest all 12 constituencies in the North. They had also requested 'that no shade of Nationalist thought will confuse the issues at stake by creating a situation similar to that created in the 1956 by-election in Mid Ulster'.[48]

But, as the *Irish News* was to report, it quickly became obvious that compared to 1955 the level of support for and activity by SF was disappointing.[49] In the end this was reflected in the results which saw the SF vote drop from 152,310 in 1955 to 73,415 in 1959, with seven of their candidates losing their deposits.[50] This outcome was quite obviously welcomed by the Nationalists, not only as an electoral setback for SF but as a justification of their decision not to enter any contest. As one of their spokesmen told the *Belfast Telegraph*, it vindicated their policy of sitting back to leave 'the field open between the Unionists and Sinn Fein', confident that the people would clearly 'reject the boys from Dublin'.[51] As Connellan had told the *Irish News*, before polling day, the 'circumstances were so exceptional that there was nothing to induce any sensible Nationalist to vote one way or other'. This was because to vote Unionist would be 'to endorse the partition of our country', and a vote for SF would be 'to give approval for a continuance of a physical force policy that has already proved disastrous'.[52] In the aftermath of the election Nationalist MPs and Senators met and agreed to try to arrange some kind of conference which would try to bring 'order out of the chaos resulting from Sinn Fein's intervention' in the recent election.[53]

But this call and the explanation given by Connellan did not appear to satisfy everyone. There were now those who saw the Nationalists as being equally to blame for a situation where again all 12 seats in Northern Ireland were held by Unionists. Some had now obviously lost patience with the party and in particular Curran's criticism of the lack of party organisation was shared by others. On 13 October a letter to the *Irish News* attacked the present leaders of the Nationalist Party for allowing the 'National cause' to reach 'rock bottom' in a political vacuum that had been allowed to develop due to the fact that 'in this area there is no organisation of any kind'.[54] A few days later another letter took up this theme and pointed to the fact that without any organisation 'Our people scattered and divided like sheep when confronted with the disciplined, efficient Unionist machine'. What was required was a new attempt to tackle the apathy that existed amongst large sections of the Catholic community especially in the 'business and professional classes'. As a result without the 'intellectual classes, organisation and leadership is extremely difficult'. A start could be made by obtaining 'premises in Belfast for a central organisation wide enough in constitution to admit Irishmen of all facets and political thought'. From this basis it would then be possible to begin to convince 'the headless ... (to make) a start pulling their weight to support and sustain our glorious heritage'.[55]

These were criticisms that obviously the Nationalist Party could not accept and O'Reilly replied to the attack in another letter to the *Irish News*. Concerning the elections, he argued, that once SF had announced their intention, they had no choice other than to try to avoid another damaging split which only 'makes it more difficult to heal the breech between the more rabid supporters of Sinn Fein and the rest of our people'. As for the Party itself, he referred to the work that had and was continuing to be done by Nationalist MPs at Stormont 'within the limits imposed by numerical inferiority aggravated by gerrymandering'. He concluded by accusing those critics who denounced them for not taking part at the recent election as being the very 'ones who are asking that the Party ... throw overboard the old traditional policy, to accept the status quo as inevitable and final, and to go into official opposition in Stormont, an act ... that would undoubtedly sound the death knell of the party'.[56]

However, this could do little to appease those who now saw the 1959 Westminster election as some kind of watershed in that if the Nationalist Party was unwilling or unable to confront SF, then the time was ripe for a fresh approach. A good example of this came with the establishment in Belfast in November of a new group called 'National Unity' (NU). As Michael McKeown, one of its founders explains, it developed through a group of people meeting over several months at the home of Dr James Scott, the Queen's lecturer, and deciding that something needed to be done 'to change the political situation in the North'. They had become 'appalled by the absence' of any organisation or grouping on the nationalist side that could 'appeal to Unionist voters or make a case on the Protestant doorstep for a united Ireland'. There was also the need for a 'political machine to exploit the enthusiasm of the young Republicans' and so attract them away from violence. However, they were reluctant to form a new political party as they felt 'Nationalist representation was already too fragmented' and so they wished to establish NU as a political study group:

> dedicated to the ideal of a united Ireland brought about by the consent of the majority of the people of Northern Ireland. It would pursue its aims by seeking to influence and rally support for the existing parties representing the nationalist people with the exception of Sinn Fein, and by promoting greater understanding of the Nationalist case within the Unionist community.[57]

The response of the Nationalist Party to such initiatives was one of indifference and there was no indication that they were about to forsake their traditional methods and approach. Instead Stewart again refuted the idea that they should accept the present constitutional position and made it clear that on this issue there could be no 'compromise'. If there were to be any, he maintained, this would be seen by people in Britain and around the world as a sign of weakness and indicate, 'that here in the North we were at one in recognising the permanency of British interference'. Whilst Nationalists remained in favour of 'good relations; harmony and friendship'; this could only be achieved if this was based 'upon a fair deal for every section. We demand that fair deal as our right, a right not to be gained by any surrender of principle on our part'.[58]

This continuing pledge to secure a 'fair deal' meant that the party had to continue to show that it could act as the protector of the interests and concerns of the nationalist community. One area that provided such an opportunity was the continuing controversy over the routing of Orange Order marches through predominantly Catholic areas. A good illustration of this was the traditional march along the Longstone Road, near Kilkeel in County Down. In 1955 holes had been blown in the road the night before to try to prevent a procession taking place but it had gone ahead accompanied by a large police presence in the area. The following year local people along the route 'fought a pitched battle' with the police to try to prevent a march taking place. By 1960 the problem still remained and at Stormont O'Reilly, the local MP, pressed for the parade to be banned. But the attitude of the government to such a plea did not change and was summed up by Brian Faulkner, then Minister of Home Affairs, who had on an earlier occasion declared that 'Orangemen would not tolerate threats about the freedom to march wherever they liked'.[59]

Later in the same year attention switched to the town of Dungiven, where a march by local Orangemen in July provoked serious disturbances.[60] This led Stewart to demand that Stormont be recalled to give Nationalist MPs a chance to raise the matter and Paddy Gormley, the local MP, denounced Faulkner for allowing the parade to take place. The Minister was also held personally responsible for the subsequent 'ill-feeling and bitterness' that the events in the town on the 10 July had provoked. Moreover, he promised to take 'this matter up at the highest level and ... have urged that we seek the recall of parliament to discuss the question of provocative parades with particular reference ... to Dungiven'. [61]

An alternative method of protest then appears to have been suggested by Healy and he proposed that a memorandum on the subject of Orange marches be presented to the authorities at Westminster. This was confirmed by McGill, in a letter to Healy, when he told him that one was being prepared and would be handed over to Mr D. Vosper, the joint parliamentary secretary at the Home Office, on his forthcoming visit to Belfast. McGill also took time to stress the importance of the issue in raising people's awareness of the work the party was doing:

> Paddy Gormley was on the phone to me ... and reports that the Party's stock in the Dungiven area ... has risen enormously by reason of our interest in the Orange procession ... even the Abstentionists are now asking "When will the MPs get a chance to get going in the Commons?" ... (his) personal stock has risen exceedingly and he is very pleased that his people approve the prompt action to expose the parade business. He tells me it is the best thing the Party has done in recent years ...[62]

The proposed meeting between Vosper and a Party delegation consisting of Stewart, McGill and Healy took place in Belfast on 13 August. At their press conference afterwards the three men spoke of their discussions and the issues they had brought to Vosper's attention. McGill, who had been present in the place of McAteer who was indisposed, presented facts in regard to the Londonderry Corporation and its alleged discrimination against the Catholic majority in the city. Gormley concentrated on the topic of Orange marches and the fact that they were 'invariably allowed, even where holding them was resented by local majorities in defined areas'. Due to this there was a 'widespread feeling among a third of the people of the six Counties that they were being denied a square deal in the matter of public rights'. As a result events had occurred 'where public resentment and anger' had boiled over into violence, a response that was welcomed only by an 'extremist wing in the Unionist camp' who were determined to 'thrive on public ill-feeling and civil commotion'. Stewart meanwhile gave general details of the discrimination suffered by the nationalist minority across the province, especially 'the permanent shutting out from those posts in the public sector to which their abilities and achievements entitled them'. Finally, he touched upon the absence of an 'effective franchise' at local government level that allowed Unionist minorities to control councils in Tyrone, Fermanagh, Armagh and Derry City.

For his part, Vosper welcomed the chance to meet a Nationalist delegation as he had come to Northern Ireland, 'to see things and meet as many people as possible ... (and) to hear their points of view'. He was certain that the Home Secretary was, 'anxious to ensure that the minority be heard' and so he would be reporting back 'all he had seen and heard'. However, as for some of the specific grievances presented to him he made it clear 'he did not accept everything he had been told' and that 'in other countries minorities felt they were not getting a fair crack of the whip, even in Britain'. With regards to Northern Ireland he therefore believed that 'every effort was being made to give the minority point of view a fair deal' and as for events in Dungiven those remained 'solely a matter for the Government of Northern Ireland'. This brought an angry riposte from Stewart who asked, 'How can you say that after what we have told you?'

Nonetheless, the Nationalist delegation seemed pleased with their work and McGill concluded that the practical result of the encounter had been the fact that:

> undoubtedly new ground has been broken and the Unionist sound barrier smashed ... Mr Vosper is now aware, and we have asked him to convey ... to ... his cabinet colleagues, that there is a case for investigation ... His visit and this meeting may well be commencement of a liaison that will blunt the edge of repression ...[63]

This higher profile being presented by the Party was also carried on at Stormont where it was again anxious to be seen at work on behalf of its constituents. A prime example of this came with the introduction of the Electoral Law Bill which Faulkner described as merely an attempt to 'consolidate into one comprehensive measure all important aspects of common law'. Yet for the Nationalist MPs it provided a chance to press their case for a reform of electoral boundaries and of the local franchise. Up to 200 amendments dealing with such matters, most of them tabled by the Nationalists were then set down for debate.[64] Over the next few weeks all the MPs with the exception of Stewart, who fell ill, attempted to force divisions on their amendments. By 24 November the *Irish News* reported that after 11 hours of debate 'less than a seventh of the 208 amendments tabled for the Committee Stage of the132 clause bill had been dealt with'.[65]

The government's response to the tactics employed by the Nationalists was to seek to speed the Bill through the House by introducing a guillotine measure to the Committee Stage. When this was done, McAteer led the protests by describing it as another step towards 'dictatorship' and an attempt 'to obliterate Parliamentary opposition altogether'. He concluded by stating, 'The way of the Nationalist MP in the House was a hard one. At times they were charged by the Government with not making full use of

Parliament, and now they were being "glanced at" ... because they were making use of ... procedure'.[66]

In spite of this apparent failure, Nationalists remained determined to carry on with their policy of providing a vociferous and constructive opposition. This was to extend into the economic field where by the late 1950s the Northern Ireland economy had begun again to experience severe difficulties. Its traditional industries of agriculture, textiles and shipbuilding were all in serious decline. The numbers employed in agriculture fell from 21,400 in 1950 to 13,100 in 1961 and in textiles from 72,800 in 1950 to 56,300 in 1961. Furthermore, in the first nine months of 1961 some 10,000 men were made redundant from Harland and Wolff.[67] To make matters worse, as Sabine Wichert concludes, 'Both the composition of her industries and the openness of her regional economy made her vulnerable to cyclical fluctuations ... The result was the region felt every decline in the UK's economic cycle more strongly than other areas'.[68]

One such period followed the election triumph of Harold Macmillan in 1959 when his Conservative government struggled to achieve the goal of all post-war administrations to secure economic 'expansion without inflation'.[69] This had been done by what became known as 'stop-go' economics. When the economy showed signs of overheating steps were taken 'to "cool it down" with strict controls which although bringing temporary unemployment would soon redress any imbalance in the 'Balance of Payments'. After a sufficient period these controls could be relaxed and 're-inflation could proceed'.[70] In the summer of 1961 the Chancellor of the Exchequer, Selwyn Lloyd, was forced to introduce an emergency budget that led to 'bank rates again hitting 7% and import controls imposing increases of 10%'.[71]

Nationalists were determined to take full advantage of the damage such measures could do to the economy in the province. McGill informed Healy that he had prepared material for Stewart ready to be launched 'once the Chancellor's restrictions are announced'. He also believed that the Party should press for parliament to be recalled in order to highlight 'the threat to living standards created by the British rise in tax intended for a Britain with full employment'.[72] At the end of July Nationalist MPs, along with those from the NILP, wrote to Lord Brookeborough to ask for parliament to be recalled in order to discuss the impact which the emergency budget could have on Northern Ireland. The refusal was denounced by Stewart in a letter to the Prime Minister and he referred to the fact that 'My party deeply deplore your decision ... (it) may be viewed by your colleagues and yourself to be good for the Unionist Party, but it is certainly not good for the pub-lic'.[73]   Further criticism came from Paddy Gormley when he accused the government of complacency and he asked Brookeborough whether or not 'the threat to our already all too low living standards of sufficient import-ance to justify recalling Stormont ? Has his government no thought for the tens of thousands unemployed or ... the uncertainty into which our farmers have been thrown'.[74]

A few days later McGill, in a letter to Healy, urged that their demand for the recall of Stormont should 'be pressed to the limit so far as publicity is concerned'. The government's reluctance to do so, he believed, was due to its fear 'that our MPs will call for a united front against the financial fan-tasies of the British Government as applied to this area ... it is surely up to us to let them see it is only the beginning'.[75] With no sign of any move being taken to grant Nationalists their wish, another option was proposed by Lennon at an AOH demonstration on 15 August. He suggested that an all party committee of MPs and Senators should be established to 'investigate the present economic crisis on the basis of non-party political considera-tions'. In the present conditions he argued it was the 'duty of all Nationalist public representatives' to assist all the people of Northern Ireland'. But it was also made quite clear that Nationalist participation would depend upon them not being asked to abandon their 'National ideals'. He emphasised that in putting forward the offer 'in your name and my own make it abun-dantly clear ... that whilst I make it with the deepest sincerity and for com-mon prosperity, we Nationalists must and do stand for a re-united, indepen-dent Ireland'.[76]

The attempt to maintain the high profile of the party continued into 1962, in the first instance with a renewed effort to obstruct and delay the Electoral Law Bill. Finally, after some 64 hours of debate and several all night sittings, forced by Nationalist MPs, the government applied its guillo-tine to close the Report Stage and so head off a further Nationalist amend-ment to ask for a third reading of the Bill. The performance and tactics of Nationalist MPs throughout the debate was defended by McAteer when he insisted that the 'Party had not wasted their time in pursuing their ... fight, as at last they had set a pattern and blueprint for the happy day when polit-ical reason came to this area'.[77]

Then in March 1962 came a major development when the party announced that it had sent a telegram to the British Home Secretary request-ing a meeting, during his visit to Belfast, in order to present evidence of 'religious discrimination and other matters concealed from you by your Unionist hosts'.[78] As a result for, the first time a Nationalist delegation, consisting of all eight MPs plus Senators O'Hare and Lennon, met a senior British government minister to submit a detailed dossier on examples of discrimination in Northern Ireland. Included in the material presented to the Home Secretary, Rab Butler, was a survey conducted by Nationalist Councillors in Derry showing the employment record of the city's corporation based on its own records. This revealed that no Catholics were employed in any of the following departments: the Town Clerk's office; the Rate Collector's office; the City's Solicitor's office, and the Welfare and Electricity departments. Of 69 administration officers only eight were Catholic and of 97 clerical officers 71 were Protestant. A similar story could be found amongst manual workers where of 25 corporation drivers only four were Catholic and of the 18 cleaners and messengers in the Guildhall all were Protestant.[79]

In a statement released after the meeting, Stewart declared that Butler had promised to consider all the matters raised and that they had also pressed him to establish an independent inquiry to investigate their grievances. The party was also now determined to keep up the pressure on this front and would be prepared to visit London for further discussions if that was felt necessary. But in spite of this initial optimism the prospects for this initiative looked bleak right from the outset. As with his colleague, Vosper, Butler pronounced that he had been happy to meet a Nationalist delegation and would study their dossier. But he would still have to 'rely on Northern Ireland ministers and departments concerned to furnish me with answers to most of what they submitted. I am not responsible for the detailed administration of Northern Ireland'.[80]

Throughout this period, therefore, the Nationalist Party had sought to present a much higher profile of itself and its activities but still this did not silence its critics. At the forefront of these was NU and at various events organised by it, the call continued to be made for radical changes in nationalist politics in Northern Ireland. For example in a letter to the *Irish News* in February, Dr Scott, outlined ideas raised at a number of NU meetings. Amongst them was again the belief that it was no longer good enough for nationalists just to sit back and complain about their mistreatment or simply wait for a united Ireland to solve all their problems. This had only resulted in frustration and apathy, particularly amongst young people who felt that nothing could be done or changed. They needed to embark on a fresh campaign to convince the unionist population that unification was not something to be feared. It was time therefore to draw up a 'blueprint' of what a united and independent Ireland should be like. This could only be done by building up a 'national organisation' capable of uniting all opposition groups or parties who believed in unity and co-ordinating their activities and policy. If this could be done the 'cynicism' of many could be overcome and by involving them in the political process a new generation of politicians could be produced.[81]

A further attack on the party came in the January edition of the magazine *Hibernia* by Ciaran McNally when he accused of it being no more than 'a collection of independent Nationalists who act as the spirit moves them'. In order to re-vitalise the anti-partition effort, he called for an organised campaign of civil disobedience through which people in Northern Ireland could 'paralyse considerable sections of the Northern administration by adopting a policy of non-payment of rates, taxes, social insurance contributions and by a discreetly applied system of non-cooperation in many aspects of government'.[82]

This constant sniping at the Nationalist Party angered people like Healy and in a reply to McNally's article and suggestions, he attacked them as being naive and unrealistic. He believed that, 'Such a plan inevitably leads to physical disobedience and force everywhere', and in any case any programme that involved the non-payment of rates and taxes would be ineffective as alternative steps would be taken to recover lost revenue.[83] As for the party's other critics, Healy rounded on them in a letter to Claude Gordon, the correspondent of the *Sunday Press* in Belfast. He argued that the:

> trouble has not often been with our own people but arises from those professing friends outside ... The latter may be of two types i.e. extremists who want to use the National position to improve their situation in the 26 Counties and who think we are not extreme enough. The others are individuals with anti-National views upon our problem, who think we don't give sufficient recognition to the permanence of Partition. They want us to drop the National opposition for one which cannot easily be distinguished from Unionism.[84]

The test of how far the Nationalists had progressed in recent years came with the calling of a Stormont election for 31 May. In its manifesto the party again re-emphasised its continuing commitment to secure a united Ireland and with a swipe at its critics made clear that this was 'not open to modification or amendment to meet any electoral breeze'.[85] This message was to be repeated throughout the campaign and in Foyle, McAteer, with reference to his Labour opponent McGonigle, stated that the people now had a 'choice between the traditional nationalism of their forefathers and the "cringing, crawling type of nationalism" that their opponents proposed'. Meanwhile in South Armagh at an election rally for Richardson, Healy was quick to deny the claim that Nationalists had failed 'to meet people's needs'. In addition, he insisted that 'whilst keeping unity and freedom of the nation at the top of their programme, they realised people had to live and nobody could ever say that their legitimate claims had not had attention from the Nationalists'.[86] He had already stressed this during an election broadcast when he outlined the work the Nationalist Party had always done in 'the interests of the common people'. For example he pointed to Devlin's attempts to secure the Old Age Pension at Westminster and that it had been them who had found 'tenant farmers on their knees to greedy ... landlords and left them standing upright, afraid of no man'.[87]

There was, therefore, not going to be any drastic change in the traditional message being given by Nationalists and this was made perfectly obvious by Healy in an election address in the *News Letter* which was simply entitled 'Unity as Ireland's Panacea'.[88] Others, too, were keen to emphasise this point, particularly at a time when the Northern Ireland economy was still experiencing difficulties. In his contribution to the election broadcast on 23 May O'Reilly stressed that until the 'national question' was solved the province's problems would continue. This was because London still controlled the North in a manner that put the interests of Britain first.[89]

As polling day approached, the party was quite pleased with their campaign and the response they had received and quietly confident that it would produce good results. In a note to Healy, McGill concluded 'All round on television ... radio ... newspaper ... our party has done better ... than ever before ... it is good to see public interest so favourable, it reflects the good work at Stormont over the past 18 months'.[90] When the results were announced this optimism was rewarded by a rise in the number of votes cast for Nationalist candidates from 36,013 in 1958 to 45,680 in 1962.[91] An added bonus came with the recapture of Mid Tyrone from the Unionists by Tom Gormley, who had on this occasion had been the only Nationalist nominee. In addition, in Foyle, as James Doherty points out, a great deal of satisfaction and pleasure was taken not only from McAteer's victory but also the sizeable increase in his majority.[92] (See Appendix 5: Election Results 1957-1963).

As an editorial in the *Irish News* concluded 'Of the parties contesting the general election, the Nationalists (are) the only one with good cause for satisfaction. It has won back Mid Tyrone an augury of unity and it has had increased majorities in its battles'.[93] The message, taken by the party from these results, was that they quite clearly continued to have the overwhelming support of the Catholic electorate. Another editorial in the *Irish News* a few days later commenting on the party's decision to again reject the role of Official Opposition, confirmed this. It stated that 'their's is the only political group that obtained a satisfactory vote of confidence. This vote is interpreted as an endorsement of their "as you were policy". Stormont will have to seek elsewhere for an Official Opposition'.[94] The evidence that this was the view of the Party came in Healy's letter to Gordon in October when he submitted that the election results 'saw us upon firm ground once more. The people showed we had their confidence'.[95]

The choice now facing the Nationalist Party was what to do with this apparent vote of 'confidence', particularly now that the IRA had been forced to call off its border campaign in February. The decision had been forced on them due to the action taken by the authorities North and South and the attitude of people 'whose minds have been deliberately distracted from the supreme issue facing the Irish people – the unity and freedom of Ireland'.[96] According to James Doherty and other sources in Derry, the feeling in Nationalist circles was that the time was right to try to seek to achieve some measure of reform without necessarily abandoning any of their principles. Instead of concentrating upon trying to expose various grievances the conviction grew that it was now opportune to see if by extending the 'hand of friendship' towards the unionist authorities some improvement in the condition of the nationalist minority would arise. At corporation level in Derry the decision was taken to relax the policy of boycotting official functions and Nationalist councillors agreed to attend the re-opening of St Columb's Cathedral. As Doherty declares, account had to be taken of the fact that for the foreseeable future they would have to live and work under Stormont. This meant that public representatives could not just sit back and allow their areas to be turned into 'economic graveyards'. It would be up to them to ensure that nationalist areas were not destroyed by the possible entry of Britain and Ireland into the European Common Market, and to try to guarantee that the government's pledge to regenerate the Northern Ireland economy would be extended to cover all districts.[97]

The first step in this process was the need to try to improve relations between the two communities in the province and it was to be McAteer who attempted to get this process underway. At a meeting of the party in Derry he proposed the establishment of direct Nationalist-Unionist talks to see if they could 'reduce religious rivalry'. While he claimed that the minority population had every right to raise examples, and protest at the discriminations under which they suffered, it was time to see if an agreement could be reached where religion was not an 'insurmountable barrier' to people obtaining a job, a house and any public or civic position. The matter was now of some urgency, he proposed, because in the changing world conditions, such as the onset of British and Irish entry into the Common Market, Northern Ireland risked being left behind. The comparison he drew was that 'we are two furiously battling mice in the path of a steam roller ... heedless of the doom that is overtaking both of us'.[98]

McAteer was keen to 'sound out' the Orange Order over his suggestion but, as Michael Foy highlights, he lacked any contacts within the organisation with whom he could begin discussions with. However, his attention was drawn to the fact that Lennon, as leader of the Nationalist Party in the Senate and vice-president of the Ancient Order of Hibernians, was on reasonably friendly terms with Senator George Clarke, Unionist leader in the Senate and Grand Master of the Orange Order in Ireland. He believed that 'if these two men could meet and discuss the problems of Ulster they might set an example that other public figures could emulate'.[99] Lennon was agreeable to the suggestion and at an AOH demonstration on 15 August he announced that he was willing to meet Clarke. He hoped that they could remove the 'stigma of religious discrimination' in Northern Ireland and attempt to create an atmosphere of 'toleration and respect'. Like McAteer, he warned of the danger if immediate action was not taken and that faced with the current critical 'unemployment conditions in this area and the unknown consequences of the advent of the Common Market, we owe it to our country as a whole to make an effort within the framework of our national aspirations to find these solutions'.[100]

Initially, the response to McAteer's initiative was mixed and Unionist opinion in Derry, whilst welcoming the idea of a meeting, reiterated that they did not believe that nationalists had any grounds for complaint. Furthermore, much of the division and mistrust in the city, they argued, had been the direct result of campaigns trying to prove something that was simply not true.[101] Clarke appeared to be more positive and offered to meet Lennon in October when he hoped 'matters relating to the goodwill of the

Ulster people as referred to in the Senator's speech may come forward for discussion'.[102] But in a note of caution an editorial in the *Irish News* entitled 'No Wind of Change', warned of too much being expected from these talks as there was yet little evidence of any 'change in Unionist Party policy towards the minority here'. It also drew attention to the cool response from Unionists to McAteer's first suggestion back in July. Equally important was the fact that, on 6 August, the Nationalist Party had received confirmation from the Home Secretary, that after consulting with the authorities at Stormont, he had decided there were no grounds for an investigation into the complaints of discrimination brought to his attention in March.[103]

In spite of these reservations both sides appeared keen that the proposed "Orange and Green" talks should be at least given a chance to get off the ground. Earlier in the year, Healy had received a number of letters from Martin Ennals, general secretary of the NCCL, informing him that the organisation was preparing to launch a wide ranging investigation into conditions in Northern Ireland.[104] Then in September McAteer had met Ennals and asked him to postpone any kind of an inquiry as it was vital to 'create the best possible climate' for the upcoming discussions between Lennon and Clarke.[105] Just over a month later, Clarke spoke of the obligation they had to all the people in the province to ensure there were better relations between the two communities and that both sides had a duty to 'strive ... to ensure a better understanding of each others problems'.[106] Finally, early in 1963 when Lennon sought to include McAteer and Healy in the talks, both men sought and received backing from Nationalist opinion in their own constituencies for the process and their involvement in it. Typical of the response which Healy received was a letter from Mr C.B. Leyden, Lisnaskea urging him to attend as any refusal to do so 'would leave you open to the charge of bigotry'.[107] At a meeting of the Nationalist Party in Derry, McAteer sought backing and advice on whether he should attend the next round of talks. The party's response was positive and informed him, that although they were aware of the risks involved for it in participating, they felt that if old rivals on continental Europe like the Germans and the French could co-operate, then it was right for the people in Northern Ireland to try to do the same.[108]

The first encounter between Clarke and Lennon took place in private on 17 October and in a short statement released afterwards they revealed that they had 'had a very wide, general discussion on the main aspects of social and economic life in Northern Ireland'. It was also announced that no further meetings were planned until after Clarke had reported back to a meeting of the Orange Order planned for December. It would then discuss the talks so far and what future steps, if any should be taken.[109]

This took place on 12 December and the *Irish News* reported that it had agreed to set up a committee to continue the discussions and invited Lennon, if he wished to take a similar step, and if that could be done both sides could meet again some time in the New Year. However, the problems facing the talks became only too apparent when at the same meeting, the Grand Orange Lodge invited Lennon to submit an agenda for the next round. Significantly this included the proviso that although this could include 'any subjects that would lead to a better understanding and goodwill between Ulster's people', it was also made clear that 'recognition of Ulster's constitutional position within the United Kingdom by Nationalists would be our choice for first discussion on such an agenda'.[110]

This prompted the *Irish News* to predict that Nationalists would find such an agenda 'completely unacceptable' although it did not rule out entirely the prospects for future talks.[111] The matter was then discussed at a meeting of Nationalist MPs and Senators on 18 December. In a statement released after the meeting they failed to give a definite opinion on whether the talks should be continued. Rather they pledged their support for discussions which it was hoped would 'promote good relations, rules of justice and equality in this part of Ireland'. It went on to point out that whilst 'wishing success to all such efforts', the 'value of the talks will be judged by results'.[112] Nonetheless, in an interview with the *News Letter* Lennon told the paper that he was determined to carry on with his 'informal tete-a-tetes', and that his party had left 'the door open for further talks and it is my intention to proceed ...'.[113]

Lennon's next step, as has already been mentioned, was to approach Healy and McAteer to assist him in drawing up an agenda and to join him for the next meeting. On 1 January he wrote to Healy 'I send you a draft letter and agenda and I would be grateful if you would ... amend them or alter them in any way you deem prudent or necessary. I have sent ... McAteer ... the same request ... how would you feel about coming with me to the meeting' ?[114] In his reply Healy agreed to attend and declared 'The agenda for the talks is excellent. It is neither such as your opponents could object to but at the same time it includes most of our grievances. These are expressed in tactful if unobjectionable terms'.[115]

A few days later, Lennon forwarded his agenda to Harold Budge, general secretary of the Orange Order, and stressed that it did not include 'anything which impinges upon any constitutional issue. In my view these talks do not provide a suitable or proper forum for any such consideration'. Rather he wanted to concentrate on five main topics:

> (1) That it is to the general good of the community that employment and advantages, especially in the public services should not depend upon considerations other than suitability and capability; (2) To consider Senior Appointments in the various public services; (3) ... to consider the membership of local authorities, statutory and semi-statutory bodies and the appointments made by them; (4) ... to consider to what extent embittered public feeling mitigates against full employment and may be responsible for the present Unemployment position; (5) ... to consider the present unsatisfactory housing position, the methods of allocation and possible improvements thereof.[116]

In his response Budge repeated that the Orange Order continued to see the constitutional issue as 'a fundamental point which must be accepted by all Ulster people if there is to be any real understanding'. With regards to Lennon's agenda, it was rejected as a basis for further discussions 'as the matters referred to by you are primarily the concerns of Parliament, where they have received frequent consideration to the satisfaction of fair-minded people'.[117] This was rejected out of hand by Lennon, who argued that he had drawn up his agenda in direct response to Clarke's invitation 'to discuss subjects that would lead to a proper understanding and good will'. He went onto challenge Budge by asking, 'whether your Committee desires to continue with the talks or to terminate them. Should your Committee be afraid to pursue the talks, and so indicate, then the matter is ended'.[118]

Clearly an impasse had been reached and although on 17 March Lennon again emphasised that Nationalists saw the proposed talks as a genuine attempt on their part to improve community relations, he also repeated that under no circumstances would they weaken their demand for a united Ireland.[119] Equally on the Unionist side attitudes had hardened and, at a meeting of the Central Committee of the Orange Order in April, it was announced that they were having difficulties in accepting Lennon's proposals as a basis for future discussions.[120] The whole process was now on the verge of collapse and in June Lennon, Healy and McAteer met to consider a letter from the Orange Order that again asked them to accept the constitutional position before the talks could resume. According to McAteer, the suggestion was akin to asking for 'unconditional surrender' and he accused 'inner Orange saboteurs' of forcing this condition on Clarke.[121] This was an allegation that Clarke refused to accept and he told the *Irish News* that from the outset he had made it clear that the Nationalist side had been informed that future progress depended on them accepting the constitutional position.[122]

In spite of this setback, McAteer remained determined to press ahead with his attempt to improve relations between the two communities. These hopes had been raised by the retirement of Brookeborough in March 1963 and his replacement as Prime Minister by Captain Terence O'Neill. From the outset, O'Neill stressed his and his government's intention to 'transform the face of Ulster'.[123] Late in October McAteer decided to test O'Neill's promise and wrote to him asking for a meeting on television in order to discuss the problems of a divided community:

> I have been wondering whether anything practical can be done to pour into concrete terms the buzzings which have been going around regarding goodwill, co-operation, wind of change ... It is evident that it would help the community as a whole ... if we met before these all seeing cameras for a frank and unscripted discussion on our hopes and complaints ... I do hope that you will ... consider the suggestion on its merits as an aid to better understanding. For my own part I ask you to believe that suggestion is born of only a desire to lift the scowl from the image of our mutually beloved North.[124]

O'Neill rejected the offer and in a reply to McAteer, his Private Secretary gave his reasons:

> The Prime Minister is entirely in agreement with you that improvements are only practical when expressed in "concrete terms". He feels, however ... that little is likely to be accomplished by further talk ... Captain O'Neill does not quite follow your reasoning when you argue that divisions ... are likely to be healed by a public confrontation between those whose views are widely different. Captain O'Neill, will of course continue to work for the best relations within the community and is glad to know that he can rely upon your practical support.[125]

In recent years one can therefore see that the Nationalist Party had sought to re-establish itself as a significant player in the political life of Northern Ireland. It was keen to show that whilst, as O'Connor stated, it had 'stood firmly by its principles' of believing in the 'unity of their country', it also accepted Paddy Gormley's point that 'they were liable to change' and remained the 'party of the future'.[126] But if Gormley's promise was going to be fulfilled it still needed to transform itself from a 'party (that) had no organisation in the country' and which continued to exist largely as 'a loose collection of individuals acting in harmony, but not in harness'.[127] This had long been a major criticism of the party from groups like NU and on the eve of the Stormont elections in May 1962 they had again appealed that the 'case for unity must be put through a common supra-national party organisation'.[128] In Derry City, where the party did have some semblance of an organisation with regular meetings and an open membership, according to men like Curran, James Doherty and Eugene O'Hare, many now felt that the time was right for the party to start organising in other areas and constituencies across the province. At a special meeting on 24 April 1963 the main topic under consideration was the 'lack of co-ordination' amongst different strands of nationalist opinion. It was agreed that the party in Derry should write to McGill '(1) expressing disappointment at the lack of routine co-ordination and discussion between the various Nationalist areas', and '(2) calling for a conference of public representatives at the earliest possible time'.[129] Similar ideas were being expressed to Healy from Maguire when he suggested the creation 'of your own Independent organisation capable of training your successors'.[130]

The attitude of the parliamentary party to these moves was one of caution and although they did not rule out the idea of creating a proper party organisation, neither was there any great rush to do so. At a party meeting in Derry members continued to press for a start to be made and suggested the calling of a conference 'on the same lines as other political parties'. In addition Alderman James Hegarty appealed for the 'MPs ... not (to) be afraid to sit down with public representatives in an attempt to get one policy for all Nationalists of the Six Counties'. This forced McAteer into denying that such an idea had been rejected by his parliamentary colleagues.[131] A few weeks later McGill, who remained as secretary of the parliamentary party, wrote to Doherty and told him that they were 'fully aware of the importance of maintaining the existing unity of purpose on policy, and in the respective constituencies, and ... will continue to avail of all opportunities ... to make it clear to all non-Nationalist sections that unity both in aim and method remains ... the constant concern of the members'.[132]

Such statements did little to satisfy members of the party in Derry and many remained convinced that the MPs and Senators remained reluctant to see any major change in the party's present structure. Suspicions centred around the fact that many of the parliamentary body were unwilling to see any interference in the way they ran their own areas or, which could threaten their personal control.[133] Whilst sources in Derry confirm that this was possibly a concern of a number of MPs, others were reluctant because of their experience with the APL. It had started with great enthusiasm, but as it had declined much of its workload had been pushed onto a few individuals. As a consequence, although they were keen to see some sort of reform and change to the way the party was structured and operated, they wanted it to be done slowly and cautiously so as to create something that would stand the test of time.[134]   Another reason why some of the MPs appeared to be so opposed to change was the fact that they did not believe there was any need for it as the results of the 1962 Stormont elections had proved. In reply to Maguire's appeal for the party to establish its 'own independent organisation', Healy had rejected the idea. He commented, 'You suggest we should spend maybe a year or two going around Sunday after Sunday organising – against what ? We are well enough organised. The last election showed our poll greater than (anything) since 1918. Why set up a new organisation – to enable all the old cranks to get a platform?'.[135]

However for Curran, O'Hare and James Doherty this reluctance of the party's MPs and Senators in taking the lead in transforming its image was frustrating. In particular they felt that the party needed to attract a new generation of people into its ranks, especially the new group of young, educated Catholics who had benefited under the 1947 Education Act. According to James Doherty this was vitally important, as across the province the party was finding it increasingly difficult to attract good quality public representatives for work that remained extremely demanding but largely went unrewarded. This was partly explained by legislation that forbade civil servants and teachers from contesting or standing for election, but equally, if not more important was the image and makeup of the parliamentary party.[136] By 1963 it was still being led by Stewart who was now 74 years old and had first been elected back in 1929. Two of its other MPs, Connellan and Healy, were 74 and 86 years old respectively, and had first entered politics in the days before partition. The other MPs and Senators were all men who had battled for many years at Stormont and local government level to uphold the rights and traditions of Northern nationalists. For a growing number of people therefore, especially in Derry, it was essential that the Nationalist Party took the lead in transforming its image and structure.

Others outside the party, like NU, however had grown to believe that they would not do this willingly. McKeown points out that in the beginning relations with Nationalist MPs and Senators were quite good and men like

Healy and Lennon had attended and taken part in many of their events. However, by 1962 relations had begun to deteriorate and had not been helped by the publication of a NU pamphlet entitled, *Unity – New Approaches to Old Problems*. As its author, McKeown, described it as mainly a 'critique of the way the national community has responded to the partitioning of the country'. He concluded 'that the calibre of the Nationalist MPs was that of adequate County Councillors' and that 'while a County Councillor might have been justifiably wounded by this, it did in fact incense the Nationalists'.[137]

Another area that was to lead to further friction was the question of what was going to happen at the next Westminster election and whether SF would again be the only choice for nationalist voters, particularly in seats such as Mid Ulster and Fermanagh and South Tyrone. Such a prospect clearly alarmed NU and with no evidence that the Nationalist Party was willing to take any action, it began to make its own position clear. In NU's bulletin in October 1962 coverage was given to the decision reached at its general meeting in September that:

> the organisation was free to contest parliamentary elections in those areas
> where it felt alternatives to the present constitutional position were not being
> clearly presented to the electorate ... We would like to stress that the decision
> ... was merely permissive and not mandatory, and whether in fact NU
> does mount the hustings will depend on the circumstances.[138]

The prospect of this happening was raised by Scott when he wrote to Healy and mentioned that while NU did not intend to nominate anyone 'against any other Nationalist candidate', it did want 'to have full co-operation and trust of whoever does stand in the next Westminster election, or if no one is in mind as a candidate, be free to make suggestions if we can find anyone we consider suitable'.[139]

By now, however, amongst Nationalist MPs like Healy there was a growing suspicion of the motives and intentions of Scott and NU. In reply to an inquiry from Maguire asking for information on NU, Healy accused it and Scott, of sharing the same views as men like Ernest Blythe, the ex-Irish cabinet minister. Over the last decade Blythe had been a constant critic of the Nationalist Party accusing it of amongst other things of failing to look after the interests of their constituents and calling for nationalists to accept the present constitutional position. Furthermore, Healy described Scott as someone who had hidden his real ambitions and who clearly 'wants to get a seat in Westminster'.[140] These were claims Scott always denied and in inviting McAteer to attend a NU function in February 1963, he again refuted the idea that it saw itself as a 'new National organisation'. Rather it still wanted to act 'as a link between all people who believe in a united Ireland'.[141]

There were now others whose patience with the Nationalist Party as a body capable of making any progress to securing its aims or improving the lot of the minority community in Northern Ireland had run out. In May 1963 in Dungannon the Homeless Citizens League (HCL) was formed under the guidance of Dr Conn McCluskey and his wife Patricia. The HCL's initial aim was to bring attention to the chronic housing shortage in the town, especially amongst working class Catholic families. This was to be achieved by the maintenance of up to date statistics on the problem and the holding of public meetings in order to draw attention to their complaints. An early success followed with an organised squat of a number of pre-fabricated houses due for demolition and when the Stormont authorities became involved a delegation from the HCL, along with Stewart, visited the Minister of Health and Local Government. As a result of these discussions a compromise was reached where the squatters were allowed to remain and, 'A new housing estate in the Nationalist ward was to be hurried to completion and the squatters were promised houses there'.[142]

In addition, as McCluskey points, out many of the people associated with this new group were also attracted to some of the ideas espoused by NU, such as 'the need to make re-unification conditional on consent, and secondly, on the need for a united opposition'.[143] McCluskey had written to McAteer and pleaded that the time had come for the Nationalist Party to change tack and to 'concentrate on getting our rights and trying to overcome gerrymandering. I feel that to mention the border just puts the Unionists backs up and some other poor devils lose their chance of a house or job'.[144] As part of this process he felt that it was essential 'for Nationalist politicians to organise a proper political party' and to ensure that SF would never again be left unopposed as the standard bearers of the minority community.[145] In both areas he was to be disappointed and in October he issued a warning to McAteer:

I am extremely concerned about the Nationalist Party. I went to see Joe Stewart about the two Westminster seats. He said you were not putting up a candidate in either. This could be understood in Tyrone and Fermanagh but in the other seats to put up no Nationalist would, I think, involve the risk of the Nationalist Party fading out. It cannot afford not to be represented.

If no Nationalist candidate went forward the next time he proclaimed, that along with others he was prepared to work with the 'Liberals and all forms of Labour' to secure an agreed nominee. Whilst he accepted that this might involve 'stopping the talk of anti-partition for the present', he believed this would be an 'excellent thing and get a bit of democracy in Northern Ireland for a change'.[146]

Notes

1. Healy to H.J. Matthews, 15 October 1957, D2991/Box 4, Healy Papers.
2. *Irish News* 6 February 1957.
3. *Irish News* 12 June 1957.
4. *Irish News* 6 October 1956.
5. *Irish News* 19 March 1958.
6. *Irish News* 13 March 1958.
7. *Irish News* 4 March 1958.
8. *Irish News* 15 March 1958.
9. *Irish News* 4 March 1958.
10. *Irish News* 26 February 1958. Plus interview with J. Doherty.
11. *Irish News* 14 and 15 March 1958.
12. *Irish News* 8 March 1958.
13. *Belfast Telegraph* 17 March and *Irish News* 15 and 18 March 1958.
14. *Belfast Telegraph* 17 March 1958.
15. *Irish News* 14 March 1958.
16. *Irish News* 13 March 1958.
17. *Irish News* 24 March 1958.
18. *Belfast Telegraph* 24 March 1958.
19. Curran, *Countdown to Disaster*, p.17
20. F. Hanna to Healy, 24 March 1958, D2991/B/3, and Diamond to Healy 25 March 1958, D2991/B/42, Healy Papers.
21. *Irish News* 31 March 1958.
22. *Belfast Telegraph* 31 March 1958.
23. Interviews with H. Diamond and P. Gormley.
24. Curran, *Countdown to Disaster*, p.17
25. *Irish News* 2 April 1958.
26. *Belfast Telegraph* 1 April 1958. Plus interviews with P. Gormley and F. Curran.
27. *Belfast Telegraph* 1 and 4 April 1958.
28. McGill to Healy, 27 March 1958, D2991/B/24, Healy Papers.
29. Ibid., F. Traynor to McGill, 11 July 1958.
30. Ibid., McGill to Healy, 28 July 1958.
31. Traynor to Healy, 24 November 1958, D2991/B/34, Healy Papers.
32. McGill to Healy, undated, D2991/B/24, Healy Papers.
33. Ibid., McGill to Healy, 27 November 1958.
34. Elliott, *Northern Ireland Parliamentary Election Results 1921-1972*, Tables 1.08 and 1.09, p.93.
35. *Irish News* 22 March 1958.
36. Healy to K. Smith, 5 September 1961, D2991/B/82, Healy Papers.

37. Interview with F. Curran.
38. R. O'Connor to Healy, 3 July 1958, and Healy to O'Connor, undated, D2991/Box 4, Healy Papers.
39. I. McAllister, 'Political Opposition in Northern Ireland: The National Democratic Party, 1965-1970'. *Economic and Social Review*, vol. 6 (1975), pp.354-355.
40. *Irish News* 4 August 1958.
41. E. Rumpf and A.C. Hepburn, *Nationalism and Socialism in Twentieth Century Ireland*, (Liverpool, 1977), p.186.
42. *Irish News* 5 August 1958.
43. *Irish News* 2 April 1959.
44. *Irish News* 28 April and 12 May 1959.
45. *Irish News* 12 August 1958.
46. *Irish News* 14 May 1959.
47. *Irish News* 9 September 1959.
48. *Irish News* 13 February 1959.
49. *Irish News* 6 October 1959.
50. *Irish Independent* 10 October 1959.
51. *Belfast Telegraph* 12 October 1959.
52. *Irish News* 7 October 1959.
53. *Irish News* 12 October 1959.
54. *Irish News* 13 October 1959.
55. *Irish News* 15 October 1959.
56. *Irish News* 24 October 1959.
57. M. McKeown, *The Greening of a Nationalist*, (Naas,1986), pp.18-19.
58. *Irish News* 18 March 1960.
59. T. McGurk, 'Nationalists' New Approach 1954-1965', *Irish Times* 9 September 1980.
60. *Irish News* 11 July 1960.
61. *Irish News* 30 July 1960.
62. McGill to Healy, 9 August 1960, D2991/B/24, Healy Papers.
63. *Irish News* 15 August 1960.
64. *Irish News* 17 August, 27 October and 10 November 1961.
65. *Irish News* 24 November 1961.
66. *Irish News* 29 November 1961.
67. Farrell, *The Orange State*, p.227.
68. Wichert, *Northern Ireland Since 1945*, p.59.
69. D. Thomson, *England in the Twentieth Century*, (London, 1965), p.261.
70. M. Pearce and G. Stewart, *British Political History 1867-1990: Democracy and Decline*, (London, 1992), p. 480.
71. Ibid. p.480.
72. McGill to Healy, 19 July 1961, D2991/B/24, Healy Papers.
73. *Irish News* 31 July 1961.
74. *Irish News* 4 August 1961.
75. McGill to Healy, 9 August 1961, D2991/B/24, Healy Papers.
76. *Irish News* 16 August 1961.
77. *Irish News* 12 January 1962.
78. *Irish News* 21 March 1962.
79. Pamphlet, *Rule by the Minority: How Democracy Works in Derry*, 10 March 1962, McAteer Collection. Plus Curran, *Countdown to Disaster*, p.21. Plus *Irish News* 9, 28 March and 1, 2 May 1962.
80. *Irish News* 24 March 1962.
81. *Irish News* 6 and 15 February 1962.

82. C. McNally, *Hibernia* January 1962, D2991/B/13, Healy Papers.
83. Letter from Healy, October 1962, D2991/B/13, Healy Papers.
84. Ibid., Healy to C. Gordon, 15 October 1962.
85. *Irish News* 17 May 1962.
86. *Irish News* 28 May 1962.
87. *Irish News* 24 May 1962.
88. *News Letter* 28 May 1962.
89. *Irish News* 24 May 1962.
90. McGill to Healy, undated, D2991/B/24, Healy Papers.
91. Elliott, *Northern Ireland Parliamentary Election Results 1921-1972*, Table 1.10, p.94.
92. Interview with J. Doherty.
93. *Irish News* 2 June 1962.
94. *Irish News* 18 June 1962.
95. Healy to Gordon, 15 October 1962, D2991/B/13, Healy Papers.
96. Coogan, *The IRA*, p.418. Plus *Irish News* 27 February 1962.
97. Interview with J. Doherty and Anonymous Sources in Derry.
98. *Irish News* 20 July 1962.
99. M. Foy, ' The Ancient Order of Hibernians: An Irish Political-Religous Pressure Group 1884-1975 ', (M. A. Thesis, Queen's University, Belfast, 1976), pp.158-159.
100. *Irish News* 16 August 1962.
101. *Irish News* 21 July 1962.
102. *Irish News* 20 August 1962.
103. *Irish News* 6 August 1962.
104. Healy to M. Ennals, June 1962 and Ennals to Healy 31 July 1962, D2991/B/85, Healy Papers.
105. *Irish News* 12 September 1962.
106. *Irish News* 10 October 1962.
107. C.B. Leyden to Healy, 8 January 1963, D2991/B/15, Healy Papers.
108. *Irish News* 8 January 1963.
109. *Irish News* 18 October 1962.
110. *Irish News* 13 December 1962.
111. Ibid.
112. *Irish News* 19 December 1962.
113. *News Letter* 19 December 1962.
114. Lennon to Healy, 1 January 1963, D2991/B/15, Healy Papers.
115. Ibid., Healy to Lennon, 2 January 1963.
116. Ibid., Lennon to H. Budge, 9 January 1963.
117. Ibid., Budge to Lennon, 19 January 1963.
118. Ibid., Lennon to Budge, 21 January 1963.
119. *Irish News* 18 March 1963.
120. *Irish News* 11 April 1963.
121. *Irish News* 19 and 21 June 1963.
122. *Irish News* 25 June 1963.
123. *The Autobiography of Terence O'Neill, Prime Minister of Northern Ireland 1963-1969*, (London, 1972), p.46.
124. McAteer to Captain T. O'Neill, 21 October 1963, (PRONI), Cab/9B/292, *Improvement of Community Relations inside Northern Ireland*.
125. Ibid., J.Y. Malley to McAteer, 24 October 1963.
126. *Irish News* 30 October 1962.
127. McAllister, ' Political Opposition in Northern Ireland ', p.356.
128. *Irish News* 24 January 1962.

129. Interviews with J. Doherty, F. Curran and Mr Eugene O'Hare 4 August 1994. Plus Minute Book of the Derry Nationalist Party 1963-1970, 24 April 1963, McAteer Collection.
130. Maguire to Healy, 12 December 1963, D2991/B/145, Healy Papers.
131. Minute Book of the Derry Nationalist Party 1963-1970, 17 July 1963, McAteer Collection.
132. McGill to J. Doherty, 5 June 1963, J. Doherty Collection.
133. Interviews with J. Doherty, F. Curran and E. O'Hare.
134. Anonymous Sources in Derry.
135. Healy to Maguire, 9 February 1963, D2991/B/145, Healy Papers.
136. Interviews with F. Curran, E. O'Hare and J. Doherty.
137. McKeown, *The Greening of a Nationalist*, pp.22-23.
138. *National Unity Bulletin*, October 1962, D2991/B/44, Healy Papers.
139. Dr J. Scott to Healy, 17 November 1962, D2991/B/15, Healy Papers.
140. Healy to Maguire, 9 February 1963, D2991/B/145, Healy Papers.
141. Dr J. Scott to McAteer, 17 February 1963, McAteer Collection.
142. C. McCluskey, *Up Off Their Knees*, (Ireland, 1989), pp.10-13.
143. Ibid., p.62.
144. Dr C. McCluskey to McAteer, 1 July 1963, McAteer Collection.
145. McCluskey, *Up Off Their Knees*, p.63.
146. McCluskey to McAteer, 3 October 1963, McAteer Collection.

5   1964-1969: Eclipse

By 1964, the Nationalist Party was beginning to find itself under increasing pressure from within its own ranks, and also from new emerging groups such as NU and the McCluskeys, to modernise its policies and image as well as transforming its structure and organisation. The task that, therefore, was to face the party throughout the 1960s was whether this could be done not only against the background of the traumatic events that were to occur, but also if it was going to be possible to come up with arrangements that would satisfy all shades of opinion. This can be seen by the establishment early in 1964 by the McCluskeys and their associates of the Campaign for Social Justice (CSJ), based on the idea that as 'we lived in a part of the United Kingdom where the British remit ran, we should seek the ordinary rights of British citizens which were so obviously denied us'.[1] On the other hand, Nationalist MPs, like Healy, maintained there was 'Nothing wrong with the Nationalist Party' apart from the fact 'that splinter groups would like to replace us', and O'Reilly reasserted 'eventual reunification' remained 'the mainspring of Nationalist policy' and the 'driving force to which all other acts are geared'.[2]

These apparent differences soon became public and the initial cause was to be a television debate between O'Reilly and Brian Faulkner in February 1964. The subject under discussion was to be the issue of religious discrimination in Northern Ireland and it seemed to offer the Nationalist Party a perfect opportunity not only to present detailed evidence of examples but also to show a wider audience that it was capable of successfully campaigning to rectify these.

This process had already got underway with the launch a month earlier by the party of 'Operation Truth and Justice' in which the aim was to visit London and place before the main political parties in Britain the 'disabilities operating against Catholics in the Six Counties'.[3] Although the Prime Minister, Sir Alec Douglas-Home, and the opposition leader Harold Wilson, refused to meet with the Nationalist MPs and Senators on their visit, some comfort was taken from their meeting with Jo Grimmond, leader of the Liberal Party. In particular there were his promises to investigate the evi-

171

dence of discrimination they had brought and to examine the constitutional position to see if anything could be done to rectify these. Thus, on their return to Belfast, McAteer commented that their trip had been 'surprisingly successful in view of the rather inadequate preparation' and that there 'is good, fruitful soil to be toiled in England'. In addition, he promised they had brought back a 'hatful of new ideas for the continuation of our campaign'.[4]

The scene appeared to be set for O'Reilly to present the Nationalist case as it had been done in London before a television audience. Unfortunately his performance against Faulkner left a lot to be desired and according to James Kelly, writing in the *Irish Independent*, it was clear that 'James O'Reilly, the able MP for Mourne, got rather the worse of his television debate with Brian Faulkner ... because his charges were diffuse and not well enough documented. He badly needed a good brief from a research team'.[5] This was a view shared by party members such as James Doherty, Eugene O'Hare and a future parliamentary colleague Austin Currie, in that even though O'Reilly was a very capable and hardworking MP he had been no match for Faulkner. For Doherty it was yet another example of the urgent need for the party to freshen up and improve on its public image.[6]

However, for long term critics of the Nationalist Party, O'Reilly's lacklustre performance was seen as the final straw and as McKeown states, it forced many people to 'reach the point of exasperation'.[7] Similarly Conn McCluskey mentions how, along with others, 'we squirmed in our seats' as 'the shrewd Mr Faulkner walked rings around O'Reilly on a subject where Faulkner would not have had a leg to stand on had he been faced by a competent adversary'.[8] In addition, as a result of the debate, McKeown points out that NU decided 'The general mood of disgust was such that it led us to ignore our original resolution that we would not intervene directly ourselves in electoral politics'. This encouraged NU in conjunction with Gerry Quigley, secretary of the Irish National Teachers Organisation (INTO), to summon a gathering of 'all the groups and lobbies National Unity had established contact with, as well as individuals and all public representatives of the nationalist community', to make arrangements 'for a properly organised nationalist political machine'.[9]

The immediate response of the Nationalist Party to such a move was one of suspicion and this was largely based upon the resolution, which was to be tabled at the proposed meeting, which declared:

That this assembly of persons convinced of the need for a Nationalist political organisation to stimulate the growth of Nationalist constituency organisations, to permit Nationalist candidates to be democratically selected and to
secure adequate representation on all public bodies – (a) calls on Nationalist
parliamentary representatives, in conjunction with other MPs who support the
National ideal, to take immediate steps to create a democratic party, ... and (b)
further declares if these steps are not taken, this assembly will undertake the
creation of such an organisation.[10]

This can be seen in McAteer's reply to the invitation to attend the conference when he mentioned that although he was always interested in 'gathering new ideas and suggestions', he believed the 'resolution for discussion
is misleading and offensive to those who have been bearing the thankless
burden of representing the Nationalist cause and it is hard to see how such
an approach can do good'.[11]

The mood on both sides became obvious when the different delegates
began to gather for the meeting in Maghery on 19 April. McKeown was to
recall the 'patronizing and ridiculing' attitude amongst 'the supporters of the
orthodox politicians', whilst in a letter to McAteer a few weeks later Conn
McCluskey expressed his shock at the 'rigid immobility of your party' and
warned that 'you are doomed if you do not move on'.[12] On the Nationalist
side, especially amongst the MPs and Senators, there remained a suspicion
that those who called the Maghery conference had a hidden agenda, which
was not to work with the party but to replace it. Even for men like O'Hare
and James Doherty, who were anxious to see the party reform itself, there
was a degree of resentment at the arrogance of the delegates present and
their "We know best attitude".[13] Thus at a meeting of the local party on 22
April, Curran paid tribute to the efforts of the 'Derry contingent' at Maghery
in that they 'had shown they wanted unity, but avoided the passage of the
original motion which would have been a serious outcome'.[14] In the end,
instead of the Maghery meeting breaking up without any agreement,
Senator Lennon proposed a compromise based on the importance of showing that there was 'unity of purpose' amongst the differing factions. As
McAteer was to tell the *Irish News* the 'keynote was unit of National forces
and the end of weak division'. Agreement was therefore reached to release
the following statement:

That this assembly of persons decides ... (1) In conjunction with Nationalist
Party representatives and ... other MPs, who support the National ideal, to

take immediate steps to create ... a National Political Front (NPF) with all the machinery of a normal political party in such areas where these do not exist. (2) In pursuance of this ... a Provisional Committee composed of all existing MPs and Senators who support the National ideal together with one delegate from each of the Westminster constituencies ... (shall be) charged with the duty of implementing part ... (1) of the resolution, and we hereby invite all National organisations to subscribe to this resolution.[15]

Although an agreement had been seemingly reached at Maghery, a question mark hung over whether the Nationalist Party was firmly committed to or believed wholeheartedly in the NPF. On 22 April McAteer told Miss Anne McFadden, later to be appointed as secretary of the NPF, that even though the Parliamentary Party had met and had decided to attend the first meeting of the Provisional Committee it was going to take 'a massive effort of charity and goodwill to launch the ship we hope for'. This was due largely to some of the 'unfortunate statements' made about the party at Maghery.[16] There were also doubts elsewhere, for example in Derry, the local party, whilst accepting the fact that the 'lack of an overall National organisation (had) created a vacuum which had caused the NPF', still harboured doubts about their involvement. At one of its meetings the Chairman, Charles McDaid, told the members present that many of those 'who attended (Maghery) had a different approach to Nationalism' and the real object 'had been to end Nationalism'.[17] Not all of the members entirely agreed with everything McDaid had said, but there was a worry, as Curran concluded, that it was wrong to ask the NPF to 'provide our policy'.[18]

Yet in spite of these misgivings, it appears as if MPs like Connellan and McAteer were at least prepared to give the NPF a chance to prove itself. At the end of April Connellan described the Maghery conference as 'an experiment from which it was greatly hoped far reaching benefits would result',[19] and when the first meeting of the Provisional Committee of the NPF was held on 5 May he was to be elected as its Chairman. McAteer, too, sought to offer the body his support and, speaking to his local party in Derry, he strongly denied the accusation that they had agreed to join any new political party. Instead, he argued they had an obligation to co-operate with any grouping provided there was 'a chance of welding it into something useful'.[20] A month later he described the work of the NPF as an attempt to find a 'common denominator' for all nationally minded groups and that the party could not simply walk away from such deliberations because some of the people involved 'did not measure up to our ideas'.[21]

The problem that was soon to confront the NPF, however, was whether it was ever going to be possible to achieve its stated aim of promoting 'the integration of all existing parties who support the National ideal into a unified political party', considering the underlying suspicions which still existed. For the Nationalist Party these continued to centre on the belief that any new grouping would seek to replace it. Matters were therefore to come to a head over the question of who should have responsibility for the nomination of candidates for the forthcoming Westminster election. As McAteer was to announce in the *Irish News*, only his party could do so and he made it clear they would find it 'impossible to abdicate our position as elected representatives in favour of people who had no claim to representation whatsoever'.[22] In addition, in a letter to Healy, McGill declared there was more at stake than just who should take a lead in calling a selection convention for Fermanagh and South Tyrone. Rather, it boiled down to the fact that, if the party allowed the NPF to take over once, 'we were all finished'.[23] Subsequently Healy and Senator O'Hare organised a convention on behalf of the Nationalist Party in Enniskillen on 1 September. By an 'overwhelming' majority the *Irish News* reported that the decision was taken not to contest the seat on the grounds that it was the only course open to them in order to try to preserve 'Nationalist' unity in the constituency in the face of intervention by SF once again.[24]

For the other elements in the NPF the behaviour of the Nationalist Party in Fermanagh and South Tyrone was inexcusable and they bitterly attacked it. In a press statement they alleged that as a result of the party's actions it had 'laid aside any claim to represent the Nationalist people of Northern Ireland' and as a result the only conclusion that could be reached was that 'as a national political party they have ceased to exist'.[25] A week later, further condemnation of the decision of the Nationalist Party was made at a special council meeting of the NPF. In particular, the move to call a convention without consulting anybody else was denounced and the decision taken by the delegates in Enniskillen on 1 September was summarised as an act of gross 'political cowardice'.[26]

These were accusations that McAteer could not accept, and he alleged that they were proof of an ongoing campaign to undermine the Nationalist Party. He revealed to a party meeting in Derry that along with his parliamentary colleagues he had turned up for the monthly gathering of the NPF in September to find that 'a typewritten motion had been prepared beforehand' which was highly critical of the party. For him it was quite evident that the 'Fermanagh and South Tyrone issue was only an excuse' and that the NPF was not going to work. It was now 'obvious that suspicion was dominant: that the Council was not going to work as a team. There were cleavages on ideals and on the constitutional position'. This was something he regretted but he maintained he was still in favour of dialogue continuing no matter how long it took and even though, 'the high hopes of the Maghery meeting are a long way from fermenting ... I am hopeful that a new Phoenix may arise from the ashes'. At some point he believed it would 'still be possible to embrace' all elements in a real 'National movement entirely free, from self-interest'.[27]

To a certain extent Maghery and the establishment of the NPF had relegated the debate, within the party itself, over proposals for internal reform and reorganisation. With the NPF initiative now seemingly at an end, attention was again focused on this process and for members in Derry they repeated their point that 'organisation of the Nationalist Party was essential'. At a meeting on 30 September, the members present agreed to 'write again to the (parliamentary) party urging the necessity for a united party in the Six Counties'.[28] This was a point now accepted by McAteer, who had become leader of the parliamentary group following the death of Stewart in May. In a note to Healy he outlined his thinking on the subject:

> Despite our inevitable severance from the so-called NPF each of us is under an urgent obligation to establish or improve constituency organisation. It is becoming harder ... to defend the quinquennial get togethers as the sole source of our authority to speak for our people.

However, McAteer remained extremely cautious on the form which this organisation might take and so he stated his preference, 'I do not myself envisage a rigid organisational pattern ... (and which indeed seems unsuited to our people) but some form of "collegiality" with interested people in the constituencies and then further afield'.[29]

But there were others who did not necessarily share McAteer's ideas on reform of the party because they did not go far enough. Amongst his parliamentary colleagues the Gormley brothers, and in particular Paddy Gormley, continued to call for a major overhaul of the party which went far beyond that advocated by McAteer. In interviews with the *Irish News* and the *Irish Press* Paddy Gormley, gave his wholehearted support for the ideals expressed at Maghery. He declared himself at one with the NPF on the need to establish a properly organised political party with a 'card-carrying membership' and an annual conference to decide policy. It was therefore essential that in the future 'National policy should not be decided solely by the elected MPs. Other people of a Nationalist persuasion, who were willing and able, to give direction should be consulted'. As part of this process it was vital for the Nationalist Party to attract into its ranks 'trained political spokesmen well-versed in economics and the social services. We would also need competent research workers to interpret the political and economic affairs of the day'.[30]

In support of his ideas it appeared as if Gormley had a possible ally in Austin Currie who had sought, and won, the East Tyrone by-election in June as a Nationalist candidate. (See Appendix 6: Election Results 1964-1969).

Currie in many ways was exactly the type of person the Nationalist Party needed to attract, not only was he young and a recent graduate from Queen's University, but his experience in student politics had given him an opportunity to sharpen his political skills and to make a name for himself through television appearances. Throughout his campaign he had stressed the necessity for a new approach to be taken by the nationalist community in Northern Ireland and he argued 'they needed unity, not only of their country but also among the national minded people of the six Counties and all over the six Counties'. To achieve this he advocated the creation of a properly organised political party based on 'left of centre policies' which would be capable of tackling and offering solutions for everyday 'bread and butter issues', such as unemployment or poor housing.[31]

With, as yet, no proper party structure to allow for differences of opinion over such issues as reorganisation and restructuring, and with Paddy Gormley continuing to pursue his own independent line, it was almost inevitable that conflict would occur. This was finally to happen during the by-election in East Tyrone when Paddy Gormley publicly backed Currie by helping to pay his deposit. He also strongly condemned his parliamentary colleagues over their moves to hold conventions in Mid Ulster and Fermanagh and South Tyrone to decide on whether the seats should be contested at the forthcoming Westminster elections. The danger in such moves, he suggested, was that by putting up Nationalist candidates against SF nominees, the party would be seen as deliberately splitting the vote. As a result there could be retaliation against Currie by republican voters in East Tyrone abstaining, and thereby damaging his chances of holding the seat. Gormley concluded by alleging that all of this was 'a deliberate attempt to "knife" young Currie in the back ... It was obvious that they did not want Currie elected. They were afraid if he was elected he would clean up Nationalist politics'. Currie, too, expressed concerns and although he did not go as far as Gormley, he commented that the moves with regards to the Westminster election were 'ill advised' at this time. Furthermore he emphasised 'Unity was essential if they were to hold East Tyrone and that anything that would divide National minded people was to be deplored'.

These were obviously claims that could not be allowed to go unchallenged and in a statement released to the *Irish News* on 19 June, the rest of the Nationalist parliamentary party dismissed Paddy Gormley's suggestions as, 'absurd and malicious' and pointed to the fact, that through his brother Tom, he had always been kept informed of the party's intentions in regards to the two Westminster seats. They also believed they were perfectly within their rights to consider opposing SF and had 'nothing but contempt for the suggestion we should conceal our intentions ... even to lure one solitary voter'.[32]

Although the dispute did not unduly affect Currie's prospects, it appears that relations remained strained throughout the rest of the summer. For instance, in September McAteer confessed to Healy that recent events had caused him great concern and as a result he was seriously reconsidering his political future:

> I am appalled at the public image which over the past few months we have shown to friends as well as enemies. It may, or may not be coincidence that this has reached a climax since I formally inherited the "leadership" but I am resolved that a change must be made soon or I will retreat behind my Derry walls.

He concluded his letter with a warning:

> It is absolutely essential that we re-combine as a fighting force or else publicly separate into agreeable groups or ... units. I do not need to elaborate ... but none of us, I am sure want the continuance of the present internal tensions. It is bad for us in every way ... (but) I still believe our party has all the authority and ability needed for the proper custody of our ... people. It is entirely up to ourselves to make good use of this wonderful privilege.[33]

This was something McAteer clearly intended the party should do and so he began to build upon the momentum created by the NPF. In November he wrote to other opposition MPs at Stormont with a proposal to create a new 'United Nationalist Party'.[34] As part of these discussions he led a delegation to meet with the Republican Labour Party (RLP) which was represented in Stormont by Diamond and Gerry Fitt, MP for Dock. Even though the talks were to end without agreement both sides stressed they were prepared to meet again. McAteer informed the *Irish News* that 'So far as our party is concerned we will endeavour to do all we can ... to promote the unity which is yearned for by the Nationalist people as a whole'. As well he promised they would do 'everything in our power to clear the path to real unity and, with goodwill on all sides, this can be achieved'.[35]

In conjunction with this, Nationalist MPs and Senators came together again to launch their party's first ever general policy statement, which became known as the "Thirty Nine Points", in Belfast on 20 November. McAteer boldly announced 'The Party is now anxious to step into the Twentieth century' and therefore saw the policy statement as 'stage one in our renewal programme. The next exercise will be to establish normal political machinery with membership, constituency bodies and annual conferences'. Support came from Paddy Gormley, who declared that due to the changed atmosphere in the North, 'We have examined ourselves from within and accepted constructive thought. For the first time in Northern Ireland there is room for the positive political action we envisage'. He also predicted, with their policy statement, the party would be in a position to start to attract the 'floating vote' which would develop as 'Religious segregation' became 'less and less' relevent.[36]

As for the actual contents of the document, McAteer asserted that they were largely a resume of what the party had been saying for years. The first article enshrined their commitment 'To hasten, by positive political action, the inevitable re-unification of Ireland and the establishment of a democratic republican form of government'. Furthermore, under the banner of improving 'community relations in Northern Ireland' and the 'maintenance of public order', undertakings were given that the party would pursue policies which would ensure the 'creation of an integrated community based on principles of social justice and mutual respect', along with the 'fullest measure of political, civil and religious liberty' for 'all citizens before the law'. This would have to involve the revocation of the Special Powers Act, the disbandment of the B Specials and the appointment of an Ombudsman to examine 'complaints of improper or unreasonable exercise of statutory powers'. In the fields of social and economic matters promises were given that the party would work to provide:

satisfactory housing for the entire population ... the promotion of industrial expansion and the development of a well balanced, mixed economy ... the creation of full employment and the use of all capital and local government resources to secure this end ... the creation of an education system in which equality of educational opportunity is a reality ... the recognition of the special place of agriculture not only in the economy but in the social structure of the community itself.[37]

The "Thirty Nine Points" not only provided the Nationalist Party with a detailed description of its aims and goals for the first time, but also provided it with a programme which could be presented as part of its continuing effort to be at the forefront of attempts to secure unity amongst the various opposition groupings. For example, in a letter to Healy, McAteer pointed out that 'a very considerable part of this was provisionally agreed to by the policy making sub committee of the NPF'. He therefore remained confident that it would 'satisfy most of our people' as it was nothing more than 'a more formal statement of the very things we have been urging for years'.[38] This is a point later confirmed by McAteer to F.W.S. Craig when he mentioned that the party's policy statement had been the 'product of a lot of Committee work in conjunction with "Nationally minded" groups such as Republican Labour, Independent Labour (Frank Hanna), National Democratic Party and ourselves'. As a result he remained hopeful that 'this document will eventually pave the way for a wider degree of unity amongst anti-Unionist forces'.[39]

One can therefore see the release of the "Thirty Nine Points" as a sign that the Nationalist Party, as Lennon was to establish during a debate at Queen's University, had now realised there was room for 'improvement in the party' and that it was 'their aim to achieve this as soon as possible'.[40] Yet the importance of this move was soon to be overshadowed by the meeting in January 1965 between Terence O'Neill and Sean Lemass, Prime Minister of the Irish Republic, at Stormont. As Wallace points out, both men seemed to represent the fact that a new generation had assumed power in Belfast and Dublin, which appeared to be anxious to break with the past. For instance, O'Neill was the first Northern premier not to have 'experienced the struggles of early Unionism which so shaped the characters of his predecessors'. In addition since coming to power he had emphasised the importance of developing Northern Ireland's economy and of improving relations between the two communities in the province. Similarly Lemass, even though a veteran of the 1916 Easter Rising and the War of

Independence, as well a long time ally of De Valera and a Minister in many of his Cabinets, was nonetheless very much a 'pragmatist intent on developing the Republic's economy'.[41] This was confirmed by a statement released after their talks when both men stressed that 'Our talks ... did not touch upon constitutional or political questions' and instead had focused upon 'matters on which there may prove to be a degree of common interest' such as economic and social matters. Agreement had been therefore reached to 'explore further what specific measures may be possible or desirable by way of practical consultation and co-operation'.[42]

Undoubtedly for O'Neill this meeting was a huge personal and political gamble, a fact recognised by his refusal to consult with all but a few close confidantes over Lemass's visit, in case it provoked serious dissension in his Cabinet. Further danger for O'Neill lay in alienating those Unionists who were already highly suspicious of his intentions, and for them the meeting with Lemass was final proof that he could not be trusted to safeguard their interests. Unfortunately for O'Neill, the development of such things as the ecumenical movement in the 1960s merely strengthened such views and gradually a figure emerged to give this growing movement the leadership it needed. This man was to be the Rev Ian Paisley, and in the years ahead he was to move from his position as head of the Free Presbyterian Church, to lead an ever burgeoning extra parliamentary opposition to the policies of O'Neill and ecumenism.

The O'Neill-Lemass meeting also presented a major challenge to the Nationalist Party in that it would have to be seen to be responding to the apparent rapprochement between Dublin and Belfast. If it did nothing it ran the risk of being marginalised by the talks and thereby possibly lose its mantle as the voice of nationalist opinion in the North. Almost immediately speculation began to mount whether in the wake of this historic meeting the Nationalist Party would accept for the first time the role of Official Opposition at Stormont. As both Currie and James Doherty were to make clear the dilemma that now faced the party was whether such a conciliatory gesture on their behalf would bring a similar response from the authorities at Stormont.[43]

This whole episode was clearly something that troubled McAteer, and in particular, he viewed it as another example of the lack of consideration shown by the authorities in Dublin towards Northern nationalists. For example he was to inform Curran:

In my role as leader of the Nationalist people, I made many trips to Dublin ... for talks and consultations with Dublin Ministers. I got hospitality but little real support.   There was less than enthusiasm to get involved ...When I returned home after my post-O'Neill talk with the Taoiseach I was more worried than ever. I got neither the encouragement nor understanding of our position ... Lemass said that it appeared to him that Catholics in the North were just as intractable as Protestants. It was hardly the reaction I expected from a Taoiseach with his Republican background to the representative of the oppressed Irish minority in the six Counties ... I came away with the conviction that as far as Sean Lemass was concerned, the Northern Irish were very much on their own.[44]

As a result McAteer was almost duty bound to act and McGill reveals that as leader of the parliamentary party he consulted his colleagues on the issue and also visited Lemass in Dublin to discuss the situation. Finally at a meeting of all MPs and Senators 'members reported on the soundings taken by them in their constituencies and declared that the ... role of Official Opposition would be acceptable to the mass of the Nationalist electorate'.[45] At a press conference on 2 February the announcement was made that the parliamentary party had reviewed the 'whole political landscape' and had reached the 'following conclusion':

> Stormont must be seen as a federal or regional Irish Parliament to continue in existence until the fears of an All Ireland parliament are finally resolved. There must be co-operation to ensure that ... the existing Parliamentary machinery operates for the common good. For all practical purposes this will mean little change in existing practice and will enable us to advance the policy programme we have already issued. Our fidelity to a United Ireland ... remains unaltered by this decision. Pursuit of this aim is an entirely lawful political objective in no way inconsistent with full community status. Co-operation will not and cannot be carried beyond the brink of national principle.[46]

Although McAteer was to receive the backing of his own party in Derry when it met on 10 February and passed a motion agreeing that the steps taken had been 'a realistic appraisal of the needs of the moment',[47] he, along with other party colleagues, had to make appeals to their supporters to give this policy a chance of producing some results. At a meeting in Newry, Connellan reiterated that people were 'greatly mistaken' if they believed that in the 'name of progress' Nationalists had 'repudiated the idea of a united Ireland'. What had to be accepted was that 'it (reunification) is something that cannot be brought about miraculously overnight. We must realise the road to be travelled is still a long road'. In the meantime 'we cannot keep harping on the same string all the time' and therefore 'one of the most immediate and urgent duties is to help in the building of prosperity, tolerance and mutual respect among all our people in the part of the country in which we live'. A similar message was delivered by McAteer when he announced that the decision to become the Official Opposition at Stormont had not changed their 'outlook or policy' and he denied it was a sign the party had lost its 'compass'. He maintained the time was right for Nationalists to observe a truce from their 'exposure campaign until we are convinced that Unionists really do not intend to admit us to full citizenship'. Whilst he was aware of the 'temporary party disadvantage which our forbearance may entail', he considered it a risk 'worth taking' in order to overcome the suggestion that 'militant Nationalist movements merely strengthen the Unionist Party to govern on in the interests of the ruling caste here'.[48]

It is therefore quite clear that McAteer was conscious of the fact that such "conciliatory gestures" ran the risk of alienating many people but, as James Doherty points out, it was a choice they felt they had to take. As a constitutional party they concluded that the onus was on them to ensure that all areas in Northern Ireland would receive the benefits from the social and economic developments which it was hoped would occur under O'Neill.[49] Nowhere was this more important than in Derry where as Curran describes 'the frustration of the Nationalist majority was immense, and they could see no prospect of the government making a real attempt to tackle Derry's problems'.[50]

These sentiments had already been publicly aired by John Hume, then a local teacher and activist in the growing Credit Union Movement, in the *Irish Times*. Like many Catholics of his generation, Hume was very much a product of the post-war education reforms that had allowed children from a relatively poor background to obtain a place at a grammar school and then possibly a place at university. For Hume this had resulted in someone from a large family living in a two bedroom house in Derry, and a father who struggled to find work, to attend St Columb's College in Derry and then graduate from Maynooth. After rejecting a career in the priesthood he had become a teacher and soon returned to St Columbs as a member of staff. As Curran concludes however, his interests soon spread beyond teaching and as 'his experience grew and his perceptions broadened ... He became a strong advocate of self-help. People, he felt, should set about using their talents to practical purpose rather than complaining about what they lacked'.[51] Such ideas were clearly evident in his two articles, simply entitled *The Northern Catholic*, and in both he was highly critical 'both of the (Nationalist) party and traditional nationalism'. For him,

> Weak opposition leads to corrupt government. Nationalists in opposition have in no way been constructive. They have ... been loud in their demands for rights, but they have remained silent and inactive about their duties ... leadership has been the comfortable leadership of flags and slogans ... There has been no attempt to be positive, to encourage the Catholic community to develop the resources ... they have in plenty to make a positive contribution in terms of community service ... the only constructive suggestion from the Nationalist side would appear to be that a removal of discrimination will be the panacea for all our ills ...

As Barry White in his book, *John Hume: Statesman of the Troubles*, points out, Hume also went onto call for the 'complete revitalisation' of the Party and in particular the 'necessity of a fully organised democratic party which can freely attract and draw upon the talents of the nationally minded community ...'.[52]

For a period, however, it appeared as if Hume was prepared to give the party a chance and in a response to an invitation by the local branch in Derry, at its meeting on 20 May 1964, to address one of its future gatherings, he became a member and over the next few months attended some meetings.[53] Throughout, his main contribution was to urge them to end what White describes as the 'head without-a-body type of party'. On 3 June he asked members to examine why it was that 'Only a few of his generation were present'.[54] Then, as the party's relationship with the NPF began to sour Hume's attendance at meetings became less frequent. In one of his last contributions during a debate on the fate of the NPF, he made it clear that although sympathetic somewhat to the party's claim 'that many in the National Unity movement may have been trying to jump into the limelight', the onus was firmly on them to take the lead. He argued that at least 'the (NU) movement had its roots in something: the Nationalist Party must examine its conscience. They should grasp the nettle, call a convention and give an image of vigour'.[55] With no sign of this occurring to the extent he desired, Hume resigned from the party and his letter of resignation was noted in the party minutes without comment.[56]

Free from any involvement in party politics, Hume returned to an area he had first identified in his articles in the *Irish Times*, when he had noted that, 'The need for action in the non-political front ... is probably greater' and, 'There exists in the North at the moment a greater wealth of talent ... than ever before, and ... growing desire to get together to pool ... talents and to tackle community problems'.[57] The opportunity for him to put this into practice came with his high profile involvement in the "non-political" campaign to ensure that the proposed new university would be sited in Derry.

This belief that Derry was the natural location for the province's new university was based partly on civic pride in the city, its long history as a centre of learning through Magee College, and its traditional position as Northern Ireland's second city. Undoubtedly the campaign that was to be organised on the issue was highly effective in promoting these ideas, but its most significant feature was the way it brought the two communities in Derry together, creating 'a city unity hitherto unknown'.[58] This was illustrated by the establishment of an inter-denominational "University for Derry" committee, with Hume as its chairman. The impact that the campaign was to have on the people of Derry was highlighted by the holding of a mass rally in the Guildhall in February 1965. This meeting saw 'Unionists and Nationalists taking their places together on the platform for the first time anyone could remember, and ... McAteer sharing a leading role with the arch-Unionist Gerald Glover'.[59]

Yet all the evidence that seemed to be emerging from the Lockwood Committee, which had been established by the government to 'report on all facets of the university question', was that the people of Derry were going to be disappointed. This was finally confirmed by the publication of the Lockwood Report on 10 February 1965 which recommended that the new university should be located in Coleraine. In one last effort to persuade the government to reject Lockwood's findings the "University for Derry" campaign planned to bring a motorcade of protestors from the city to Stormont. Once again Nationalist and Unionist politicians like McAteer and the Mayor, Albert Anderson, took part and when it finally reached parliament buildings an estimated 25,000 people were present. Such an appeal however failed to persuade the government and in an often bitter and acrimonious debate which took place on 3 and 4 March the Lockwood Report was approved by 27 votes to 19.[60]

Although the local Nationalist Party pledged its support for the campaign and McAteer was involved in bringing the protest to Stormont,[61] it was to be Hume in the long term who was to benefit most of all. This was to be particularly important because, as Curran argues, for the Catholic population of the city the university issue was part of a much wider question, namely the attitude of the Stormont government towards Derry and its future development. Whilst people could grudgingly accept that the government could not force new industry to locate in the area, they believed it could and should have a significant say in where a new university should be sited. As Curran concludes 'The denial of the university really awakened even the politically dormant, and inspired the beginning of more questioning about the nature of the Northern state'. Its importance was also later recognised by Hume himself when he told Curran:

> The university decision electrified the people on the nationalist side, and I think was really the spark that ignited the civil rights movement, though I suppose nobody could have articulated it in those terms then. And when the university went to Coleraine, the chance of orderly change in Northern Ireland probably disappeared. It became clear to me certainly that change could only be affected by positive political action.[62]

All of this, however, was still some time off and in 1965 the pressure continued to mount from both outside and within the Nationalist Party to follow up its policy statement with its plans to establish a political organisation which would encompass the whole province. In Belfast, in February, up to 200 delegates from South Antrim, North Down, North Armagh and Belfast met to establish the National Party. According to its new chairman Gerry Quigley the 'Overwhelming conviction among the various groups represented was of the tremendous necessity to secure unity. That was the keynote of the meeting'. With Lennon and McAteer present at the meeting as observers, the new grouping pledged itself to link up 'with the reorganised associations in the rural areas to form a united political party'.[63] By June, however, the National Party had grown tired of waiting and at a special conference it decided to transform itself into the National Democratic Party (NDP). The change was made, it was stated, in response to the failure of the Nationalist Parliamentary Party to put into 'effect the proposed merger' or 'to put into operation the democratic machinery which they had committed themselves publicly to establish'. Furthermore, the NDP expressed its belief in the need for a 'broadly based, democratically organised political party to unite all those who accepted the National ideal' and its intention 'to extend its activities to all areas where there is a demand for democratic organisation'.[64]

There was also a growing impatience amongst party members in Derry at the speed of reform and at its monthly meeting in May, O'Hare renewed his demand for an 'energetic attempt to obtain a proper party organisation'. He then threatened to introduce a motion criticising the Parliamentary Party for lacking any kind of 'a policy' on this important matter. Curran, too, drew attention to the fact that 'Organisation had been promised at Maghery' and accused the MPs and Senators of having 'a lack of confidence' and 'a fear that organisation would endanger them'. Finally, along with O'Hare he suggested that they should be given a 'last chance' and the meeting agreed to send a letter to McGill requesting he 'take immediate steps to hold a Nationalist Party convention ... with a view to setting up a party organisation'.[65]

When McGill's reply was placed before the next meeting in June, it did nothing to allay fears that it was the Parliamentary Party which was attempting to stall the progress towards greater party organisation. Instead, McGill urged caution and argued against the holding of 'a premature general convention' which he assumed would only produce 'newspaper copy for our opponents'. Rather, he suggested, that change should be restricted to the idea of 'organisation (being) tightened up at a local level'. If this reply was considered unsatisfactory, what really angered members was McAteer's announcement that the letter they had sent in May had not been placed before the parliamentary group for discussion. The mood of many was summed up by Alderman James Hegarty when he pronounced that it was obvious that 'many MP's did not want organisation'. In the end, however, it was decided this time to write to each MP and Senator individually asking them for their 'co-operation and views' on the need for party organisation.[66] It appears that at last this mounting pressure was having some impact and at a meeting in Derry, on 30 June, McAteer announced that the parliamentary party had unanimously accepted the 'principle of constituency organisation and an informal convention'. This had clearly been shown by his presence at a meeting in Newry, on 23 June, which had been called to address these concerns and his intention to be present at a similar gathering scheduled for Crossmaglen early in July. Then later in the year he informed members in Derry that the party's first 'get together' was scheduled for November.[67]

In spite of his apparent support for this process of modernising the party, McAteer in private continued to have doubts about it and his lack of enthusiasm can be noted in a letter to Healy in September. On the subject

of the holding a party convention he remarked 'I think that it might be a useful exercise even if it only meant disarming our critics of one weapon'.[68]
Not all of his parliamentary colleagues shared McAteer's cautious approach
and, as has already been noted, the Gormley brothers had long been advo-
cates of the need for the party to become an effective, modern political
machine capable of taking on unionism. Since his election back in 1964,
Currie had been closely associated with the Gormleys' and their ideas by the
press but he had always been keen to establish that he was "his own man"
and had his own agenda to follow. At first he moved slowly, anxious to
avoid the accusation that he was a "radical" who wanted to "rock the boat"
by "barnstorming" the parliamentary party with his ideas.[69] It was therefore,
not until the summer of 1965 that he felt confident enough in himself to start
actively campaigning for the type of party he wanted to see develop. On 27
August the *Irish News* reported that he intended to call a public meeting to
establish a 'proper political organisation' in his own constituency. Currie
told the paper he had always argued for the creation of 'a democratic organisation to which every interested person can belong and in which he can
play a part'. This was vital as the 'National movement has for too long been
frustrated by divisions amongst those whose hopes for Ireland's future are
fundamentally the same', and the 'absence of a solid and properly organised
party machine' had resulted in the lack of 'effective political action'. He
concluded that for 'far too long the National movement has been on the
defensive. It is now time to go on the attack. A broad based democratic
organisation is a necessary prerequisite for the great surge forward'.[70] The
following day, before an audience of 350 people, Currie picked up the same
theme and urged those present to ensure that East Tyrone took the lead in
creating a 'New party ... built up from the grass roots ... with an annual conference, central offices, a card carrying membership and a professional
organisation'. In addition, its main function should not be as the Nationalist
Party had become, namely a body that merely contested elections, but a
'forum for ideas and policies ... a training ground for the youth and politicians of the future and as a unifying factor among the adherents of a particular political philosophy'. Now was the time Currie urged for them to
'take as our maxim the words "Sinn Fein" and help ourselves. A proper ...
organisation, attracting as it will, the most energetic and able people, can be
the basis of "self help" efforts'.[71]

   Such views, however contrasted, sharply with the path that other, more
senior members of the party wanted to take. At a meeting in

Newtownbutler, McAteer expressed 'doubts as to whether the spirit of Nationalism was improved by being encased in a tight organisation'. It seemed a better idea at this time 'to content themselves by calling for the establishment of "alert posts" in as many districts as possible so as to pool and exchange ideas'.[72]   Similarly, McGill favoured a more cautious approach and in a note to McAteer advocated:

> As for ourselves, we must organise on our lines. A constituency Executive, springing from local branches in electoral divisions or towns. Each executive to send ... delegates to an annual conference. No cards, no fees, all voluntary. In a card carrying membership, remember, you appear to exclude those who are too shy or unwilling to ask for cards.

He also rejected out of hand the suggestion that their party should consider 'fusion' with the NDP and warned that there was a widespread feeling amongst many people in 'Mourne, South Down, West Tyrone ... South Fermanagh and South Armagh' that 'fusion' would be seen as simply a 'take-over'. Whilst, along with others he was prepared to see closer ties with the NDP, it was vital to stress 'we are ourselves, not a branch, co-ordinator or otherwise of any hierarchical structure thought up by ... Belfast ... or assimilated by what Lennon rightly calls "Johnny come latelies" '.[73]

Before the Nationalist Party could hold its own conference, which had been scheduled for 14 November, the event was postponed by an election called by O'Neill and polling day was set for 25 November. Although McAteer described its calling as a 'needless waste of money' and an attempt by the Prime Minister 'to resolve an internal Cabinet difference', he predicted 'We (Nationalists) will certainly give ... a good account of ourselves'.[74] To try to ensure that this happened the party announced, during the election campaign, that it would be 'maintaining the closest possible contact and liaison' with the NDP. This involved the mutual endorsement of each other's candidates and the exchange of speakers between both parties.[75] Yet even this level of co-operation worried some members of the party in Derry and McAteer sought to reassure them by pointing out that the NDP had been 'joint authors of the 39 Points' and had agreed to stay out of 'traditional Nationalist constituencies'. Eventually a motion proposed by O'Hare supporting the 'efforts to bring a rapport between the NDP and our party' was approved.[76]

Overall, the campaign was a relatively low key affair with only four Nationalist MPs facing contests: McAteer by a Labour nominee,

Richardson by an Independent Republican, whilst Connellan and O'Reilly faced Unionist opponents. As a result the party's electoral message was an attempt to balance tradition with a pledge that it was open to new ideas and thinking. A perfect example of this came from O'Reilly and McAteer during the campaign. During an election rally, O'Reilly asserted that under no circumstances would the party listen to the 'siren voices' urging the 'Nationalist people to abandon some of ... that heritage their forefathers had held' and reaffirmed the 'basic principle of the Nationalist Party despite all the sneers remained their right to form part of a free and unfettered Ireland'.[77] At the same time launching the party's manifesto, which was based largely on the 39 Points, McAteer again emphasised that they were aware of the criticism made of them and promised that change and reform was under way. Equally, they were only too aware of the responsibilities placed on them as public representatives to remove 'bitterness and hatred which had disfigured the community for so long'.[78] In the end the steps taken by the party in recent years were put before the electorate and in all four seats the sitting Nationalist MP was returned with a comfortable majority. (See Appendix 6: Election Results 1964-1969).

With the election now over and the Nationalist Party according to the *Irish News* having 'stood firm',[79] with nine MPs returned, the long awaited party conference was scheduled for 12 December in Belfast. In the run up to it McGill again emphasised the need for caution and warned McAteer 'we must be careful not to allow any changes that would cause trouble'. This meant in particular 'details of card carrying etc. can be left until there is a structure, and then it can be discussed. Merger with the NDP cannot arise ... If they want unity they can unite in one existing Nationalist Party'.[80]

In the end, it appears that the cautious approach, favoured by the leadership prevailed, at the gathering and at the press conference afterwards McAteer stressed that the party would follow its own agenda and reject the 'sudden zeal of a hostile section of the press to see us reform in this way or that way'. He strongly rejected the accusations being made that the party had somehow lost contact with its electorate and instead referred to the fact 'In our own quiet way we have always kept in close touch with the people'. To ensure this was maintained he did not want to see any structure created which might lead to a 'barrier (being) created against the people who have opinions to express to us regarding events or trends'. Although he was keen to see the party's newly established Co-ordinating Committee 'undertake the removal of the "closed shop" image with which the party has been labelled in the past', it was also vital 'to make our party easy to join'. His chief concern remained that 'too formal or rigid organisation ... might repel people from joining' and therefore as a result agreement had been reached where even though an 'official party membership will be organised' its members would not 'necessarily be issued with cards'. Finally, he announced that the new 23-man Co-ordinating Committee, consisting of himself along with two other MPs and Senators plus two representatives from each of the nine Nationalist held constituencies, would examine and report back on the proposal to hold the first ever party conference sometime next year.[81]

Although disappointed at the outcome, Currie was not completely surprised at the slow pace and the limited extent of the reforms being proposed. In any case as the party was to remain very loosely based, this allowed him the freedom to continue with his own plans. As a first step be began to create an organisation within his own constituency along the lines he had already advocated.[82] This measure of independence was also carried into other areas, such as his call for the party to broaden its electoral appeal. During a debate in Belfast in February 1966, Currie insisted it was time for the party to start to deal with the 'economic facts of life' and to position itself politically 'left of centre'. In addition it was essential for Nationalists to rid themselves of the label of "Green Tories" or as the "party of publicans", and to offer a new 'radical and positive alternative to Unionism'. This could only be done by correcting 'one of the misrepresentations of the ultimate aim of the Nationalist Party. It was not (just in favour of) reunification because when reunification came it would not be the end of all our problems'. Rather he believed 'a party with leftish views could be the only effective opposition to the Unionist Government'.[83] In pursuit of this he carried on with his efforts to establish a democratic organisation in East Tyrone and at the founding of a new branch in Cookstown he spoke of the 'importance of obtaining unity among all the Nationalist people'.[84]

The same message was also continuing to be expressed by Paddy Gormley, notably, in an interview with the *Sunday Press* in August. He told the paper it was extremely disappointing to find that many people still considered the party to be a 'Catholic or Hibs Party' made up of 'Green Tories'. The time was, therefore, ripe for a new political alignment more broadly based than the Nationalist Party. This new grouping would have to include 'progressive elements' which could offer the electorate a 'new and virile alternative to the Unionist Party'.[85]

Such sentiments ran completely contrary, as has already been pointed out, to the views of senior party colleagues such as McGill who remained

steadfastly opposed to the direction men like Currie and the Gormley brothers wanted to take the party. On Paddy Gormley's demands for a 'United
Anti-Unionist Front' he dismissively told McAteer that the 'whole thing is
a nonsense' and asked him to 'remember (that) whatever new pattern would
emerge it would bode no good for us, individually or otherwise'.[86] Earlier
in the year, in a series of letters to Healy, McGill returned to voice his concerns at the moves towards greater organisation within the party. For him
the problem was that 'enthusiasm is difficult to sustain, and if the initial
promise is not speedily followed by performance, disillusionment fol-
lows'.[87] Then, on the eve of the party's first annual conference, he summed
up all his concerns:

> The trouble is, as I think you pointed out on one occasion, that one starts off
> very well but that it is difficult to sustain the tempo and there is inevitably a
> reaction. We had this in the APL and I suppose ... it will manifest in this lat-
> est effort too.

Despite these deep-seated reservations McGill, as McAteer before
him, had come to realise that the mood for change from both within and outside the party was such that some kind of steps had to be taken. As a result
he accepted them, if such moves resulted 'in creating some organisational
structure that will give our people a base against the emergence of Liberal
and Labour elements ... then something at any rate will have been done'.[88]
This meant that the process begun in 1965, continued and on 6
February 1966 over 60 delegates representing all nine Stormont-held constituencies met to consider the report of the Co-ordinating Committee on the
prospects for the party holding an annual conference. It was subsequently
accepted in full and a provisional date of 22 May was set. Such developments were most welcomed by the local party in Derry which had long been
calling for such a development. At its meeting on 23 February O'Hare, a
member of the Co-ordinating Committee, gave a report of its work and rec-
ommendations. He informed the members present that up to nine delegates,
from the constituency parties already in existence, which basically covered
the areas represented by the party's MPs, would be invited to the proposed
conference. In addition attempts would be made to include areas such as
North Tyrone where as yet no organisation existed. At the same time an
undertaking had been given that the party would not attempt to organise in
areas 'where seats were held by like-minded people'. Elsewhere it appears
as if the cautious approach outlined by McAteer in December 1965 towards

the reorganisation of the party was acceptable to the members in Derry. O'Hare announced, without any criticism from any one, that 'the basis of organisation would be an elected executive in each constituency ... and an open membership', and that there 'would also be a party and executive as distinct from the parliamentary party'.[89] For James Doherty these changes represented the fact that the party had taken on board the criticism of it, and was now inviting new members to join and to take the process further, if that was what people wanted.[90]

Yet the holding of the party's first annual conference was still warmly received by the *Irish News* as a sign that McAteer's promise to 're-fashion, reorganise, and strengthen' the Nationalist Party was underway and also meant the 'days of the caucus meeting – always calculated to scare off those who wanted to be fully identified with the party and its role – are over'.[91] This was also something the party itself wanted to dispel and so resolutions were tabled for debate on issues ranging from education, rural development, housing and calls for the introduction of an electoral system in Northern Ireland comparable to those in Britain and the Irish Republic.[92] Later in the year this need was repeated in an appeal for funds which declared:

> This decision to fully and vigorously organise on a more widespread basis and to further positive and practical policies as far as possible, means we will need resources vastly greater than anything hitherto ... Our progress will be in accordance with the backing we get and in this most important foundation year we ask for your most generous financial support.[93]

Whilst much time and effort had gone into trying to bring the party into the "twentieth century" in terms of its structure and organisation, the party also wanted to ensure that in the process it did not abandon its role as defending the rights of the minority community in Northern Ireland. In the hope that some improvement could be achieved in this field, the party had accepted the role of Official Opposition at Stormont, but with as yet no sign of this happening, the position soon came under review. As early as February 1966 McAteer had warned 'If we don't get some token from the Unionists that they are going to normalise conditions here, we might have to take our troubles to Westminster again'.[94] This was a point he returned to during his address to the party conference in May, when he concluded:

> In our efforts to find and co-operate on matters of general good we find much misunderstanding. The Government seem reluctant to accept any ideas aris-

ing outside the narrow limits of their own Front Bench and I am wondering lately whether they really want parliamentary opposition. At times they seem to be yearning for the good old days of growl and glare ... Perhaps we will some time have to review this brave experiment in normalisation.[95]

1966

By the summer it looked as if this point had been reached when McAteer announced he was to visit London to meet the Labour Home Secretary, Roy Jenkins, in order to end the 'system whereby Stormont Ministers are the sole official reporters of events here'. He also hoped to 'establish direct channels of communication between the Opposition's Shadow Ministers and the British Government', and so remind the 'Home Secretary of the true state of affairs' in the province.[96]

Nationalist politicians had already sought to interest the authorities in Britain, as well as public opinion, in Northern Ireland affairs without any success for many years. This was largely due to the fact that on the whole, no matter what government had been in power in Westminster, there had been a marked reluctance to intervene in any matters which came under the remit of the Stormont Parliament. Thus, by the 1960s this had reached a stage where there was little interest in Northern Ireland affairs. The extent of this is noted by Ken Bloomfield in his book *Stormont in Crisis: A Memoir*, when he mentions the fact that the Home Office in London which had the 'responsibility for oversight of Northern Ireland', consisted of 'a small department that also handled relations with the Channel Islands and the Isle of Man, the regulation of London taxi cabs, and other functions of a stimulating kind'.[97]

In spite of this, the return of a Labour government following the 1964 Westminster election, albeit with a small majority, had encouraged Healy and Senator O'Hare to write to Harold Wilson, the new Prime Minister, asking him to investigate alleged discrimination in housing allocations by local councils in Fermanagh. The advice Wilson received, however, from his civil servants was to repeat the answers he had given in the past to such queries. For example in reply to an earlier letter from Healy he had stated:

> I share your desire to see remedial action taken when discriminatory practices are believed to exist. But I went on to say that in view of the constitutional position, it would not be proper for me to comment on the matters to which you draw attention, or seek to intervene in them. I am sure you will understand that in those circumstances it will not be possible for me ... to discuss questions within the fields of responsibility of the Northern Ireland Government and Parliament.[98]

Yet within 18 months of the return to power of the Labour Party there were signs that this attitude could possibly change in the future. This was largely due to the increasing resentment felt by Labour back bench MPs at the presence of the 12 Unionist MPs at Westminster who continued to follow the Conservative whip, and thus threaten a government with a small working majority. In May 1965, the *Irish News* drew attention to the widespread anger felt by many Labour MPs at the narrow passage of a bill renationalising the steel industry which had almost been defeated by Unionists voting en masse with the opposition. The paper reported the growing animosity at a situation where Northern Ireland MPs' could influence affairs in Britain, whilst British MPs' had little say in matters regarding Northern Ireland. One possible consequence of these concerns, the paper reported, was the rumour that Wilson was considering possible changes to the voting rights of Northern Ireland MPs.[99]

Although these were charges strenuously denied at the time by Wilson, in his memoirs *The Labour Government 1964-1970: A Personal Record* he records that the 'Westminster Parliament and ... many of our 1964 and 1966 entrants, was deeply concerned about human rights. It seemed inconsistent to assert human rights in Africa or the darkest areas of Europe when they were being patently denied in Ulster, a part of the United Kingdom'.[100] These concerns had eventually led to the establishment of the Campaign for Democracy in Ulster (CDU) by Labour MPs in the summer of 1965 and amongst its stated aims were:

(1) to secure a full and impartial inquiry into the administration of the Government of Northern Ireland and into allegations of discrimination in the fields of housing and employment; (2) to bring electoral law in Northern Ireland into line with that of the rest of United Kingdom and to examine electoral boundaries with a view to providing fair representation for all sections of the community; (3) to press for the application of the Race Relations Act to ... Northern Ireland and that it be amended to include religious discrimination and incitement.[101]

Then, early in 1966, up to 40 Labour MPs associated with the CDU tabled a motion at Westminster calling for the establishment of a Royal Commission to inquire into the working of the Government of Ireland Act 1920.[102] For Wilson it was clearly now time for him to be seen taking a tougher line on Northern Ireland and accordingly, on 5 August, along with Roy Jenkins, his Home Secretary, he met O'Neill for their 'most important meeting up to that time'. Wilson emphasised that 'without constitutional reform and more liberal policies it was becoming more difficult to justify to MPs and to some members of the Cabinet, the large sums we were being asked to vote' for Northern Ireland. The meeting ended with Wilson, as he records himself, content with its outcome and satisfied with O'Neill's promises that his reforms in the province would continue.[103]

In the wake of these talks McAteer, as has already been pointed out, had judged that the time was right for Nationalists to once again press their claims for a much wider and extensive reform package. On 10 August he met Jenkins and Quentin Hogg, the Shadow Home Secretary, in London and as a result seemed to hold out the promise that progress was at last on its way. He informed the *Irish News* the talks 'went like a bomb ... I now know there is a great interest in both sides of Westminster in Northern Ireland affairs'. He had also taken the opportunity to bring to their attention the case of Derry and, in particular, to study it and see 'democracy at its worst'. Furthermore, as a politician who remained firmly committed to peaceful, constitutional change, he was quietly optimistic of the future, 'It may seem we have stepped forward once and stepped back twice, but change is on the way and I think my visit today might accelerate this change'. The onus, he concluded, was now on the British Government and 'having assumed ownership of Northern Ireland they should assume responsibility for it as well'.[104]

Yet, by 1967, the task that still lay ahead of the Nationalist Party was still an extremely daunting one. Not only was there a need to convince the authorities at Westminster and Stormont that a major programme of reform was essential to improve conditions in the province, but it had still also to satisfy the minority community in the North that the party had the ability and talent to carry this out. An opportunity to try to achieve these goals seemed to present itself with the launch in April 1967 of an inquiry into Northern Ireland by a group of lawyers in Britain who had connections or sympathy with the Labour Party. On 8 April this body which became known as the Labour Lawyers Inquiry (LLI), and consisted of S. Silkin, P. Archer, Sir E. Jones, I. Richard, Lord Gifford and C. Thornberry, invited political organisations in the province to submit written evidence to them. It would be then 'the Committee's duty to inquire into and report on the workings of the Government of Ireland Act and other legal and constitutional provisions affecting the Stormont administration'.[105]

The first reaction of the Nationalist Party to the initiative by the LLI was not one of great enthusiasm and rather there were suspicions that it would have an adverse affect on their efforts. As McGill told McAteer, 'There is, as we both know, a real dilemma here, not least being my feeling that Mr Wilson has approved this way out of absolving himself from mounting an official inquiry'. At the same time, McGill argued 'it is clear we must not ignore it' and cautioned that 'if we don't do it some other crowd will'. He therefore concluded:

> I would have preferred an Official Inquiry – such as we sought – instead of this semi-put off by Wilson who, cleverer than Douglas-Home, does not turn it down outright but comes at it glancingly; but this being the best offering at the moment, we must ... turn it as much into a Nationalist indictment as we can.[106]

McAteer was also wary of the LLI and he immediately made it clear that he was not optimistic the inquiry would produce any immediate results. He repeated that his preferred option remained the same, 'How much simpler it would be ... for Mr O'Neill to perform an act of real statesmanship and invite representatives of the minority to sit around the table and hammer out a solution to our problems'.[107] In spite of these reservations it was agreed, as McGill had urged, to work with the inquiry and on 13 April the LLI wrote to McAteer stating they were 'very pleased to learn that your party will ... cooperate with us in our inquiry'.[108] This had already begun in Derry, where at a meeting of the local party, James Doherty announced that Eugene O'Hare was already preparing a 'dossier on electoral discrimination' and invited others to prepare material on matters such as the provision of jobs and housing by the city's Corporation. A few weeks later it was announced that Alderman Hegarty and Councillor Brian Friel were 'working on up to date figures on job allocations', whilst Doherty 'reported he was preparing figures for house allocations'. In addition members were informed that 'L. McCollum (barrister) had agreed to put our case in "lawyer-like language" '.[109] Once these were nearing completion McAteer sent a letter to Thornberry, Secretary of the LLI, on 12 May with the first dossier on 'municipal employment in Derry' and promised 'Dossiers on other aspects will follow shortly'.[110]

Elsewhere, in other areas of the province, other representatives of the party also began to collate evidence to present to the inquiry team. In Fermanagh John Carron, who had gained Healy's seat at Stormont following his retirement at the 1965 election, agreed to establish a small commit-

tee to gather material. Carron wrote to Healy requesting that 'If at all possible I would like yourself ... for your knowledge is invaluable with O'Hare,
M. Mahon, Traynor and P. Maguire'.[111] By September Healy was in a position to tell the LLI 'Fermanagh County is getting ready the evidence as to
the gerrymandered electoral areas, the property vote, and discrimination in
housing, public posts and work generally'.[112]   Similarly, McGill had
informed McAteer 'I have this minute sent off ... about the Omagh and West
Tyrone discrimination facts, being prepared in an arrangement made by
you'.[113]

It is important to point out again that the significance of the LLI for the
Nationalist Party lay not in any great expectations that it would produce any
great results but in the need, as McGill had emphasised, 'to strengthen the
public image for the party'.[114] This was now critical for the party as after
two years in the role of Official Opposition at Stormont nothing had been
gained. As McAteer was to state 'We took this calculated, risky decision ...
based on the hope Captain O'Neill was indeed ... earnest about reform. In
fact we have been bluffed so far because there has been no reform'.[115] The
frustration that this was now producing can be identified in an editorial in
the *Irish News* which drew attention to recent government appointments to
a number of statutory bodies:

> they have not hesitated to offer another insult to the minority by finding all
> but a few of them in default of the qualities needed to serve on the Youth
> Employment Service Board ... two out of 33; on the Hospitals Authority two
> out of 22 .. on the General Health Services Board two out of 24.[116]

Nowhere however was this mounting anger more evident than in
Derry, where since the loss of the new university to Coleraine, followed by
other instances of the government allegedly ignoring the city, had according
to Curran given 'credence to the theory that a policy to down-grade Derry
was being insidiously and painstakingly pursued from Stormont'.[117]
Examples had included the Benson Report which proposed that the Great
Northern and LMS railways should be cut from Derry so ending the city's
direct train routes to Dublin and Belfast; the government's decision to concentrate its economic development plan around the building of a new city
between Lurgan and Portadown; or the siting by the Michelin Tyre
Company of their new factory in Ballymena rather than Derry. With regards
to the new city of Craigavon for many, 'It was obvious that such a concep-
tion could only be undertaken at the expense of Derry' and as a result

'Nationalists bitterly accused the government of starving Derry industrially and strangling it politically, and the local Unionists of collusion in the two-pronged assault'.[118]

If this feeling of resentment was not bad enough, the fact of the matter was that for the city 'expansion, not only economically, but physically had become a matter of life and death. Over 50,000 people were crammed into an area of just over 2,000 acres within a city boundary that had been unchanged for a century and a quarter'.[119] The obvious solution to this problem appeared to be simply to extend the city's boundaries and throughout 1966 the local party in Derry had agreed to press for such a policy.[120] Support also came for this particular strategy from non-political bodies such as the Londonderry Junior Chamber of Commerce which published a pamphlet, Thoughts on *Boundary Extension*, which stated 'Londonderry requires urgent expansion and the best form would be an enlarged county borough'.[121] A similar conclusion was then reached by two reports which also looked into the issue, one by the Chief Officers of the Corporation, and the other from a group of planning consultants employed by the Corporation to come up with an outline plan for the development of the Waterside area. When, however, the extension of boundary extension was raised in the Corporation, much to the annoyance of Nationalist councillors, the Unionist majority voted en masse to reject the idea. Even when the reports from the City's Officers and the firm of planning consultants were published Unionist councillors 'still managed to reject a proposal that the Reports be sent to the Ministry of Development for comment; instead they ordered them to be pigeon-holed and forbade their publication'. Such a move prompted Seamus Deeny, a local Nationalist councillor, to cynically conclude, 'We have made history. We are the only city in the North where the Council has refused to extend the city boundary; we are the only city where some of the citizens have murdered their own city'.[122]

With signs of increasing frustration at the lack of progress towards meaningful reform, it is hardly surprising to find that some in the Nationalist Parliamentary Party continued to view with suspicion the growth in the profile and support for the new figures and groupings, who were also seeking to raise the grievances of the minority community. As Currie points out this was based on the belief that such people had a secret agenda in mind which was to usurp and eventually replace the Nationalist Party.[123] Attention has already been drawn to McGill's comments to McAteer that they needed to involve themselves fully in the LLI or otherwise 'some other crowd will' and so ensure that 'our political clothes are not stolen'. A few days later he further suggested, 'I think you ought to consider passing word to John Carron or Pat O'Hare to collaborate with Cahir and get out the Nationalist Party case for Fermanagh and that will settle the CSJ effort to ... take the credit'.[124]

Suspicions had also grown over the possible impact being made at Westminster by Fitt and what he intended to do, if anything, with the high profile his work there had brought him. Since his election as MP for West Belfast in 1966 Fitt had forged close links with the growing number of Labour backbenchers who had shown a greater interest in Northern Ireland affairs. This had been skillfully done by his use of material produced by the CSJ and his own political background which made him a natural ally of the Labour government. He had left his humble surroundings in Belfast to serve in the British merchant navy for 12 years between 1941 and 1953. Whilst at sea according to W.D. Flackes he had 'educated himself in law and politics' and when he left the service 'devoted himself to grass roots politics in his native Dock' area. He soon established himself as a 'personality in local politics', emphasising the need to tackle bread and butter issues, such as unemployment and poor housing.[125] As Purdie points out he considered himself to be a 'Connolly socialist', who believed that the 'Irish socialism that James Connolly had envisaged had not evolved because of partition'. The only solution Fitt argued was to 'integrate the Labour movements on both sides of the border'. All of this, as Purdie suggests, was by no means 'particularly original' as Connolly 'was a favourite icon of the Irish left in the 1960s and was often used to provide a nationalist slant for socialist social and economic policies'. Rather, Purdie saw Fitt's skill in using all of this, 'to present just the right degree of non-sectarian imagery to wrong foot his opponents and rivals, while not straying too far from what was acceptable to his core support among Catholic Belfast voters'.[126]

As Rumpf and Hepburn conclude, the danger posed by Fitt to the Nationalist Party lay in the possibility that he could surpass McAteer as the 'spokesman for Ulster Catholics'.[127] This was to surface after a visit of a number of Labour MPs, organised by Fitt, to Northern Ireland to enable them to see for themselves the grievances people had in such areas as Derry and Strabane, and their subsequent call for a 'united front' amongst the various opposition parties in the province.[128] Such a call alarmed McGill and he told McAteer that all this talk 'about NDP, Republican Labour, NILP and "Nationalists" all to combine to form one party – this is ... an extension of the United Nationalist Front concept of last year ... (and) a regurgitation of the Gormley thesis – all against the Union'. What had disappointed him even more was the impression from the newspaper reports 'that some of our men have been encouraging this latest move and (it is) clear that Fitt's tour was intended to advance it. We have come to a nice pass when unity can be undertaken on the say so of three British Labour MPs'. He now urged McAteer to think carefully of the future:

> position: what is projected is a united movement headed by it
> r whom, probably Fitt ... If we as a party give into this then as a
> sunk ... I am inclined to the belief that the time is coming when
> must find out who is with you and who is not, and if you have
> en take those and stand firm on the bastion. Co-operation yes,
> Unionists if it brings practical results; but amalgamation and
> fment no. You can be sure of all the fellows except the obvi-

The onus was, therefore, very clearly upon the Nationalist Party to show that the recent advances it had made to modernise its image and structure had worked and now provided it with an organisation capable of going on the "offensive" against the Unionist government. Unfortunately, the impression remains that a great deal of work remained to be done and a perfect example of this was to be in Derry, which if anything was the party's stronghold. Early in 1967 the local party had begun to consider the possibility of putting up candidates outside the South Ward in the forthcoming local government elections. At a meeting, on 8 March, delegates from the recently established Young Nationalist section, which was affiliated to the party, put forward a proposal that candidates should be nominated for the two Unionist held wards. James Doherty agreed that this should be a long term goal in order to ensure that it was clear to everyone of the party's intention to one day secure a majority on the corporation.[130] Over the next few weeks, however, the practical problems of attempting to do this immediately were discussed and in the end the conclusion was reached that it was not in their interest to do so at this juncture. On 26 April a lengthy discussion took place on the issue and McAteer finally proposed a motion, which was seconded by Alderman Hegarty, that the party should 'confine ourselves to the South Ward'. The minutes of the meeting record that the decision which was taken was based largely on the lack of self confidence and internal party organisation, and therefore, it was 'Generally felt within the party that we lacked the candidates, finance and organisations to fight these wards' and so McAteer's motion was passed by 13 votes to seven.[131]

In addition, in spite of the efforts that had been made to convey the message that the party was now a province wide organisation with a membership able to come together at an annual conference to debate policy, all the signs seemed to indicate that members of the Parliamentary Party continued to pursue their own agenda. This is perfectly illustrated by the continuing activities of the Gormley brothers: in May, Tom became the first Nationalist MP to attend a Royal function by attending a garden party at Hillsborough,[132] whilst Paddy kept up his calls for the creation of a 'united opposition' with the 'common objective' of fighting the 'mismanagement by the Unionist Party'. He maintained '40 shades of green existed' because there were '40 different ideologies' and if 'there was more attention paid to practical politics there would be no room for ideological differences'.[133]

Underlying all these problems lay the harsh fact that in spite of the long years of campaigning and active opposition in and out of Stormont nothing as yet had been won. The role of Official Opposition had been accepted back in 1965 in the hope that some practical results would be achieved but two years later the minority community was still waiting for a reform package capable of satisfying their demands. As McAteer was forced to admit during his speech to the party's annual conference in July 'the past year had been one of patient expectations when Nationalists had looked for some remedy ... But that hope had not yet been fulfilled'.[134] As a result he had warned throughout the year that without some kind of response from the government 'we will certainly have to reconsider our position'.[135] Yet if such a step was to be taken the question that had to be asked was what then was the alternative. That one was needed was clear by the tone of an editorial in the *Irish News* which contrasted O'Neill's promise that his tenure in office marked the 'inauguration of a community happier and politically more progressive and a liberal era. Fair words and conciliatory gestures ... lent colour to these hopes ... Time, alas, would seem to be showing that the image was all wrong', and had proved to be a 'mirage'.[136]

One thing was certain however, and that was that McAteer remained firmly committed to the ideal that under his leadership the party would not deviate from its 'traditional path'.[137] For Currie this amounted to no more than a pledge to continue with existing parliamentary and constitutional means to reduce the growing tension in the community and thus avoid the possibility of violence.[138] McAteer persevered with his efforts to persuade either the authorities at Westminster or Stormont to take immediate steps to try to ease the situation by way of some guarantee that reforms were on the way. In September he had again visited London to meet with Jenkins and Hogg to let them know 'what is cooking as far as Northern Ireland affairs are concerned'. It was also vital he pointed out to again remind them 'that there had been precious little practical improvement in the plight of the minority so far', and that they were still waiting for 'remedies' for the 'things they so frequently complained about ... discrimination against Catholics in jobs and housing', and the continuing 'failure to endow us with the One Man, One Vote system in local government'.[139] Such visits did not however bring any sign of a breakthrough and more often than not McAteer's queries were met by the now standard answer from politicians in Britain, 'The irritants of which complaint is made relate to matters which lie wholly within the constitutional ambit of the Parliament and Government of Northern Ireland and I would not consider it proper on my part to intervene ...'.[140]

Similarly McAteer tried to interest O'Neill into beginning a process where through negotiations some kind of a reform package to improve community relations could be agreed upon. In November he asked the Prime Minister for a private meeting in the hope that it would bring about an 'honest attempt to try to find some basis of progress without either of us playing to the gallery'. Yet here too he was rebuffed, and the meeting lasted a mere ten minutes with McAteer's disappointment mirrored by the *Irish News* which commented that 'McAteer, like many of us, must now be moving from disenchantment to disdain'.[141]

In spite of all these setbacks McAteer remained determined that his efforts to bring about conciliation would continue even if it ran the risk of alienating members of his own party and its supporters. Thus in June 1967 he approached James Dillon, National President of the AOH, with a suggestion that in order to improve community relations his organisation should make the 'supreme sacrifice in going out of existence' in the hope the Orange Order would respond by taking the same course of action.[142] This was rejected out of hand by Dillon as being completely impractical and unacceptable as the Orange Order would simply use the opportunity to justify their claims that the AOH had always 'promoted acrimony and ill will'.[143] Lennon, who was also Vice President of the AOH, appealed to McAteer to reconsider his proposal and argued it would not produce the results he desired. Rather, Lennon warned of the danger it could do to the

continuing relationship between the Nationalist Party and the Hibs, especially in the rural areas where the AOH 'has always been at the service of
Nationalist candidates'. Furthermore, he was concerned that 'both in the
United States of America and Scotland where there is a very substantial
membership of the AOH this suggestion would simply not be understood
and would be considered as a hostile act on your part'.[144]

Along with the suggestion for the AOH to dissolve itself, McAteer
managed to stir up further controversy with an offer to turn the LLI into a
'court of conciliation' and he made public his belief that the 'Labour
Lawyers would only be to glad to give their services in making out a peace
plan'.[145] This led to the editor of the *Irish News*, T.P. O'Keeffe, to write to
Healy to inform him that McAteer's suggestion on the LLI was completely
wrong and could be 'used by the Unionists to confuse the issue'. Instead,
O'Keeffe insisted, 'would it not be better to establish ... that discrimination
does exist in the various fields and produce the proof, once and for all. This
done we could then talk all we want about conciliation'. O'Keeffe then
appealed to Healy that if he agreed with this assessment, he should write an
article giving his reasons, which the *Irish News* would print.[146] The offer was
accepted, and in the paper on 28 August, Healy expressed his surprise at
McAteer's suggestion to turn the LLI into a 'court of conciliation' and his
worries that the whole process could be cancelled 'seemingly at our
request'. His opposition was based solely on his experience with the failed
Orange and Green talks and he therefore concluded 'A conciliation group of
wishful thinkers would leave us as we stand, witness the result of the
Orange and Green group set up a few years ago in which Mr McAteer himself co-operated and which was eventually called off by the Orange Order'.
Any such move he believed would be seen as 'acting contrary to what the
public expect and what we have been arguing for years', namely the 'truth
brought out by an independent legal tribunal of the Westminster parliament'.[147]

For others, like Currie, such controversy was by now a side issue to the
main problem which remained the fact that the minority community in
Northern Ireland was still awaiting a meaningful reform package. Currie,
was not yet sure how this could be won, but the lack of urgency from both
Stormont and Westminster seemed to suggest that other means had to be
tried. What this would involve had not been settled upon but one thing was
certain, the reforms so far introduced had not gone far enough.[148] For
instance, in December 1966 the Queen's Speech at Stormont had, amongst

other things, proposed the abolition of the business vote for Stormont elections, four new parliamentary seats to replace those still held by Queen's University and an investigation into the nature and role of local government.[149] Over the next year, however, as government plans began to take shape, particularly with regard to local government, it became clear that this would not satisfy Nationalist demands. Although the Minister of Home Affairs announced that the existing local government structure would be replaced by 18 new area councils, he also made it clear that no review of the local government franchise would take place until the 'streamlining of the present system' had been completed.[150]

Throughout 1967 Currie had begun to pick up on the plight of Catholic families, especially in areas in Tyrone, who were having great difficulties in obtaining houses from Unionist controlled councils. By October in Stormont he was pointing to the recent cases of squatting in the Caledon area of Dungannon Rural District Council by homeless Catholic families as an example of the 'growing desperation and frustration' and he wanted to inform people that it was capable of producing some 'real anger in Northern Ireland politics'.[151] As his own patience with O'Neill ran out, he launched a bitter attack on the Prime Minister and his government during a speech at Magee College in Derry. He alleged that O'Neill had 'not even begun to tackle any of the main problems which cripple this community' and furthermore in spite of his 'expressions of pious hopes and well intentioned phrases ... Down in the grass roots nothing stirs'. For him the forthcoming White Paper on local government reform presented a final 'opportunity to translate hopes into achievements' and warned that another year of 'growing frustration and anger' would 'make a real impact on politics in this area'. In particular he predicted 'There will be more squatting, more acts of civil disobedience, more emphasis on the "other means" and less on traditional parliamentary methods'. If this was to happen then 'Terence O'Neill and his Government must carry the reponsibility'.[152]

The views expressed by Currie in this speech on the subject of civil disobedience however were not shared by other party colleagues especially those in Derry, who had been involved in the street protests of 1951 and 1952. After such experiences they were reluctant to adopt any kind of a strategy which involved taking people onto the streets again due to the inherent risks involved, namely that it would inevitably end in serious public disturbances. The chief concern of the party in Derry remained the fact that anything other than a strictly constitutional approach could produce a period of turmoil. As a result, therefore, as "responsible" politicians it was felt that it was their duty to take an active and constructive part in politics, and to ensure that the interests of the nationalist population of the city were properly looked after.[153] This was illustrated by their belief in the need for them to have an input into the development plan announced for Derry in March 1968. The plan not only proposed that it remain as Northern Ireland's second city but included undertakings to build up to 10,000 new houses, encourage major industrial growth by improving communications and for the provision of new schools and recreational facilities. At the local party's annual general meeting in May, whilst the secretary attacked the plan as another 'gerrymander', James Doherty 'explained the necessity of the plan and the benefits it would bring'.[154]

By this stage Currie had decided that only direct action by the nationalist population themselves would bring about any improvement in their conditions. As 1968 progressed he began more and more to follow his own course which seemed to take him further away from his party colleagues.[155] Early in the year, in Stormont he had defended his support for the squatters in Caledon and repeated 'If doing what he had done was called being a supporter of civil disobedience then he was an unrepentant supporter of civil disobedience'.[156] A few months later he followed this with a pledge that 'We will have justice or we will make a government system based on injustice unworkable' and to achieve this he called for 'all weapons in the arsenal of non-violence and civil disobedience' to be used.[157] The chance to put some of these ideas into action finally was to come in June with the eviction of the squatters in Caledon and his subsequent condemnation of the move which led to his expulsion from the chamber. Having been unable to persuade the government or the Minister of Development to intervene on the issue Currie concluded that this marked 'a failure of traditional Parliamentary representation' and along with a number of his supporters began his own squat in Caledon.[158] A month after this, Currie then appealed to the Northern Ireland Civil Rights Association (NICRA), which according to Farrell had been established in 1967 as 'a multi-party lobbying organisation on civil rights issues', to hold a protest march from Coalisland to Dungannon to highlight the situation even further. After some discussion a decision was finally reached and Currie's proposed march was set for 24 August.[159]

Whilst Currie had pursued his own course, McAteer had continued on with his efforts to try to secure change solely by constitutional means and so avoid the threat of violence which direct action could provoke. With his family background, his brother Hugh had been Chief of Staff of the IRA for a time in 1941, and long experience in politics, he was by 1968 only too aware of the growing frustration and anger amongst many in the nationalist community.[160] His aim, therefore, was to continue to endeavour to persuade the government to act quickly before the situation deteriorated any further. For instance, during a debate on local government reform at Stormont in February, he urged O'Neill to involve the opposition parties in the process so as to avoid sowing 'the seeds of further recrimination in the years ahead'.[161] This warning was then further developed in May when he warned O'Neill and his government that he could detect a growing 'smell of sulphur' in the air.[162]

As McAteer sought to ensure that change within Northern Ireland came about by peaceful means, the pressure for a reform package to be introduced immediately continued to grow. In August the interim report of the LLI was published and pointed to a number of areas where 'grievances' had been identified. Amongst these were the local government franchise, the gerrymandering of electoral boundaries particularly those at local government level, and discrimination against Catholics in the allocation of local authority housing and employment. For McAteer the report was proof, if proof was needed, that 'something is rotten in the state of Northern Ireland', and for the need for urgent action to be taken to restore 'democracy in this part of Ireland'.[163]

Unlike Currie, however, McAteer still considered that the best way to quicken the reform process was not by direct action, such as squatting or organising public marches, but persuading through negotiation the authorities, at either Stormont or Westminster to act. In July he had again written to the Home Office in London to ask for a meeting with the Home Secretary, and hopefully Wilson, in order to convey to them 'the anxious position which is fermenting here' and stressed even 'a brief meeting would have an important deterrent effect here'.[164] At the same time, McAteer sought another private session with O'Neill 'to impress on him the sense of frustration and disillusionment felt by the Nationalist people'.[165]

Yet, as in the past, he appeared to gain little for his efforts and on both fronts the answers remained unchanged. On a visit to Belfast Lord Stoneham, the Home Office Minister responsible for the province, made it clear once again that Westminster would not intervene over issues 'such as discrimination, plural voting or gerrymandering' as these areas remained the sole responsibility of Stormont. In addition the present Labour administration under Wilson held out the hope that 'as far as possible ... the Government of Northern Ireland would make changes, if necessary, to ensure there is no possible basis for (such) accusations'.[166] Similarly in his meeting with O'Neill, McAteer appealed to the Prime Minister to take significant steps immediately and although he was 'not fussy' what came first he felt 'local authority administration was the nettle to grasp'. The response from O'Neill was disappointing and McAteer, on leaving the meeting ruefully commented, 'This time it lasted ten minutes instead of eight minutes the last time, so I suppose this is a 20% improvement in relations'.[167]

With little indication of any sign of movement, Currie attempted to persuade the Nationalist Party to commit itself to the ideas and suggestions he had adopted in order to try to secure meaningful reforms. At the party's annual conference on 23 June he tabled a motion which stated:

> This conference reaffirming the dedication of the Party to the ideal of Social Justice for all ... and recording its disappointment ... with the so-called "Pace of Change" declares its willingness to support a policy of non-violent disobedience to wreck a system which has as its basis the deliberate policy of denying equal treatment and free opportunities for all.[168]

The possibility of such a motion ever gaining the support of the whole party was remote due to the reservations many people had about any such campaign staying non-violent. As McGill was to state, 'emphasis upon civil disobedience movements is really a conditioning of the populace towards the unknown – and unworkable unless everyone takes to the streets – (which) then makes a nonsense of passive civil disobedience'.[169] During his address as party leader to the delegates, McAteer, whilst recognising the 'deep disillusionment with the lack of progress which has been made in abolishing the second class citizenship label which is hung around the necks of our people', renewed his appeal for calm and argued 'we must not allow ourselves to be goaded into precipitate action which indeed might not be fully supported by the body of our people'. Although Currie and his supporters from East Tyrone argued forcibly for the motion to be adopted, the majority of the other delegates came out against it. In particular what concerned many was the feeling that the policy had not been properly thought through on what it could possibly lead to.

With no agreement in sight, Lennon proposed a compromise 'that the Conference was not sufficiently informed' to reach a decision and suggested it be sent back to the Executive with the direction to examine it fully and report back to a Special Conference in six months'. In the end, even though Lennon's suggestion was accepted unanimously, it did nothing to alter Currie's view of the proceedings. As the minutes of the conference record he was 'surprised and appalled at the attitude of some of the delegates' and believed that the impression this would give was 'we want justice for our people, but we do not want it all that much'. For him the decision reached that day was the final missed opportunity for the Nationalist Party to be seen at the forefront of a renewed campaign to secure "civil rights" for all. Yet as with previous disagreements within the Party, in the end it made no difference to him, nor did it change his mind on what his next steps should be. For him there was now no turning back on a campaign of non-violent civil disobedience which had already involved him squatting in Caledon or his presence on the first Coalisland to Dungannon march.[170]

The Nationalist Party's rejection of Currie's motion produced a mixed response. An editorial in the *Irish News* welcomed the decision and suggested that such a policy was quite 'rightly a matter for deep consideration' as it was still full of 'loopholes' which the paper claimed could easily play into the hands of 'disruptive elements'.[171] This view was not shared by Fred Heatley, a leading Republican and member of the executive of the NICRA, who concluded that the decision was a clear sign the party had 'abrogated its claim to lead the people who are being victimised under the existing conditions here in the North'.[172] Unfortunately, there were growing signs for the Nationalist Party, that this view was gathering strength in places like Derry. Throughout 1968 the Derry Housing Action Committee (DHAC), a left wing pressure group containing both labour and republican elements, and under the erstwhile leadership of Eamon McCann, had launched a campaign with the 'object of highlighting the problem of the homeless by creating havoc, as publicly as possible'.[173] As McCann concludes in his book *War in an Irish Town* the 'decision to select the Corporation as the primary target ... was in itself a minor political master-stroke'. Its meetings were picketed by supporters of the DHAC and other protests carried out, such as the blocking of the Lecky Road in the city, to highlight the grievances people had over the Corporation's housing policy.[174] Within a few months McCann began to think that 'such activities seemed to be bearing some fruit' and whilst many people objected to their 'political ideals' this was balanced by the fact that 'we were at least getting things done'.[175] The DHAC, however, had another target in its sights and as well as the Corporation it alleged

that the Nationalist Party itself was another symptom of the problems facing the people of Derry. In one of its pamphlets this point was clearly established:

> The great mass of the people continue, for historical reasons to see religion,
> not class, as the basic divide in our society. Thus sectarian consciousness is
> reinforced ... The machinations of Catholic and Protestant Tories such as
> McAteer, Glover, Anderson and Hegarty are carefully calculated to maintain
> the status quo ... People in Derry are worried about housing and jobs and the
> denial of civil rights. The question before us is: how best can the discontent
> arising from each issue be gathered together and directed against the root
> cause – i.e. the political and economic set up?[176]

In normal circumstances the activities of an organisation like the
DHAC would have probably had little impact but as Curran indicates by the
summer of 1968 in Derry, 'Internal pressures were forcing the temperature
up steadily'. Accordingly at a James Connolly commemoration march in
the city Fitt, 'echoing the increasingly militant atmosphere', told the crowd,
'If constitutional methods do not bring justice, if they do not bring democracy to the North, I am quite prepared to go outside constitutional methods'.[177] McAteer was only too aware of this growing sense of anger in the
city and in August he made one last trip to London to meet the Home
Secretary to highlight the seriousness of the situation. He referred to 'the
feeling of frustration and disillusionment among the minority' which had
been caused by the 'sense of disappointment' O'Neill had caused by raising
expectations which remained largely unfilled. This had now produced an
extremely 'dangerous' and volatile position.[178]

It was not long before this final warning from McAteer became a reality with the serious public disturbances which followed the holding of a
civil rights march in Derry on 5 October. This was, after all, to be the event
which finally drew the attention of the rest of the world to Northern Ireland.
In order to try to understand why the events of that day took on such significance it is necessary to highlight the tensions that had been building in
both communities for a considerable period of time.

On the unionist side O'Neill was faced with an ever growing threat to
his authority and this began from within his own cabinet. Members, such
as the Minister of Commerce, Brian Faulkner, were increasingly concerned
with the path the Prime Minister was taking. At this stage Faulkner's opposition was based largely on style and not substance, but it clearly signalled

the dangers that existed for O'Neill. In particular Faulkner was concerned that:

> O'Neill was making the main plank of his premiership the improvement of community relations, and I welcomed his efforts in this direction. But the methods he used were no substitute for real action and only raised hopes that were not being fulfilled ... In 1967 I made a speech referring to the "change in the air" ... But I stressed this should be "a gradual process, developing deep roots, undisturbed by too much probing and not forced up by the spotlights".[179]

In expressing such a view, Faulkner was obviously aware that O'Neill's strategy was causing alarm in the wider Unionist community. His worry was that:

> Too much publicity about our wish to change only fed the fears which Ian Paisley was beginning to exploit: fears that better North/South relations might undermine Ulster's position as part of the United Kingdom; fears that the South was only trying to find a new way of effecting its claim on our territory; fears aroused by the massive republican celebrations of the fiftieth anniversary of the 1916 rising; and fears that the ecumenical movement was in Northern Ireland designed to reduce opposition to a takeover by the Catholic Irish Republic.[180]

Recent months had only illustrated this point, as Paisley had begun to organise counter demonstrations against the growing civil rights movement. For example at the Coalisland-Dungannon march he had led several thousand protestors in an occupation of Dungannon town centre in a clear exhibition of the fact that they believed that 'ecumenism ... combined with political tolerance and even encouragement of Catholics ... appeared to endanger all they stood for ... their religious and political inheritance'.[181]

As for the nationalist community, not only was its patience with O'Neill reaching breaking point, but it also appeared as if it had lost faith in the Nationalist Party. For men like Currie the party's rejection of his call for a campaign of non-violent civil disobedience had been a grave error. As Curran was to conclude, the decision had 'cast away the Nationalists' last chance to reassert their dominant role in deciding what direction the energies of the North's Catholics should be directed'.[182] In recent times this role had been taken over by, and would eventually be controlled by a diverse group of young, largely educated Catholics, who refused to accept any longer what they conceived to be their status as second class citizens. For many in this group, the 1960s had ushered in a new era, and they had watched, and taken encouragement from television coverage of the campaign by Black Americans to end segregation in the Southern States and thus obtain their basic civil rights.[183]

By October 1968, therefore, all that was needed was something to ignite an already tense situation and it came with the civil rights march planned for Derry. The route, submitted by the local organisers, was by its very nature designed to provoke controversy, as it involved areas within the city's historic walls which had been traditionally restricted to Orange processions. When, on 1 October the Apprentice Boys announced their intention to hold an "annual parade" over the same route William Craig, Minister of Home Affairs, took the opportunity to act. On 3 October he banned the demonstration planned by the Apprentice Boys, and announced that the civil rights march would not be allowed 'within the walled city or in the Waterside Ward'.[184]

Even for McAteer, Craig's move was considered to be the final humiliation and as he told the Cameron Commission, which was later established to inquire into the background of events leading up to 5 October, 'I tried to persuade him (Craig) that this was a foolish thing to do ... but he treated me in so cavalier a manner that I decided that I would be at the march'.[185] Others shared McAteer's frustration and according to Paddy Doherty the Minister's decision transformed the attitude of people in Derry to the march. Whilst many had initially been very wary and suspicious of the real intentions of march organisers, like Eamon McCann, the ban changed all of this. As Paddy Doherty's son told him 'Craig's challenge is not only to the civil rights movement but to all Catholics in Derry, because he has identified them as the same people. He has to be confronted or we will never get off our knees'.[186]

As McAteer was to correctly conclude at the time, the aftermath of these events were undoubtedly going to usher in 'a new phase in six County politics'[187] and the question that now confronted the Nationalist Party was what its role was going to be. The dilemma facing the party was to be perfectly illustrated by its contradictory attitude towards the civil rights campaign. Although it was anxious to give its support to the goal of securing "civil rights" for all, the party was still reluctant to commit itself to the campaign currently underway. To begin with, it remained opposed to the methods being used, as the party felt street protests and public demonstrations would ultimately lead to conflict. In addition, as with the attempt to bring the new university to Derry, the party took a conscious decision not to become actively involved, in case their presence was used to try to discount the claims that were being made that the call for "civil rights" was a non-political issue. As a result, when marches were being organised in Dungannon in August and Derry in October members were asked to attend as individuals and not as representatives of the party.[188] The problem that this was going to create, however, was that if these marches and protests appeared to quicken the reform process who would gain the plaudits? Furthermore, would people remember the long years of fruitless opposition carried out by the Nationalist Party?

It comes as no surprise to find that after the events of 5 October O'Neill found himself under enormous pressure from Wilson to take imme-diate steps to end the crisis in Northern Ireland. At a meeting between the two men on 4 November Wilson emphasised that 'only speedy reform could avert the irresistible pressure for legislation at Westminster – under rights explicitly reserved by Section 75 of the Government of Ireland Act – inter-vening in Irish affairs'. In particular, Wilson suggested a number of areas which needed to be tackled straight away: reform of the local government franchise; action over the allocation of housing; the appointment of a Parliamentary Ombudsman to investigate claims of maladministration by Stormont; and an investigation of certain aspects of the SPA.[189] O'Neill was in no position to disagree and a few weeks later announced a five point reform package which covered most of the topics raised by Wilson and which far exceeded anything that the Nationalist Party had been able to gain in over 40 years. This was to involve the following: the abolition of the Londonderry Corporation and its replacement by an appointed Development Commission; an Ombudsman to be appointed to investigate any grievances against central government; the repeal of those sections of the SPA which 'conflicted with Britain's international obligations'; all local authorities to be encouraged to allocate housing by a fair and equitable points system; and a major overhaul of the structure of local government which would involve such things, as the abolition of the Company Vote and consideration of the introduction of a universal adult franchise for local elections.[190]

This reform package was announced just at a time when the Nationalist Party was seeking to regain the ground it had lost in recent months to the new, emerging leadership which had grown out of the civil rights move-ment. On 12 October the party's executive had met and James Doherty, as

Chairman, declared in a sombre tone, which Lennon suggested he do in order to emphasise the seriousness of the decision, that it would ask the parliamentary party to withdraw from its position as Official Opposition at Stormont.[191] A few days later this was confirmed, when Nationalist MPs and Senators met to proclaim that they would 'cease to function as the Official Opposition until such times as the Government gives further concrete evidence of its sincere desire to remedy the present situation'.[192] Then, just over a month later, the special conference promised back in June was convened and the decision taken unanimously that the party should give its backing for a policy of non-violent civil disobedience. For Currie the message was clear 'Today the Nationalist Party serves notice on the Government of its determination to keep up the fight until social justice for all is insured ... We have served notice ... that our patience is at an end'.[193]

Yet it soon became obvious that this attempt by the Nationalist Party to re-establish itself as a potent political force still had to overcome the fact that many within its ranks now wanted a period of consolidation and not further confrontation. As James Doherty was to state the overriding aim of the party was now to build on the reforms that had been won and not to plunge the province into further chaos.[194] This was evident at a party meeting in Derry on 6 November when it was agreed to recommend that instead of a 'uniform' policy of civil disobedience across the province it should be left up to each individual constituency to decide which way to act. Subsequently, therefore, at the special conference in Dungannon on 17 November although the decision was taken to adopt a programme of non-violent civil disobedience no details were given as to how or where it would be carried out.[195]

In addition, opinions within the party as a whole were split over how it should react to the package of reforms announced by O'Neill at Stormont on 22 November. McAteer firmly believed it was time that the community recognised the problems the Prime Minister faced especially from within his own ranks, and therefore he pronounced 'I would like to give it a chance. It is half a loaf'.[196] This assessment was supported by James Doherty during a debate at a party meeting in Derry on the newly established Development Commission. Whilst some members argued that it was no more than an attempt to prevent the nationalist majority in the city gaining power he insisted it would help to start to solve many of their grievances. The onus was therefore on them to ensure that it was 'fair, and composed of well qualified and objective men'.[197]

This apparent acceptance of O'Neill's belated good intentions, how-

ever, did not meet with the unanimous approval from all of McAteer's parliamentary colleagues. According to Tom Gormley, they were nothing more
than a 'smoke screen' designed to buy the Unionist cause some time until
Wilson fell from office and was replaced by their Conservative allies. From
Michael Keogh, who had succeeded Connellan as MP for South Down in
1967, there was a great deal of scepticism in that 'anything in the nature of
reforms which had the unanimous approval of the Unionist Party must be
treated with the deepest suspicion ... One could come to the conclusion that
nothing was being given away'.[198] These views were also shared by Currie
and for him McAteer's "half a loaf" statement was a major blunder, as it further tarnished the party's already damaged image amongst large sections of
the community, for whom O'Neill's announcement had come "too little, too
late".[199]

This had been perfectly illustrated by the fact that people continued to
take to the streets in protest throughout November and December. By this
stage, their demands had gone beyond the reforms announced by O'Neill on
22 November, to include such things as: the immediate introduction of One
Man, One Vote for all elections; the complete repeal of the Special Powers
Act; the dismissal of Craig, the Minister of Home Affairs; and the establishment of an independent inquiry into the events surrounding the march
on 5 October.[200] Faced by the growing threat of civil unrest and from mounting opposition from within his own party O'Neill made a final appeal for
calm on television on 9 December. He began with the by now famous
words "Ulster stands at the crossroads" and went on to speak 'of the need
for justice to all sections of the community and the inevitability of intervention if Northern Ireland did not put its own house in order'.[201] In his
response the following day, McAteer again repeated the necessity for a period of calm and concurred with O'Neill's warning that the province could
slip into civil war. Whilst he recognised the fact that the government had
still a long way to go 'I take the Prime Minister's point that the Civil Rights
message has been received and understood'. As a result he remained optimistic that the 'good seed will not again fall on stony ground'.[202]

In the end, however, this appeal and further attempts by the government to try to meet the demands of the civil rights movement proved to be
unsuccessful. The Prime Minister followed up his appeal with a further set
of concessions which involved the sacking of Craig, the appointment of an
Ombudsman to investigate grievances at a local government level and a
general amnesty for all those charged over the disturbances of the past few
months, but it was not long before the situation deteriorated even further.[203]

The next potential flash point came with the announcement in December by Peoples Democracy (PD), 'a leftish, student based civil rights organisation', that it had organised a march between Belfast and Derry over the New Year period.[204] The danger that such a march could ignite an already tense situation led McAteer to urge those involved to abide by a statement by the NICRA calling for a "truce" over the Christmas period. Furthermore, he considered it opportune to 'publicly ... express my thanks to the wise heads in the Cabinet who decided on the so-called amnesty in connection with the Civil Rights ... Some time has been bought and the feeling of truce is in the air ... (it) must not be wasted'. Thus, his advice to the PD was simple 'I think it isn't good marching weather in more senses than one and I feel the public has become browned off with marches and that they have lost their novelty'.[205]

It is therefore quite clear that since 5 October McAteer had sought to ensure that the Nationalist Party remained a voice of moderation in what were troubled times. This theme was developed in a number of speeches he was to make on the current state of affairs in the province. At a local party meeting in Derry he had issued a new challenge to those present:

> If indeed the ugly discrimination era is nearing its end, what are our reactions, what are our new attitudes then? ... Yes, there will be startling amendments to Nationalist thinking. What of it? Nationalism has already changed greatly in fifty years – further accelerated change is natural and to be expected. If Belfast is in Ireland, would it be treasonable to work towards rule from Belfast rather from Dublin? Could a two-piece Ireland not be fitted into a sort of little United Nations grouping of these islands? I have no cut and dried answers. But we must think ... and open our minds to the hurricane of change which beats upon us all.[206]

Equally revealing was his address to a meeting of the United Ireland Association (the UIA had emerged from the remnants of the APL in Britain in the 1960s) in London when he referred to the fact it was vitally important that, 'We who are engaged in the laborious work of modernising the North have an obligation in conscience to look for practical results as distinct from winning laurels for our own Party brows'. In addition, he revealed his distaste for 'the no-quarter-go for the groin kind of politics, though that is the treatment which has been meted out to me'. At the present time he considered that 'my task ... is to say as little as possible ... a difficult task for a politician. I do not want to say or do anything that would endanger the prospect of an honourable peace in the North ... To me an ounce of progress ... is worth a ton of publicity'.[207]

The problem however that now confronted McAteer and the Nationalist Party was that conditions in Northern Ireland had deteriorated to such an extent that such a message was lost in the violence which followed the Belfast-Derry march organised by the PD. Once again the spotlight had fallen on the party with regards to its attitude and position on the recent events in the province. Bitter attacks were made on it and typical of these was a letter to the *Irish News*, which stated 'If anyone had listened to McAteer, the deprived citizens of Derry and indeed of Northern Ireland, would still be dispirited, frustrated and paralysed under ... Stormont'.[208] In addition, for many people in Derry McAteer's pronouncement that "half a loaf" was better than nothing was taken as final proof that the party had lost touch with a community that had decided it had enough of Stormont and all it stood for.[209]

These criticisms then lead onto the accusation that the Nationalist Party had failed to provide the minority community with strong leadership at a time of major upheaval. In particular, critics pointed to the failure of the party to fulfil the promises it had made back in 1965 to create a vibrant and viable province-wide organisation capable of providing strong opposition to unionism. As far back as the party's decision in Fermanagh not to contest the Lisnaskea by-election in February 1968 the *Irish News* had accused it of failing to implement the reforms it had promised, such as a card carrying membership or to establish itself in areas where there was not a substantial nationalist vote.[210] Later in May the NDP pointed to the fact that attempts to get the two organisations to work towards a unified party had foundered. This was due largely to their reluctance to accept the claim that simply because a constituency had a Nationalist MP meant it was properly 'organised' by the Nationalist Party. According to the NDP there was still a lack of any party organisation in many areas especially at local government level.[211]

The critical position that the party now faced only became too apparent when O'Neill decided to call a general election early in February 1969, with polling day set for 24 February. Although McAteer could attempt to dismiss the election as no more than an attempt 'to paper over the ever-widening cracks in the Unionist Party', across the province his party faced opponents who were seeking to offer an alternative to the nationalist electorate. In three constituencies Foyle, Mid Derry and South Armagh men such as Hume, Ivan Cooper and Paddy O'Hanlon, who had all emerged out of the civil rights movement made clear their intentions to stand. Then in South Fermanagh and South Down candidates from the PD were nominated against sitting Nationalist MPs. Finally, in Mid Tyrone Tom Gormley, was to be opposed by Tom McDonald of the newly established People's Progressive Party, which believed in the 'socialism of James Connolly', backing for the civil rights campaign and a pledge not 'to accept any longer the mealy mouthed crumbs from Stormont'.[212]   Elsewhere, in Mourne, O'Reilly faced a Unionist opponent and in West Tyrone, in spite of much speculation that a PD nominee would stand, O'Connor was returned unopposed.

As for Currie it is significant that from the outset it was apparent that he was not to face a rival candidate from the nationalist community. This he believed could be explained by the fact that in recent times he had pursued his own agenda which had placed him firmly in the civil rights campaign and as a result had distanced himself from the Nationalist Party. For instance, in a speech in Dublin in January 1969 he had spoken of the important impact the civil rights movement had had on opposition politics in the North. In particular it had 'shown the inadequacy both of abstention and timorous attendance and ... the necessity for a new alignment of political forces in the North'. There was also great encouragement in the way in which the campaign for civil rights had helped to 'capture the idealism of the young' and had allowed for the emergence of a 'new leadership ... few of whom will be prepared to play a part within the pre-Civil Rights political framework'. Now was the time therefore for the creation of a 'new united political movement' and as far as he was concerned 'the sooner the better'.[213]   On accepting the nomination of his local party in East Tyrone Currie vowed 'to vigorously follow up those policies which he had consistently advocated since first being elected' and especially 'to work for the formation of a new political organisation of which he would then become a member'.[214]

Of all the contests probably the most important and the one with the greatest significance was in Foyle where Hume was attempting to defeat McAteer, in what was after all the main stronghold of the Nationalist Party. The prospect of a clash between the two men was not something that was overtly welcomed by either of them, but by 1969 the feeling had grown in Derry that it was something which was almost inevitable.[215]   After all, Hume had come close to running in 1965, when men like Paddy Doherty, Dr Jim

Cosgrove and Michael Canavan had hoped to persuade to him stand to provide new leadership for the nationalist community. Yet in 1965 Hume had turned them down, as he had been unsure whether he could defeat McAteer and also because he had been reluctant to resign from his teaching job.[216] Now, however, as Curran concludes the election 'was his rubicon. He had either to fight McAteer for the leadership of the Nationalist people or abdicate to him'. Still the decision was not an easy one to take and Hume told Curran 'I was reluctant to stand ... but I felt that a more progressive political attitude and movement was vital. I had the feeling that the movement on the streets had attained its immediate objective, and must now be consolidated by political advance'.[217]

Equally for McAteer the prospect of a bruising contest was not one he was about to relish and in any case after almost 25 years in politics he was keen to retire in order to devote more time to his family and business. Such an admission shocked the local party and at a meeting called for 5 February to nominate him, McAteer confirmed he was not seeking to go forward again. Frantic efforts were then made to try to get him to reconsider and the meeting was adjourned to the following evening to allow this to continue. Finally the pressure on McAteer proved to be too much and in the end he agreed to accept the party's nomination.[218]

In spite of all this uncertainty, once campaigning got underway it quickly became obvious that the Nationalists welcomed the opportunity to put their case and as James Doherty informed Paddy Doherty 'I feel like an old war horse who is excited by the smell of battle. The Nationalist Party will fight and win this election'.[219] The party was anxious to stress, that although it welcomed the reforms that had been introduced in recent months, their main aim and guiding principle remained the commitment to a united and independent Ireland.[220] As Curran concludes the campaign allowed them to highlight 'the degree of discomfort felt by traditional nationalists within the civil rights movement', and in their belief 'that the Hume line was too six-County orientated, and that the importance of the border issue had been down-graded'. An example of this was McAteer's assertion that even though he recognised the need to ensure 'unity of action' amongst all sections of the community, in order to create a 'framework of such a broad movement to deal with the problems of the future', he would refuse to change the 'colour of my coat from one door step to another'.[221]

Others were quick to defend the work carried out by McAteer and the party for the people of the city down through the years. According to Dr

Jim McCabe, 'In the last 20 years they have each had hundreds of personal talks with the people of Derry ... We have knocked on their doors and they knocked on our doors'.[222]   Finally, in spite of the promises made that it would be a clean fight, almost inevitably Hume became a target for the Nationalist Party. Alderman Hegarty alleged he could have 'no reasonable defence against the allegation he was endeavouring to make political capital out of the popularity gained in the Civil Rights Movement'. This attack was supported by O'Hare who rebutted Hume's claims that he was attempting to bring people together and, instead, argued his decision to seek 'a personal mandate to form a new party' was tantamount to increasing division. For O'Hare the issue was simple 'My idea of unity is to bridge gaps not to widen them; to embrace all, not to attempt to destroy large sections'.[223]

By its very nature Hume's campaign was inevitably going to focus upon the record and performance of the Nationalist Party. For him, and for many of those involved in its planning and operation, such as Paddy Doherty, the ultimate aim was to see McAteer and his party replaced with a new, vibrant organisation.[224] This was a point picked up frequently by Hume when he argued that the issues raised in the election were straight forward, 'It's about opposition and strong opposition to Unionist policy'. He believed it was no longer enough simply 'to raise the flag of Ireland once every five years by using it as a political emblem ... while doing nothing about the basic problems of the people'. It was evident that people had been forced onto the streets because of their 'disillusionment with the existing political attitudes to the problems of social justice' and the abject 'failure of existing opposition to force the Unionist Government to abandon their policies which offend ...'.[225] Thus, what Hume was asking for was a new 'mandate' to allow him to take a different approach to tackle the problems facing them and this was outlined in his manifesto. He undertook to:

(1) ... work for the formation of a new political movement based on social democratic principles, with open membership, and an elected executive to allow the people full involvement in the process of decision making. (2) The movement must provide ... strong and energetic opposition to conservatism ... pursuing radical, social and economic policies. (3) The movement must be completely non-sectarian and must root out a fundamental evil in our society, sectarian division. (4) The movement must be committed to the ideal that the future of Northern Ireland should be decided by its people, and no constitutional changes accepted except by the consent of its people.[226]

When the results were announced it was quite obvious that the Nationalist Party had suffered a severe setback with three seats Foyle, Mid Derry, South Armagh lost and South Down retained by only 200 votes. (See Appendix 6: Election Results 1964-1969).

McAteer himself summed up the results perfectly when, commenting on his own defeat, he mentioned 'It's a dull day for a funeral'.[227] Yet, although bitterly disappointed at the outcome, he made it clear to Brian Friel that he still firmly believed that the party and the ideals it stood for would survive and flourish again. His immediate reaction to the party's poor showing was to look for answers largely outside their control. He told Friel, 'I have a throaty feeling that so many of our people seem to have turned their backs on that lovely ... thing which I mean by Nationalism', but he held out the hope they would return when they have 'filled themselves with the mess of "British rights and welfare benefits" '.[228] With regards to the party's loss of three seats, McAteer informed others that, whilst he could accept the 'possibility we may have failed to change with the times', he firmly believed that elements within the civil rights movement had exploited it for their own purposes. In particular, he pointed out, that a lot 'of which we hear so much at present is simply an efficient takeover of the work which has been carried on for many years by us'. This 'takeover' had largely been 'helped by the folly of ... Craig' and 'our own lack of guile in thinking the civil rights movement was really non-political'.[229]

As the local party gathered after the election, these points were to be picked up on as an explanation for why the seat had been lost. According to James Doherty, important lessons had to be learnt especially the fact that their opponents by means of 'a well financed team' and 'good advertising' had 'sold a mediocre product in preference to one of better quality'. Along with other members a call therefore went out for the party to come up with a set of 'well defined policies' and a determination to 'sell ourselves to the public'. In order for this to happen the meeting agreed to establish a new party executive with the task to prepare 'the framework of the new look party'.[230] A week later this new body was formally established, and as James Doherty announced, it was to be given the task of attracting a younger element to the party ranks and the production of detailed 'social and economic policies' in order to 'show the electorate we need not aspire to be citizens of one of the depressed areas of Britain'.[231]

This job of trying to re-establish the party not only in Derry but across the province was going to be an immense one as the nature of politics had changed and would continue to do so in the months ahead in Northern Ireland. McGill had recognised this when commenting on the election results to Healy, when he had stated 'The trouble all round is that the wave of emotion consequent on recent events on the streets rose and swamped all before it'.[232] As the *Irish News* had concluded in the wake of the election:

> the demand for Civil Rights is now to be carried from the streets into Stormont ... Since the emergence of the Civil Rights Campaign and street marches, the Nationalist Party has been subjected to close scrutiny and its weaknesses and human failings continually cited in support of its ultimate disappearance by those, who could not remember, nor wanted to be told of the party's thankless efforts to keep alive national ideals and to resist, however impotently, the heavy hand of Official Unionist domination.[233]

Notes

1. McCluskey, *Up Off Their Knees*, p.16.
2. Healy to Professor J. Scott, Undated 1964, D2991/B/13, Healy Papers. Plus *Irish News* 24 July 1964.
3. Irish News 1 January 1964.
4. *Irish News* 31 January and 3 February 1964.
5. *Irish Independent* 9 March 1964.
6. Interviews with J. Doherty, E. O'Hare and A. Currie.
7. McKeown to M. Vinney, *Irish Times* 5 May 1964.
8. McCluskey, *Up Off Their Knees*, p.63.
9. McKeown, *The Greening of a Nationalist*, p.25.
10. Note containing the Resolution for debate at the Maghery Conference, McAteer Collection.
11. McAteer to Miss A. McFadden, 16 April 1964, McAteer Collection.
12. McKeown, *The Greening of a Nationalist*, p.26. Plus C. McCluskey to McAteer, 8 May 1964, McAteer Collection.
13. Interviews with E. O'Hare, J. Doherty and Anonymous Sources in Derry.
14. Minute Book of the Derry Nationalist Party 1963-1970, 22 April 1964, McAteer Collection.
15. *Irish News* 20 April 1964.
16. McAteer to Miss A. McFadden, 22 April 1964, McAteer Collection.
17. Minute Book of the Derry Nationalist Party 1963-1970, 3 and 24 June 1964, McAteer Collection.
18. Minute Book of the Derry Nationalist Party 1963-1970, 24 June 1964, McAteer Collection.
19. *Irish News* 29 April 1964.
20. Minute Book of the Derry Nationalist Party 1963-1970, 20 May 1964, McAteer Collection.
21. Minute Book of the Derry Nationalist Party 1963-1970, 24 June 1964, McAteer Collection.

22. *Irish News* 9 September 1964.
23. McGill to Healy, Undated, D2991/B/24, Healy Papers.
24. *Irish News* 2 September 1964.
25. *Irish News* 3 September 1964.
26. *Irish News* 9 September 1964.
27. Minute Book of the Derry Nationalist Party 1963-1970, 30 September 1964, McAteer Collection. Plus *Irish News* 9 September 1964.
28. Minute Book of the Derry Nationalist Party 1963-1970, 30 September 1964, McAteer Collection.
29. McAteer to Healy, 28 September 1964, D2991/B/21, Healy Papers.
30. *Irish News* 20 June 1964 and Clipping from *Irish Press* 31 May 1964, McAteer Collection. Plus G. Thayer, *The British Political Fringe: A Profile*, (London, 1965), pp.215-216.
31. *Irish News* 20 June 1964 and Interview with A. Currie.
32. *Irish News* 18 and 19 June 1964.
33. McAteer to Healy, 28 September 1964, D2991/B/21, Healy Papers.
34. *Irish News* 3 November 1964.
35. *Irish News* 7 December 1964.
36. *Irish News* 21 November 1964.
37. Nationalist Party – Statement of Policy, (1964), McAteer Collection.
38. McAteer to Healy, 5 November 1964, D2991/B/21, Healy Papers.
39. McAteer to F.W. S. Craig, 21 June 1966, McAteer Collection.
40. *Irish News* 17 November 1964.
41. M. Wallace, *British Government in Northern Ireland : From Devolution to Direct Rule*, (Newton Abbot, 182), p.26.
42. *Irish News* 15 January 1965.
43. Interviews with J. Doherty and A. Currie.
44. Curran, *Countdown to Disaster*, pp.37-38.
45. P. McGill, 'The Senate in Nortern Ireland, 1921-1962', (Ph.D. Thesis, Queen's University, Belfast, 1965), p.111.
46. *Irish News* 3 February 1965.
47. Minute Book of the *Derry Nationalist Party 1963-1970*, 10 February 1965, McAteer Collection.
48. *Irish News* 24 June 1965.
49. Interviews with J. Doherty and Anonymous Sources in Derry.
50. Curran, *Countdown to Disaster,* p.26.
51. Ibid., pp.39-40. Plus B. White, *John Hume: Statesman of the Troubles*, (Belfast, 1984), pp.5-28.
52. *Irish Times* 18 and 19 May 1964. Plus Curran, *Countdown to Disaster*, p.41 and White, *Hume: Statesman of the Troubles*, pp.42-43.
53. Minute Book of the Derry Nationalist Party 1963-1970, 20 May 1964, McAteer Collection.
54. White, *Hume: Statesman of the Troubles*, p.45. Plus Minute Book of the Derry Nationalist Party 1963-1970, 3 June 1964, McAteer Collection.
55. Minute Book of the Derry Nationalist Party 1963-1970, 30 September 1964, McAteer Collection.
56. Minute Book of the Derry Nationalist Party 1963-1970, 18 October 1965, McAteer Collection.
57. *Irish Times* 19 May 1964.
58. Curran, *Countdown to Disaster*, p.30
59. White, *Hume: Statesman of the Troubles*, p.38.

60. Curran, *Countdown to Disaster*, pp.27-39. Plus White, *Hume: Statesman of the Troubles*, pp.38-39.
61. Minute Book of the Derry Nationalist Party 1963-1970, 10 February 1965, McAteer Collection. Plus *Irish News* 6, 9, 11, 13 and 18 February 1965.
62. Curran, *Countdown to Disaster*, pp.42-43. Plus interview with F. Curran.
63. *Irish News* 8 February 1965.
64. *Irish News* 21 June 1965.
65. Minute Book of the Derry Nationalist Party 1963-1970, 19 May 1965, McAteer Collection.
66. Minute Book of the Derry Nationalist Party 1963-1970, 16 June 1965, McAteer Collection.
67. Minute Book of the Derry Nationalist Party 1963-1970, 30 June 1965 and 18 October 1965, McAteer Collection. Plus *Irish News* 24 June 1965 and 9 July 1965.
68. McAteer to Healy, 7 September 1965, D2291/B/21, Healy Papers.
69. Interview with A. Currie.
70. *Irish News* 27 August 1965.
71. *Irish News* 28 August 1965.
72. *Irish News* 31 July 1965.
73. McGill to McAteer, 30 November 1965, McAteer Collection.
74. *Irish News* 28 October 1965.
75. *Irish News* 1 and 5 November 1965. Plus O'Reilly's endorsement of D. Rice, NDP candidate in East Down, (PRONI), D231/2/61.
76. Minute Book of the Derry Nationalist Party 1963-1970, 3 November 1965, McAteer Collection.
77. *Irish News* 22 November 1965.
78. *Irish News* 20 November 1965.
79. *Irish News* 27 November 1965.
80. McGill to McAteer, 6 December 1965, McAteer Collection.
81. *Irish News* 13 December 1965.
82. Interview with A. Currie.
83. *Irish News* 3 February 1966.
84. *Irish News* 30 April 1966.
85. Clipping from the *Sunday Press* 21 August 1966, McAteer Collection.
86. McGill to McAteer, 29 September 1966, McAteer Collection.
87. McGill to Healy, 23 January 1966, D2991/B/24, Healy Papers.
88. McGill to Healy, 22 April 1966, D2991/B/24, Healy Papers.
89. Minute Book of the Derry Nationalist Party 1963-1970, 23 February 1966, McAteer Collection.
90. Interview with J. Doherty.
91. *Irish News* 25 May 1966.
92. Programme of the First Annual Conference of the Nationalist Party, 22 May 1966, McAteer Collection.
93. Nationalist Party Appeal for Funds, McAteer Collection.
94. *Irish News* 7 February 1966.
95. Programme of the First Annual Conference of the Nationalist Party, 22 May 1966, McAteer Collection.
96. *Irish News* 5 August 1966.
97. K. Bloomfield, *Stormont in Crisis: A Memoir*, (Belfast, 1994), pp.87.
98. Letter from Healy and Senator O'Hare to H. Wilson, 20 October 1964; Wilson to Healy, 13 January 1964; and Healy and Senator O'Hare to Wilson, 7 January 1965, (PRONI), HO/5/186.

99. *Irish News* 29 March, 1 April, 23 April and 7 May 1965.
100. H. Wilson, *The Labour Government 1964-1970: A Personal Record*, (London, 1971), p.270.
101. *Irish News* 17 February 1966.
102. Ibid.
103. Wilson, *The Labour Government 1964-1970*, p.270.
104. *Irish News* 11 August 1966.
105. *Irish News* 8 April 1967.
106. McGill to McAteer, 10 April 1967, McAteer Collection.
107. *Irish News* 8 April 1967.
108. Labour Lawyers Inquiry to McAteer, 13 April 1967, McAteer Collection.
109. Minute Book of the Derry Nationalist Party 1963-1970, 12 April and 26 April 1967, McAteer Collection.
110. McAteer to C. Thornberry, Secretary of LLI, 12 May 1967, McAteer Collection.
111. J. Carron to Healy, Undated, D2991/B/87, Healy Papers.
112. Healy to LLI, 17 September 1967, D2991/B/87, Healy Papers.
113. McGill to McAteer, 19 April 1967, McAteer Collection.
114. Ibid.
115. *Irish News* 12 April 1967.
116. *Irish News* 26 September 1967.
117. Curran, *Countdown to Disaster*, p.25.
118. Curran, *Countdown to Disaster*, p.25 and p.40. Plus *Irish News* 23 and 26 August 1967.
119. Curran, *Countdown to Disaster*, p.47.
120. Minute Book of the Derry Nationalist Party 1963-1970 – the topic of boundary extension was debated throughout 1966, McAteer Collection.
121. Curran, *Countdown to Disaster*, pp.47-48.
122. Ibid., pp.50-51.
123. Interview with A. Currie.
124. McGill to McAteer, 10 and 19 April 1967, McAteer Collection.
125. W.D. Flackes, *Northern Ireland: A Political Directory, 1968-1979*, (Dublin, 1980), pp.60-61.
126. B. Purdie, *Politics in the Streets: The Origins of the Civil Rights Movement in Northern Ireland*, (Belfast, 1990), p.61.
127. Rumpf and Hepburn, *Nationalism and Socialism in Twentieth Century Ireland*, p.192.
128. *Irish News* 19 April 1967.
129. McGill to McAteer, 19 April 1967, McAteer Collection.
130. Minute Book of the Derry Nationalist Party 1963-1970, 8 March 1967, McAteer Collection.
131. Minute Book of the Derry Nationalist Party 1963-1970, 26 April 1967, McAteer Collection.
132. *Irish News* 25 May 1967. Plus Purdie, *Politics in the Streets*, pp.58-59.
133. *Irish News* 17 January 1967.
134. *Irish News* 2 July 1967.
135. *Irish News* 12 April 1967.
136. *Irish News* 4 November 1967.
137. Interviews with J. Doherty and Anonymous Sources in Derry.
138. Interview with A. Currie.
139. *Irish News* 29 August, 6 September and 12 September 1967.
140. R. Jenkins to McAteer, 28 November 1967, McAteer Collection.
141. *Irish News* 28, 29 and 30 November 1967.
142. McAteer to J. Dillon, 17 June 1967, McAteer Collection.

143. Dillon to McAteer, 21 June 1967, McAteer Collection.
144. Lennon to McAteer, 26 June 1967, McAteer Collection.
145. Undated Note from McAteer, D2991/B/87, Healy Papers.
146. T.P. O'Keeffe to Healy, 10 August 1967, D2991/B/87, Healy Papers.
147. *Irish News* 28 August 1967.
148. Interview with A. Currie.
149. *Irish News* 14 December 1966.
150. *Irish News* 21 December 1967.
151. *Irish News* 13 September, 19 and 20 October 1967.
152. *Irish News* 24 October 1967.
153. Interviews with E. O'Hare, J. Doherty and Anonymous Sources in Derry.
154. *Irish News* 5 March 1968. Plus Minute Book of the Derry Nationalist Party 1963-1970, 8 May 1968, McAteer Collection.
155. Interview with A. Currie.
156. *Irish News* 24 January 1968.
157. *Irish News* 22 April 1968.
158. Interview with A. Currie. Plus *Irish News* 19, 20 and 21 June 1968.
159. Interview with A. Currie. Plus Purdie, *Politics on the Streets*, p.135 and Farrell, *The Orange State*, pp.245-246 and p.357.
160. Interviews with Anonymous Sources in Derry.
161. *Irish News* 22 February 1968.
162. *Irish News* 8 May 1968.
163. *Irish News* 23 August 1968. .
164. McAteer to the Home Office, 5 July 1968, McAteer Collection.
165. *Irish News* 26 June 1968.
166. *Irish News* 7 June 1968.
167. *Irish News* 26 June 1968.
168. Programme of the Third Annual Conference of the Nationalist Party, 23 June 1968, McAteer Collection.
169. McGill to McAteer, 4 September 1968, McAteer Collection.
170. Interviews with A. Currie, E. O'Hare, F. Curran and J. Doherty. Plus *Irish News* 24 June 1968 and Programme of the Third Annual Conference of the Nationalist Party, McAteer Collection.
171. *Irish News* 24 June 1968.
172. *Irish News* 27 June 1968.
173. White, *Hume: Statesman of the Troubles*, p.61.
174. E. McCann, *War in an Irish Town*, (London,1974), p.28 and pp.27-36.
175. Ibid., p.33.
176. Ibid., p.30.
177. Curran, *Countdown to Disaster*, p.65 and p.68. Plus *Irish News* 22 July 1968.
178. *Irish News* 21 August 1968 and Interviews with Anonymous Sources in Derry.
179. B. Faulkner, *Memoirs of a Statesman*, (London, 1978), p.42.
180. Ibid., pp.42-43.
181. Wichert, *Northern Ireland Since 1945*, p.94.
182. Curran, *Countdown to Disaster*, p.68.
183. Interview with A. Currie.
184. Farrell, *The Orange State*, pp.245-247. Plus Purdie, *Politics in the Streets*, pp.138-141.
185. Statement of E. McAteer to the Cameron Commission, 6 May 1969, McAteer Collection.

186. Interview with Mr P. Doherty 18 August 1994. Plus P. Doherty, *Bogside of the Bitter Zeal*, (unpublished), p.55.
187. *Irish News* 7 October 1968.
188. Interview with J. Doherty. Plus *Irish News* 21 August 1968 and Minute Book of the Derry Nationalist Party 1963-1970, 25 September 1968, McAteer Collection.
189. Wilson, *Labour Government 1964-1970*, p.672.
190. *Irish News* 23 November 1968. Plus White, *Hume: Statesman of the Troubles*, p.68 and Farrell, *The Orange State*, p.248.
191. Interview with J. Doherty. Plus *Irish News* 12 October 1968.
192. *Irish News* 16 October 1968.
193. *Irish News* 18 November 1968.
194. Interview with J. Doherty.
195. Minute Book of the Derry Nationalist Party 1963-1970, 6 November 1968, McAteer Collection. Plus *Irish News* 18 November 1968.
196. *Irish News* 23 November 1968.
197. *Minute Book of the Derry Nationalist Party 1963-1970*, 4 December 1968, McAteer Collection.
198. *Irish News* 25 November 1968.
199. Interview with A. Currie.
200. *Irish News* 11 December 1968.
201. Bloomfield, *Stormont in Crisis*, p.101.
202. *Irish News* 10 December 1968.
203. *Irish News* 12 and 18 December 1968.
204. Farrell, *The Orange State*, p.358 and pp.249-250.
205. *Irish News* 18 and 30 December 1968.
206. Curran, *Countdown to Disaster*, p.92.
207. Address by McAteer to UIA, 14 November 1968, McAteer Collection.
208. *Irish News* 2 January 1969.
209. Interviews with F. Curran and P. Doherty.
210. *Irish News* 11 March 1968.
211. *Irish News* 30 May 1968.
212. *Irish Times* 20 February 1969.
213. Interview with A. Currie. Plus *Irish News* 16 January 1969.
214. *Irish News* 10 February 1969.
215. Interviews with J. Doherty, P. Doherty and F. Curran.
216. Curran, *Countdown to Disaster*, pp.43-45. Plus White, *Hume: Statesman of the Troubles*, pp.53-55.
217. Curran, *Countdown to Disaster*, pp.115-116.
218. Minute Book of the Derry Nationalist Party 1963-1970, 5 and 6 February 1969, McAteer Collection. Plus Interviews with J. Doherty and Anonymous Sources in Derry.
219. P. Doherty, *Bogside of the Bitter Zeal*, p.34.
220. Interview with J. Doherty.
221. Curran, *Countdown to Disaster*, p.115. Plus *Irish News* 7 and 17 February 1969.
222. *Irish News* 24 February 1969.
223. *Irish News* 17 and 24 February 1969.
224. Interview with P. Doherty.
225. *Irish News* 17 and 24 February 1969.
226. Curran, *Countdown to Disaster*, p.115.
227. *Irish News* 26 February 1969.
228. McAteer to B. Friel, 27 February 1969, McAteer Collection.

229. *Irish News* 26 February 1969. Plus McAteer to Mrs C. Philpott, 24 March 1969, McAteer Collection.
230. Minute Book of the Derry Nationalist Party 1963-1970, 5 March 1969, McAteer Collection.
231. Minute Book of the Derry Nationalist Party 1963-1970, 12 March 1969, McAteer Collection.
232. McGill to Healy, 14 May 1969, D2991/B/24, Healy Papers.
233. *Irish News* 27 February 1969.

Conclusion

After the crushing blows inflicted on it by the election results of February 1969 the demise of the Nationalist Party was being talked about and predicted. Yet in the immediate aftermath many of its members remained determined to ensure that the party and the ideals for which it stood for should survive.[1] This was also the message delivered by O'Connor, who had succeeded McAteer as leader of the remaining group of Nationalist MPs and Senators at Stormont in October 1969, at the party's annual conference in Newry on 23 November. He told the delegates present that they should discount the claims now being made that their party was finished and pointed to the fact that he had heard that 'twenty years ago and more from the Minister of Home Affairs'. Instead he emphasised that it was still 'alive and vigorous' and furthermore, remained the only party 'that has openly and clearly declared its principles', which were simply to stand 'clearly and solidly for the unity and independence of this country'.[2]

Ultimately such a goal was to prove illusive and the results of the next set of elections in Northern Ireland clearly showed that the Nationalist Party, instead of undergoing any kind of a recovery, had continued on into terminal decline. In the first contests for the newly established 26 district council areas in May 1973, only in Derry City had the party survived. Even in this area, which after all had once been the party's stronghold, only three of its ten candidates were returned and its share of the first preference votes only amounted to around 9%.[3] Worse was to follow a month later when elections for the new Northern Ireland Assembly saw only two candidates stand as Nationalists, McAteer in Londonderry and McGill in Mid Ulster. Together they polled 8,270 first preference votes and obtained only 1.2% of the votes cast. As W.D. Flackes and S. Elliott point out this marked the first time in the history of Northern Ireland that no Nationalist member had been returned to Stormont.[4] All of this therefore begs the question as to how and why a party, which had for almost fifty years been seen as the voice of Northern Nationalism, had virtually ceased to exist.

In trying to understand how this happened the most obvious place to start is to refer back to the fact that the party could never really be considered as the sole, authoritative voice of the entire nationalist community in the province. Since 1946 it had almost exclusively been restricted to West of the Bann and those areas where there was a built in nationalist majority. After the loss of Belfast, Central following the resignation of T.J. Campbell, it never again attempted, never mind held, a Belfast parliamentary seat at either Westminster or Stormont. In effect this meant that the party had turned its back on those Catholic, working class areas of the city, which had been party bastions under Joe Devlin. As a result a huge number of potential nationalist voters were abandoned and left to be represented by men like Fitt and Diamond who tried to follow a line based on 'non-violent republicanism, linked to socialist objectives'.[5] As Rumpf and Hepburn suggests, this trend, had been developing for some time as relations between city and rural areas had never been particularly good. It had proved 'Difficult during the depression years, for a party lacking in dynamism as Nationalists of that period' to 'find common cause in the grievances of small farmers ... and the unemployed and unskilled Catholics of the city slums'.[6] This pattern is borne out by the profile of the Nationalist Parliamentary Party in the post-war period when the majority of MPs and Senators were still being drawn from rural backgrounds and from occupations which were largely the 'orthodox ones indulged in by the Catholic community, such as farming, law, insurance and the managing of public houses'. Furthermore, as McAllister suggests, such occupations also need to be 'interpreted as being connected with the brokerage and mediating roles, a pattern endemic to the political structure of Irish rural areas'.[7]

This lack of a presence in the East of the province was something which continued to haunt the party and remained a problem which was never seriously tackled although it was recognised as such. For instance, in a reply from a query from someone in the Lisburn area Healy was forced to admit that the lack of organisation in such areas was a 'distinct weakness', and if 'groups or branches' could be 'set up in such places', he believed they 'could keep us in touch with many matters of which we are ignorant of at the moment'.[8] Yet nothing concrete was ever done to remedy this and even when the party attempted to reform and modernise itself in the 1960s, it never moved outside its traditional areas. The reasons for this were partly due to the agreements with other groups such as RLP and NDP that no one would attempt to organise in areas traditionally held by others, and what can only be seen as a continuing lack of ambition and confidence. As Healy was to declare 'We have no branches in Lisburn where seemingly we have not much chance of representation on either Local Boards or Parliament'.[9]

Such a drawback could have possibly been manageable if the Nationalist Party had ever been in complete control of those areas which were supposed to have been under its domination. This, however, was never completely the case as the party continued to be challenged by republican/abstentionist elements. The contest was renewed with an increased vigour after the introduction of the Ireland Act 1949 which strengthened the province's position within the United Kingdom and clearly marked the failure of the APL to succeed in making any headway towards ending partition. Throughout the 1950s Nationalists continued to argue that the only way to achieve progress was by using both Westminster and Stormont to help get across their anti-partition message. This policy, however, never convinced those who believed that only by abstention and refusing to take their seats, if elected, could Northern Nationalists show the rest of the world that they would never accept partition. Attempts to find a compromise between these opposing views, such as the frequent appeals to the authorities in Dublin to allow the representatives of nationalist opinion in Northern Ireland to sit in the Dail, never succeeded as Irish governments made it plain that the plan was completely impractical. Even the attempts by Healy, Mulvey and O'Neill to try to adopt a policy of "modified abstention" from Westminster and use it only when the opportunity arose, to raise nationalist grievances and put forward the anti-partition cause also failed. In the end the growing frustration at the lack of headway in ending partition and the feeling that they had been abandoned by the Dublin government, put paid to Nationalist attempts to hold onto their Westminster seats. This was to be illustrated firstly at the Stormont elections of October 1953 when Abstentionist fought Nationalist in a number of constituencies and then two years later when SF candidates triumphed in Mid Ulster and Fermanagh and South Tyrone at the Imperial elections in May 1955. The final humiliation for the Nationalist Party then followed at the by-election in Mid Ulster a year later when its decision to enter the contest was met by its election workers being heckled, physically attacked and thus, forcing them to abandon their campaign. The result which saw O'Neill pushed into a distant third place behind SF and the Unionist victor, George Forrest, showed the 'alienation of the Northern Nationalist population'.[10]

In addition the campaign in Mid Ulster had once again highlighted the fact that not only was nationalist opinion divided but it lacked any kind of a properly organised political machine or structure. The APL had been established in the hope that it would provide this but since the Ireland Act it had gone into decline and by the mid 1950s was no longer a credible force. Without any organisation behind them individual Nationalist MPs were left, as they had been in the past, to manage and direct their own affairs as they saw fit. The only real assistance they were to receive came from local Registration Committees but these bodies were strictly non-political and their sole task was to look after the electoral register. The isolation of MPs was further increased by the declining links between the party and the AOH, which had been at its height when Joe Devlin was in virtual control of both organisations in the early 1900s. Although Senator Lennon was national Vice-President of the AOH, the only other member of the parliamentary party who was also a leading Hib was Joe Stewart. It is therefore an 'illusion' according to Michael Foy to suggest that the 'AOH wielded great influence on the Nationalist Party'. Compared with the days when the Hibs had been of great assistance to Devlin's United Irish League (UIL):

> 'Membership(of the AOH) was infinitely smaller than in the days of the UIL, the AOH did not as a body provide funds for the party and though the AOH representatives attended conventions which selected Nationalist MPs, there was no longer the army of candidates to help in their campaigns.[11]

By the 1960s however the role and activity of the Nationalist Party was coming under scrutiny and being debated by elements within the wider nationalist community. Eventually groups like NU, plus the McCluskeys and their associates in the Dungannon area, began to pinpoint what they saw as the main faults and failings of the party as it currently existed. In particular, they focused on the decision of the party not to contest the Westminster elections of 1959 and 1964, which they viewed as leaving thousands of voters with no alternative to voting for SF. This seemed to indicate to them that the Nationalist Party was failing to provide people with the leadership it needed. Allied to this was their anger at the lack of a province wide political party open to all and which could represent all shades of nationalist opinion. It looked to them as if Nationalist MPs treated 'their constituencies-like dioceses and they were like Bishops, answerable to no-one and answering to no-one'.[12] It comes as no surprise to find that relations with the party quickly deteriorated and their anger was perfectly summed up after one meeting when they had been told to 'go home, learn Irish and build up the population'.[13]

The pressure on the Nationalist Party from both outside and within its ranks to begin to take steps to create a modern, constituency based organisation continued to grow and finally by the mid 1960s there was an admission that some change had to come. As a first step in this process a general policy statement was published in 1964, an annual party conference was organised for May 1966, and an undertaking was given to establish a party machine with local branches and membership open to anyone interested in joining. Yet all the evidence suggests that senior figures in the Parliamentary Party remained wary of the whole idea, as many of them remembered their bitter experience with previous failed attempts to create and maintain a viable political organisation. The changes that were introduced therefore did not suddenly transform the party and even in Derry City, one of the party's strongholds where some semblance of organisation already existed, there was no radical departure in the way it went about its business or faced up to problems such its perilous financial position.

But by this time this was not the only criticism the party had to face, for questions were being raised at its inability to secure, in over 40 years, any significant reform package from the Unionist Government. In a way this was to be further highlighted by Terence O'Neill's tenure as Prime Minister when his promises to improve social and economic conditions as well as community relations only raised expectations. As a result therefore, in places like Derry, when results were not immediately forthcoming and where instead government decisions like the choice of Coleraine as the site of the province's new University, were perceived as a sign that nothing was going to change, frustration began to grow. This disillusionment applied not only to O'Neill but in an increasing way to the Nationalist Party as well. Into such a situation emerged a relatively new grouping but one which was to have a significant impact on events in Northern Ireland over the next few years. Although its importance can sometimes be over emphasised there is no getting away from the fact that at this time a growing number of young, educated Catholics, who had benefited from the post-war education reforms, began to take a greater interest in politics. What probably characterised this diverse group was their determination no longer to accept what they saw as the second class citizenship endured by their parents. If this meant challenging the existing political status quo, such as providing the minority community in the province with a new more vigorous and active opposition than that being currently offered by the Nationalist Party, then that was something which some were prepared to do.

Eventually this strategy led to the adoption, following the example of recent events in the United States of a non-violent civil disobedience campaign, in order to bring to the fore the alleged lack of 'Civil Rights' for Northern Catholics. For the Nationalist Party such a tactic was considered to be seriously flawed and potentially dangerous as it could lead to conflict. At its party conference in June 1968 Currie attempted to persuade the party to adopt such a plan. But the majority of the delegates were opposed to it and McAteer urged them to think carefully before 'going home and taking up the pike ... We must not allow ourselves to be goaded into precipitate action'.[14]

Instead under the leadership of McAteer the party continued to try to ensure that any reforms would be won by strictly constitutional means and so he carried on with his frantic efforts to persuade either the authorities at Westminster or Stormont to act before it was too late. What happened in Derry on 5 October 1968, and the subsequent events in the weeks and months ahead seemed to indicate that only direct action appeared to bring about the desired results. Furthermore, the momentum and initiative which had been seized by the civil rights movement and the new leaders it had thrown up was to be confirmed by the election in February 1969. These results confirmed that the reward had gone to those who had been credited with winning in recent 'times more than Catholics had won in 47 years of parliamentary opposition' under the Nationalist Party.[15]

Thus, any chance the party had of a recovery after this setback seemed remote and if anything deteriorated in the months ahead as Northern Ireland plunged in a period of civil unrest and political turmoil. The problem now was that the party had to find some sort of role for itself in these new conditions. Within the party in Derry what its attitude should be towards the escalation in street violence began to produce friction. Some believed that it was being counter-productive and was only making a dangerous situation worse, whilst there were those who refused to consider any condemnation which might be construed as a criticism of those engaged in trying to protect their areas from sectarian attack. Finally in October 1970 after the local branch rejected a motion condemning the outbreak of rioting in Belfast, the "moderate element" that included stalwarts such as James Doherty, Eugene O'Hare and Thomas McDonnell, the local party chairman, all resigned and severed all links with their former colleagues.[16]

As for the rest of the parliamentary party, its condition was further weakened as Currie and then Tom Gormley gradually distanced themselves from it. According to Currie the mood of the period was very much in favour, as he had long advocated, of the need to create a new political party.

This had to be able to encompass the broad range of opposition groupings that now existed at Stormont, from a former Nationalist like himself to Independents like John Hume, Ivan Cooper and Paddy O'Hanlon, as well as Fitt in Belfast.[17]

Although this process was to take some time and did not reach fruition until the formation of the Social Democratic and Labour Party (SDLP) in August 1970, throughout the period the effort always received the powerful backing of the *Irish News*. At the time of the creation of an "Opposition Alliance" at Stormont, the paper threw its weight behind the move and suggested that this was vital not only 'in the defence of minority rights', but 'in the pursuit of the government as it seeks to implement a reform programme'. In addition the editorial went on to state that 'In adopting this new stance, they are meeting the changing mood of the minority which has decided that effective opposition is felt to be destroyed by the futility of action by separate groups'.[18]

Such talk was viewed with a great deal of scepticism from what remained of the Nationalist Party. The reaction to the growing demands for one single opposition party was attacked and as McAteer informed the *Irish News*, whilst they would welcome the 'unity of all elements working towards' a united Ireland, he argued it would be 'a barren unity to seek to cement together those whose views differ on this important, basic question'.[19] To a certain extent, however, McAteer's concerns went unheeded as by this stage those individuals, like Currie, working to establish this "unity", had already decided to count the Nationalist Party out of their deliberations. This was done in order to try to ensure that the new organisation when it was launched was not seen as "old wine in new bottles". Accordingly of the four remaining Nationalist MPs only James O'Reilly and John Carron were approached to join the new party, but in the end both decided against as they both felt that as they had been elected as Nationalists they could just not "jump ship".[20] The successful launch of the SDLP was not fully tested until its first major electoral tests in 1973 and these results merely emphasised its overwhelming superiority over the remnants of the Nationalist Party. In the local council elections in May the SDLP polled 92,600 first preference votes, accounted for 13.4% of the total poll, and emerged as the single largest party in three council areas: Down, Londonderry, and Newry and Mourne. A month later at the Assembly elections it became the third largest party with 19 seats having polled 159,773 first preference votes and recorded 22.1% of the popular vote.[21]

Not surprisingly with the elimination of the Nationalist Party from the political scene in Northern Ireland there was a degree of bitterness from within its ranks. This applied especially towards those who had chosen to ignore the contribution it had made in trying to uphold and protect the rights of the minority community in the province. A good example of this comes in part of O'Connor's speech to the last party conference in November 1969 when he drew attention to the fact that, 'They had done all the things that had received so much publicity of recent months'. The only difference had been that, 'When they were trying to accomplish these things in an atmosphere which was not always friendly', they had neither the 'advantage of television cameras, or an interested or impartial press'. In spite of all of this the party had 'continued down through the years to serve the people who expected them to do so'.[22] At the same time, however there was also an acknowledgement that the nature of politics had undergone a significant change within Northern Ireland in recent times. Much of this had had an adverse effect on the party's image, making it look outdated and belonging to a bygone era. For McGill there was much regret and longing for the 'days when we had our compact party with our meetings and understandings'. Whilst there had always been 'little tiffs and minor misunderstandings and clashes due to temperament ... in general we all worked for one another ... This is all changed ...'.[23]

In the end it would appear as if that after half a century of effort the Nationalist Party had little to show in terms of advancing the cause of a United Ireland, or in significantly improving the lot of the minority community. Undoubtedly men like Healy, McAteer, McGill and James Doherty were men of integrity and honesty who had worked for many years, unselfishly and largely without reward, to serve the people they represented. But in the end their party's passing left them with little to show for all their work and effort. Yet this apparent failing was something that many within the party, after much consideration, eventually began to accept. Asked to come up with an appropriate epitaph for the party, McAteer declared:

> I'll tell you how we should be remembered. In this country of historic monuments the most important of all is missing to the unsung heroes of Irish politics ... the hard working, forgotten ranks of the Secretaries-to this and that Organisation. The quiet little men who kept the minutes, rode the country roads on bicycles in all weathers and all hours. They were the unsung heroes. If the Nationalist Party is to be remembered, we were the Secretaries. Like them we were never cut out for the limelight of the political life ... yet down

through the years kept a flame alive. We took the minutes, posted the invitations and rode the country roads.[24]

1. Interview with J. Doherty.
2. *Irish News* 24 November 1969.
3. *Derry Journal* 31 May and 4 June 1973.
4. W.D. Flackes and S. Elliott (eds.), *Northern Ireland: A Political Directory, 1968-1988*, (Belfast, 1989), p.315-319. Plus B. Walker (ed.), *Parliamentary Election Results in Ireland 1918-1992*, (Dublin, 1992), pp.82-86.
5. Flackes and Elliott, *A Political Directory*, p.245.
6. Rumpf and Hepburn, *Nationalism and Socialism in Twentieth Century Ireland*, p.188.
7. I. McAllister, *The Northern Ireland Social Democratic and Labour Party, Political Opposition in a Divided Society*, (London, 1977), pp.76-77.
8. Healy to J.B. Fitzpatrick, Undated, D2991/B/24, Healy Papers.
9. Ibid.
10. J. Bowyer Bell, *The Secret Army, The IRA 1916-1979*, (Dublin, 1989), p.269.
11. Foy, ' The Ancient Order of Hibernians', p.158.
12. McAllister, ' The National Democratic Party ', p.356.
13. M. McKeown to M. Viney, ' A Journey North' , *Irish Times* 5 May 1964.
14. *Irish News* 24 June 1964.
15. R. Rose, ' Discord in Ulster ', *New Community 1: 2*, (1971), p.124, quoted by McAllister, *The Northern Ireland Social Democratic and Labour Party*, p.21.
16. Interview with J. Doherty. Plus *Irish News* 16 and 17 October 1970.
17. Interview with A. Currie.
18. *Irish News* 4 December 1969.
19. *Irish News* 19 January 1970.
20. Interview with Currie. Plus P. Devlin, *Straight Left: An Autobiography*, (Belfast, 1993), pp.134-142.
21. Flackes and Elliott, *A Political Directory*, pp.315-319.
22. *Irish News* 24 November 1969.
23. McGill to Healy, 30 June 1969, D2991/B/24, Healy Papers.
24. *Irish Times* 11 September 1980.

Appendix 1: Profile of the Nationalist Parliamentary Party 1945-1972

Stormont

Thomas J. Campbell: Barrister and former Editor of the *Irish News* 1895-1900. Member of the Northern Ireland Senate, 1929-1934. MP for Belfast Central 1934-1946 following the death of Joe Devlin. Along with Richard Byrne, MP for Belfast Falls until his death in 1942, Campbell continued to attend Stormont after the 1938 election when other Nationalist MPs largely abstained. Involved in the establishment of the APL in November 1945 but almost immediately he plunged it into a crisis when he resigned as an MP to become a County Court Judge. He was the last Nationalist MP to represent a parliamentary seat in Belfast.

John Carron: Farmer and Publican. MP for South Fermanagh 1965-1972. Although he did not become a member of the Parliamentary Party until 1965 following the retirement of Cahir Healy, Carron had been actively involved in Nationalist politics in the County for a considerable period of time. In May 1946 he had helped to form a branch of the APL in Lisnaskea and had become its Vice Chairman. Then at the 1949 election he had stood unsuccessfully as an APL candidate against Sir Basil Brooke in the constituency of Lisnaskea. In addition he remained a member of Lisnaskea Rural District Council and Chairman of the Enniskillen Fisheries Board. Was approached to join the SDLP but he rejected the offer and continued to hold his seat as a Nationalist MP until Stormont was abolished in 1972.

Malachy Conlon: Farmer and Journalist. MP for South Armagh 1945-1950. Along with Eddie McAteer he took the initiative in launching the APL in November 1945. He became Secretary of the organisation and as part of the renewed anti-partition campaign visited the United States in 1949 with Paddy Maxwell. After he returned home he fell ill and died early in 1950.

Joseph Connellan: Journalist and former Editor of the *Frontier Sentinel*. MP for South Armagh 1929-1933 and South Down 1949-1967. His political career began in the days before partition when he was involved with various organisations such as SF, the Gaelic League and the Gaelic Athletic Association (GAA). From 1920-1922 he was a SF member of the Newry Board of Governors and along with his colleagues was forced to resign their positions due to their non-recognition of the Government of Ireland Act 1920. Connellan became a member of the NLN and although he took his seat in Stormont in 1929, he was never fully committed to Devlin's parliamentary strategy of attendance. After leaving parliament in 1933 he remained actively engaged in politics and served several terms as a member of Newry Urban District Council. Up until his death in 1967 he was still active in politics serving as Chairman of the short-lived NPF in 1964 and after the Nationalist Party became the Official Opposition in February 1965 he was appointed as Shadow Minister of Education.

Austin Currie: MP for East Tyrone 1964-1972. Graduated from Queen's University Belfast in 1963 and left Northern Ireland to take up a teaching post in England. Returned in the summer of 1964 after being approached to stand as Nationalist candidate in the East Tyrone by-election following the death of Joe Stewart. He was successful and became the youngest ever Stormont MP at the age of 25. Right from the outset however, he advocated the need for the Nationalist Party to transform itself into a modern political party with a card-carrying membership, a centralised organisation and an annual conference to debate policy. As he became disillusioned with the lack of reform under Terence O'Neill he moved towards the newly emerging civil rights movement. Currie was to take part in a squat in Calendon, Co. Tyrone in 1968 and then helped organise the first civil rights march between Coalisland and Dungannon. He attempted to get the Nationalist Party to adopt a campaign of non-violent civil disobedience at its annual conference in July 1968 but his motion was rejected. After this decision he continued to distance himself from the rest of his party colleagues and stood basically on his own manifesto at the 1969 election, which called for the creation of a united opposition party. Once the election was over he worked to achieve this goal and was one of the founding members of the SDLP in 1970.

Alex Donnelly: Solicitor. First elected as an MP in 1925 for Fermanagh-Tyrone but did not take his seat until October 1927. After boundary changes he became MP for West Tyrone in 1929 and held the seat until his retirement in 1949. In addition in the local government field he was Chairman of Tyrone County Council from 1920-1924 and served as a member of Omagh Urban District Council. His first involvement in politics came with his part in the establishment of SF in Tyrone in 1916 and after its split over the Anglo-Irish Treaty, along with Healy, James McHugh and Basil McGuckian he supported the pro-treaty faction. He was also actively involved in the ongoing efforts to unite nationalist opinion in Northern Ireland through initiatives such as the NLN and the APL.

Paddy Gormley: Potato Merchant. MP for Mid Derry 1953-1969. Entered politics in 1945 when he was elected to Derry County Council and served as a member of its Education Committee. At the 1953 Stormont election Gormley decided to stand as an Independent Nationalist and was determined to try to base his appeal on the need for practical politics rather than one based solely on ideology. This was to remain his political philosophy throughout his time at Stormont and therefore, not surprisingly, this independent line frequently got him into trouble with some of his colleagues. For example, in 1964 he accused the parliamentary party of deliberately sabotaging Currie's election chances by announcing their intention to contest the forthcoming Westminster election. This was being done he suggested, because, they feared what impact Currie could have on the party, particularly in light of his suggestions to modernise it. In November 1965 Gormley was involved in a car accident which left him seriously injured and although he recovered, he lost his seat to Ivan Cooper at the election in February 1969.

Thomas Gormley: Farmer. MP for Mid Tyrone 1962-1972. Like others he began his political career in local government where he was a member of Tyrone County Council. He shared the same political philosophy as his brother Paddy and in 1958 he stood for election in Mid Tyrone on a "Farmers" ticket. With the assistance of his brother, they advocated the creation of a policy broad enough to represent all shades of opposition opinion. He failed however, to win the seat as a split in the vote caused by F. McConnell standing as a "Nationalist", ensured that the Unionist nominee was successful. After his election in 1962 he followed the independent line of his brother and became the first Nationalist MP to attend a Royal Garden Party in May 1965. Following the election of 1969 he too distanced himself from the party and formally resigned from it in November 1969 as a protest against its lack of enthusiasm for a united opposition party. However, he refused to join the SDLP and after remaining as an Independent Nationalist MP for some time, he became a member of the Alliance Party.

Cahir Healy: Journalist and Insurance Agent. MP for South Fermanagh 1929-1965. First elected as a MP in 1925 for Fermanagh-Tyrone and after the boundary changes switched to South Fermanagh in 1929 and held the seat until his retirement in 1965. He had also a number of spells as a Westminster MP: for Fermanagh-Tyrone 1923-1924 and 1931-1935; and then after this twin constituency was divided, he held Fermanagh and South Tyrone from 1950-1951 and 1951-1955, when he made clear his intention to retire from Westminster. His political career dates back to his association with Arthur Griffith and the founding of the SF organisation in the early 1900s. This involvement was to lead eventually to his internment by the Northern Ireland government in 1922. Although initially after partition Healy remained on the pro-treaty side of SF he quickly realised that division amongst nationalist opinion in Northern Ireland only weakened their position. As a result therefore, he worked throughout his political career to try to bring the opposing factions together. For example in 1928 he was instrumental in the formation of the NLN and at the end of the Second World War, he was extremely active in the APL. Even though an early supporter of SF's policy of abstention towards the Northern authorities, Healy eventually reached the conclusion that such a policy was counter-productive. He believed that Nationalist representatives had a duty to defend the interests of their constituents, and to promote the national ideal by using parliamentary means where possible. Not surprisingly he was vehemently opposed to abstentionist candidates at both Stormont and Westminster elections.

Michael Keogh: Journalist and Editor of the *Frontier Sentinel*. MP for South Down 1967-1972. Became involved in politics through his participation in Peter Murney's NCU based in Newry and was Secretary of the local branch. He was to go on to hold a similar post with the APL when it was launched. After its demise he remained active in politics through local government and for nine years he was elected Chairman of Newry

Urban District Council. In the 1960s Keogh was involved in the effort to re-organise the Nationalist Party and became a member of the Co-ordinating Committee established in 1965 and then Secretary of the party executive established in 1966. His involvement in politics almost ended at the 1969 election when he only held his seat by around 200 votes. He was not invited to become a member of the SDLP and remained simply as a Nationalist MP until the demise of Stormont in 1972.

Eddie McAteer: Accountant. MP for Mid Derry 1945-1953 and for Foyle 1953-1969. Also a member of Londonderry Corporation 1952-1958. His first foray into politics came with his acceptance to be Nationalist candidate for Mid Derry and after eight years as its MP, he chose not to seek nomination again. Instead he sought and won the nomination for Foyle against the sitting MP Paddy Maxwell. This decision was based on his wish, along with others in Derry, to provide a more vigorous opposition to the Unionist domination of the city, rather than simply the abstentionist line followed by Maxwell. McAteer quickly established himself in the hierarchy of the Nationalist Party by playing a part in the establishment of the APL and became one of its Vice-Chairmen in 1947 and succeeding James McSparran as its Chairman in 1953. In 1958 he became deputy leader of the parliamentary party and eventually in 1964 following the death of Joe Stewart he became leader. Whilst in favour of the party modernising itself he wanted to move cautiously and this same approach characterised his attitude to the whole question of street protests in the 1960s. McAteer wanted to try to ensure that change came about through constitutional means and in the end, he and his party, were to suffer the consequences of the failure to achieve this at the elections in February 1969. After his defeat at the hands of John Hume he attempted to ensure that the party remained a viable alternative but this was ultimately to prove an impossible task.

Edward V. McCullagh: Farmer. MP for Mid Tyrone 1948-1953. Was returned unopposed at the by-election following the death of M. McGurk in June 1948. His political roots were very much in the constituency with his father having played a prominent role in various national movements in the locality. McCullagh was also a member of Omagh Rural District Council as well as being an important figure in local GAA circles. Like his predecessor his chief concern was in farming and rural issues. He lost his seat to Liam Kelly, an abstentionist candidate, at the 1953 election.

Michael McGurk: Farmer. MP for Mid Tyrone 1941-1948. His political career began with his involvement in the campaign for Home Rule early in the 1900s and moved on into local government where he served on Tyrone County Council and Cookstown Rural District Council. Had been returned unopposed for Mid Tyrone following the death of H. McAleer in 1941 and throughout his time at Stormont frequently raised concerns over agricultural matters.

Charles McGleenan: Farmer and Apple Grower. MP for South Armagh 1950-1958. Former member of the old IRA as well as various other national and cultural organisations. He joined the APL when it was formed and became Chairman of the County Armagh Executive and served on the national executive for a number of years. McGleenan stood in the by-election following the death of Conlon in 1950 as an abstentionist and made it clear he had no intention of taking his seat at Stormont. Instead he was at the forefront of the efforts to secure representation in the Dail for Northern Nationalists. Even when this goal was not achieved he still refused to take his seat at Stormont and at the election in 1958 he did not stand as recent legislation prevented him from standing as an abstentionist.

James McSparran: Barrister. MP for Mourne 1945-1958. During the 1945 election campaign he was a frequent advocate of the need for a united effort amongst Northern Nationalists. When Conlon and McAteer called a convention for this purpose in November 1945 he took the chair and subsequently became Chairman of the APL. In this role McSparran was heavily involved in the activities of the League in Britain and Ireland in the post-war period. He served as Chairman until 1953 when pressure of work forced him to accept the honorary title of President, with McAteer succeeding him. Finally he was also the erstwhile leader of the Nationalist parliamentary party from 1945 up until his retirement from active politics at the 1958 election.

Paddy Maxwell: Solicitor. MP for Foyle 1937-1953. He began his political career by being elected to the Londonderry Corporation in 1934 and by 1938 he had become leader of the Nationalist group of councillors. Succeeded J.J. McCarroll as an MP in 1937 and as a firm supporter of the abstentionist line he boycotted Stormont, along with other parliamentary colleagues during the war. After the election in 1945 he did attend for a time but was largely absent from 1946 onwards. This preference for abstention upset elements in Derry and at the 1953 election he was challenged by McAteer. When he lost the Nationalist nomination he went forward as an Independent and with his defeat he bowed out of politics.

Peter Murney: Farmer. MP for South Down 1945-1949. Member of the pre-truce Old IRA and then an anti-treaty republican with close ties to De Valera and Frank Aiken. In 1926 he helped to launch the National Defence Association which campaigned against any recognition of the Northern Parliament. Murney remained firmly committed to the policy of abstention and in 1937 formed the NCU which called for De Valera's new constitution to be applied throughout Ireland as the first step towards unification. A year later the NCU appealed for a complete boycott of the 1938 election and in three constituencies no Nationalist candidate was nominated. After the war he was involved with the APL but his relations with the rest of his parliamentary colleagues were strained due to their refusal to condemn Campbell's acceptance of a post as a county court judge. At the 1949 election he sought nomination again but at the selection convention he was defeated by Connellan.

Roderick O'Connor: Solicitor and Director of the *Ulster Herald* chain of newspapers. MP for West Tyrone 1949-1972. Although O'Connor did not enter Stormont until 1949 his first involvement in politics came with his participation in the Westminster election campaign of 1935. Once elected he quickly became established within the Parliamentary Party and in 1958 he supported McAteer in resisting any attempts to persuade it to become the Official Opposition. When this role was finally adopted by the party following the O'Neill-Lemass meeting 1965, O'Connor was appointed to the senior positions of Opposition Chief Whip and Shadow Minister of Home Affairs. After the 1969 election he succeeded McAteer as Chairman of the Nationalist parliamentary party and continued to make it clear that the party would survive and regain its former glories. He was, therefore, opposed to any moves towards a united opposition party and refused to participate in the Opposition Alliance formed at Stormont at the end of 1969. Not surprisingly he was not interested or approached to become a member of the SDLP and until the dissolution of Stormont continued to sit as a Nationalist MP.

James O'Reilly: Farmer. MP for Mourne 1958-1972. As a member of Kilkeel Rural District Council he sought the nomination for the seat left vacant following the retirement of McSparran. He became a prominent figure in the 1960s when he represented local nationalist opinion in their efforts to persuade the authorities at Stormont to re-route Orange marches away from the Longstone Road near Kilkeel. Although he was firmly committed to the party and the ideals for which it stood, he participated in the short-lived Opposition Alliance at Stormont and became its Chief Whip. O'Reilly was invited to join the SDLP but refused the offer and remained a Nationalist MP.

Eddie Richardson: Bricklayer and Farmer. MP for South Armagh 1958-1969. His first attempt to win the nomination for this seat came in 1945 when he was one of several candidates defeated by Conlon. Richardson however, remained active in politics through local government, where he was a member of Armagh County Council. By the time of the 1958 election with the collapse of the APL and with McGleenan not standing a search began for a candidate. At an early stage Richardson announced his intention to stand and if elected, he promised to take his seat at Stormont. When a Nationalist selection convention failed to nominate a candidate he stood as an Independent Nationalist and won the seat. He held it until the election of 1969 when Paddy O'Hanlon, who had emerged from the civil rights movement, defeated him.

Joe Stewart: Auctioneer, Publican and Undertaker. President of the AOH in Co. Tyrone. MP for East Tyrone 1929-1964. He also had a spell as an MP at Westminster for Fermanagh-Tyrone from 1934-1935 following the death of Devlin. First became involved in politics in East Tyrone when he acted as election agent for T.M. Kettle and then was closely involved at local government level. He served on the Dungannon Board of Governors from 1923-1948, until it was dissolved; and was a member of Tyrone County Council; and Dungannon Urban District Council. After the election of 1945 he participated fully in the activities of the APL and served in various capacities on its national executive. Following the retirement of McSparran in 1958 he became Chairman of the Nationalist parliamentary party and held the post until his death in 1964.

Northern Ireland Senate

James G. Lennon: Solicitor. Senator from 1944-1972. He also held a prominent position in the AOH and served as its National Vice-President from 1951-1975, when he was appointed National President. First involvement in politics came when he stood as the unsuccessful NLN candidate in South Armagh in the 1933 general election. In the post-war period he became heavily involved in the activities of the APL and served in various positions on its national executive. Lennon came to prominence in 1962-1963 when he held a series of talks with Sir George Clarke, Grand Master of the Orange Order. The aim of these meetings, which became known as the "Orange and Green Talks", was to try to improve community relations within Northern Ireland. However, they soon collapsed as neither side could agree upon an agenda. When the Nationalist Party accepted the position of Official Opposition, following the meeting of O'Neill and Lemass, Lennon was appointed party leader in the Senate.

Paddy McGill: Journalist and Editor-in-chief of the *Ulster Herald* group of newspapers. Senator 1953-1972. He became Secretary of the APL in 1953 and from this position he was nominated to the Senate by a number of MPs who felt it was desirable he be given a public post. After the collapse of the APL, McGill became Secretary of the parliamentary party and he continued to hold this post into the 1960s. It is evident that in this role he favoured a cautious approach to be taken on the question of modernising the party's image and structure.

Paddy O'Hare: Journalist and Editor of the *Fermanagh Herald*. Senator from 1949-1972. He was also closely involved with the APL helping to establish it in County Fermanagh and serving on its national executive. When the Nationalist Party became the Official Opposition he was appointed as Chief Whip.

Westminster

Paddy Cunningham: Dairy Farmer. MP for Fermanagh-Tyrone, 1935-1950. He was selected along with Anthony Mulvey in 1935 in a last minute compromise to avoid a split in the vote between rival Nationalist and Republican candidates. On his nomination he made his position clear, 'I am a farmer. Being a MP does not interest me'. As part of the arrangement neither Cunningham nor Mulvey took their seat between 1935-1945. They did not take their seats until after the 1945 election when a joint convention recommended they take their seats. However, Cunningham did not attend on a frequent basis and at the 1950 election announced his wish to retire.

Anthony Mulvey: Editor of the *Ulster Herald*. MP for Fermanagh-Tyrone, 1935-1950 and after boundary changes for Mid Ulster, 1950-1951. He came very much from a Republican background having been a member of the IRB and participated in the 1916 rising in Wexford. After partition he maintained close links with De Valera and his FF party. In 1937 he linked up with Murney to establish the NCU and fully supported its abstentionist line. This can be seen in his statement on the 1935 election when he announced, 'We held no election campaign. We simply issued a statement saying that if elected we would not go to Westminster'. Following the 1945 election he took his seat and played an important part in the APL's campaign in Britain. He believed that his presence at Westminster was of the upmost importance to this effort and at a selection convention for the 1950 election he refused to stand if he was going to be tied to an abstentionist policy. Eventually he only agreed to go forward as the only candidate considered capable of holding the seat. After his victory he sought to recall the convention so as to allow him to attend Westminster when he saw fit. This was done in May and he returned to London early in 1951 to take his seat in order to contribute to a debate on Ireland. However, by the time of the next election in October 1951 he had decided to retire due to ill-health.

Michael O'Neill: Farmer. MP for Mid Ulster, 1951-1955. His involvement in politics began in local government where he had been a member of Omagh Rural District Council, 1939-1949 and then of Tyrone County Council, 1950-1957. In addition O'Neill was prominent in GAA circles in Tyrone and was a member of the national executive of the APL. After his election he took his seat at Westminster along with Healy with the specific goal of using it to promote the cause of Irish unity. Furthermore, he was also active in the APL's campaign across Britain. His tenure as an MP ended however, at the 1955 election when the selection convention decided against nominating anyone to oppose a SF candidate. He made one last effort to regain the seat at the by-election in May 1956 but he could only manage to come in third.

Appendix 2: Profile of Interviewees

Frank Curran: Journalist and former Editor of the *Derry Journal*. His participation and interest in Nationalist politics date back to his membership of the local branch of the APL. On his own initiative he published *Ireland's Fascist City* which attempted to detail the long history of Unionist gerrymandering in Derry City. After the collapse of the APL he remained a member of the local Nationalist Party which maintained some kind of an organisation and structure with an open membership and monthly meetings. Curran continued to attend on a regular basis and by the 1960s he was at the forefront of the demands for the party to establish itself as a properly constituted province-wide organisation. Later his second book *Derry: Countdown to Disaster*, attempted to give an account of the growing frustration amongst the Nationalist population of Derry which was to culminate with the events of October 1968.

Harry Diamond: Fitter. He became involved in politics at an early age in his native West Belfast where his debating skills brought him to the attention of Joe Devlin and he became a close associate of the veteran Nationalist politician. Then in 1929 Diamond was elected as a Nationalist member of the Belfast Board of Governors for the Smithfield ward. However, as Devlin's health deteriorated he grew disillusioned with the Nationalist Party in the city as he felt it was coming under the control of businessmen who were using it to pursue their own interests. As a result he stood against Campbell in the by-election in Central which followed the death of Devlin. Soon after he left the city to look for work in Britain and whilst there took part in the anti-partition campaign which was organised at the end of the 1930s. On his return to Belfast after the end of the war he was approached to stand as a candidate for the Falls constituency at the Stormont election in 1945. He successfully won the seat as a Socialist Republican and held it until he was defeated by Paddy Devlin at the 1969 election. His political philosophy throughout his political career can be described as a mixture of non-violent Republicanism with socialist objectives'.

James Doherty: After graduating from the National University of Ireland in 1945 with a First Class Honours Degree in Arts and Commerce, Doherty returned to Derry to take up a career in the family meat business. With a father who had been a member of the Londonderry Corporation he was deeply interested in politics and joined the local branch of the APL and soon had risen to become Secretary of its local Steering Committee. His involvement in politics deepened further in 1950 when he gained a seat on the Corporation and he was to hold this until 1969. Through his membership of the APL he struck up a close working relationship with McAteer and when in 1953 McAteer challenged the sitting MP for Foyle, Paddy Maxwell, Doherty was to be a confidant as well as his election agent. After the collapse of the APL following this election the local branch simply became known as the Nationalist Party again and Doherty served as both its Secretary and Chairman over a number of years. Along with others he called for the party to establish itself as a proper constituency based organisation with branches across the province. In support of this process he was appointed to the Co-ordinating Committee which had been established in 1965 and then in 1966 he became Chairman of the party's national executive, a position he retained until his resignation in 1970. Despite the rise of the civil rights movement he remained loyal to the party and its ideals and as McAteer's election agent campaigned vigorously against Hume in the 1969 election. In the immediate aftermath of McAteer's defeat he was at the forefront of moves within the party in Derry to lay the foundations for its recovery. However, as conditions deteriorated in Northern Ireland he grew increasingly disillusioned with the situation and finally resigned from the party in 1970 when the local branch in Derry failed to support a motion which condemned all forms of violence.

Paddy Doherty: Builder and Managing Director of the Inner City Trust in Derry. His interest in politics came about through an incident in 1958 when his application for a house from the Corporation was rejected. He decided to build his own house on wasteland in Westland Street and this led him to believe that if he could do something like this, then other Catholic families should be encouraged to follow suit. Along with others in the city like Hume and Michael Canavan he was attracted to the Credit Union Movement and played a part in its development. Doherty's relationship with the Nationalist Party was never particularly good as he regarded it as impotent and incapable of providing the leadership that the Catholic community needed. This was to be illustrated with his opposition to the plans of the Corporation to build a complex of high rise flats in the Rossville area. Nationalist councillors were prepared to back this scheme to ease the housing crisis even though it was widely accepted that the plan was an attempt to ensure that the growing Catholic population did not spill out of the South Ward. Doherty's lack of faith in the Nationalist Party led him to join others in attempting to persuade Hume to stand against McAteer in the 1965 election and he was bitterly disappointed when nothing came of this. However, by the time of the next election in 1969 Hume was ready to take on McAteer and Doherty played an active part in his campaign. After the contest Doherty did not remain part of Hume's entourage and instead with the outbreak of serious disturbances in 1969 he became Vice-Chairman of the Citizens Action Committee in Derry. In this role he later earned himself the title of "Paddy Bogside" for his part in organising the defence of the area in the summer of 1969.

Eugene O'Hare: Chemist. He did not become involved in politics until 1963 when after encouragement from his close friend, Frank Curran, he began to attend meetings of the Nationalist Party in Derry and eventually he joined the party. In 1964 O'Hare was nominated as a candidate for the local government elections and held a seat on the Corporation until its abolition in 1969. Along with other members in Derry he was anxious that the party should modernise its image and structure and establish itself branches throughout the province. When this process finally got underway in 1965 O'Hare served on the Co-ordinating Committee which had been established to begin this task. A year later he was appointed as Treasurer of the party's national executive and this was a post he held until his resignation in 1970. As with James Doherty he remained committed to the party through the rise of the civil rights movement and McAteer's defeat at the 1969 election. However, by 1970 he had become convinced that the party had lost its way and when it refused to pass a motion condemning all acts of violence in October he resigned along with James Doherty and Tom McDonnell.

Appendix 3: Election Results 1945-1949

Stormont Parliamentary Election: Polling Day 14 June 1945

Armagh, South[1]

Electors	Turnout %	Candidate	Party	Votes	%
16,815	64.6	M. Conlon	Nationalist	6,720	61.9
		P. Agnew	NILP	4,143	38.1
				2,577	**23.8**

Belfast, Falls[2]

Electors	Turnout %	Candidate	Party	Votes	%
18,610	62.8	H. Diamond	Soc. Rep	5,016	42.9
		J.H. Collins	Fed. Labour	3,912	33.5
		J.A. McGlade	Nationalist	2,766	23.6
				1,104	**9.4**

Down, Mourne[3]

Electors	Turnout %	Candidate	Party	Votes	%
15,639	85.2	J. McSparran	Nationalist	7,784	58.4
		J. Brown	Unionist	5,544	41.6
				2,240	**12.8**

Londonderry, Foyle[5]

Electors	Turnout %	Candidate	Party	Votes	%
16,071	69.6	P. Maxwell	Nationalist	6,270	56.0
		P. Fox	Ind. Labour	<u>4,920</u>	<u>44.0</u>
				1,350	**12.0**

Westminster Parliamentary Election: 5 July 1945

Fermanagh-Tyrone[6]

Electors	Turnout %	Candidate	Party	Votes	%
114,977	88.4	P. Cunningham	Nationalist	55,373	27.3
		A. Mulvey	Nationalist	55,144	27.1
		T. Lyons	Conservative	46,392	22.8
		N.A. Cooper	Conservative	<u>46,260</u>	<u>22.8</u>
				8,752	**4.3**

Londonderry[7]

Electors	Turnout %	Candidate	Party	Votes	%
89,979	88.1	Sir R.D. Ross	Conservative	40,214	50.7
		Dr D.J. Cavanagh	Nationalist	37,056	47.4
		M.W. Gordon	NILP	<u>1,471</u>	<u>1.9</u>
				2,653	**3.3**

Belfast Corporation Election: 14 August 1947

Smithfield Ward[8]

Candidate	Party	Votes
T. Watson	Labour	1,398
P. McDonnell	Nationalist	631
T. Ferran	Working Peoples Party	73
		767

Notes

1. Elliott, *Northern Ireland Parliamentary Election Results 1921-1971*, p.63.
2. Ibid., p.40.
3. Ibid., p.70.
4. Ibid., p.72.
5. Ibid., p.78.
6. F.W.S. Craig, *British Parliamentary Election Results 1918-1949*, (London, 1977), p.660.
7. Ibid., p.661.
8. *Irish News* 15 August 1947.

Appendix 4: Election Results 1950-1956

Westminster Parliamentary Election: 23 February 1950

Fermanagh and South Tyrone[1]

Electors	Turnout %	Candidate	Party	Votes	%
67,424	92.1	C. Healy	Nationalist	32,188	51.9
		H.S.C. Richardson	Conservative	29,877	48.1
				2,311	**3.8**

Mid-Ulster[2]

Electors	Turnout %	Candidate	Party	Votes	%
68,535	91.6	A. Mulvey	Nationalist	33,023	52.6
		J.M. Shearer	Conservative	29,721	47.4
				3,302	**5.2**

Coatbridge[3]

Candidate	Party	Votes
Mrs J. Mann	Labour	23,339
Mr J. McMullan	Conservative	16,552
Mr T.P. O'Callaghan	I.A.P.L.	1,315
		6,787

Gorbals[4]

Candidate	Party	Votes
Mrs A. Cullen	Labour	24,010
Mr J. Young	Conservative	13,013
Mr J. Kerrigan	Communist	2,426
Mr W. McGuinness	I.A.P.L.	1,920
		10,997

Greenock[5]

Candidate	Party	Votes
Mr T.H. McNeil	Labour	20,548
Mr I. McColl	Liberal	11,639
Mr J.S. Thompson	Independent	6,458
Mr J.R. Campbell	Communist	1,228
Mr O. Brown	I.A.P.L. and Scottish Nationalist	<u>718</u>
		8,909

Bootle[6]

Candidate	Party	Votes
Mr J. Kinley	Labour	25,472
Mr W. Hill	Conservative	21,673
Mr B. McGinnity	I.A.P.L.	<u>1,092</u>
		3,799

Stormont Parliamentary By-Election: 6 December 1950

South Armagh[7]

Electors	Turnout %	Candidate	Party	Votes	%
17,496	46.5	C. McGleenan	APL	5581	68.6
		S. McKearney	Irish Labour Party	<u>2555</u>	<u>31.4</u>
				3026	**37.2**

Belfast Corporation Election: 17 July 1951

Smithfield[8]

Candidate	Party	Votes
J. Beattie	Irish Labour	1,402
H. Diamond	Irish Labour	312
J. McGivern	Anti-Partition	148
		1190

Westminster Parliamentary Election: 25 October 1951

Mid Ulster[9]

Electors	Turnout %	Candidate	Party	Votes	%
68,412	91.8	M. O'Neill	Nationalist	33,094	52.7
		J.M. Shearer	Conservative	29,701	47.3
				3,393	**5.4**

Fermanagh and South Tyrone[10]

Electors	Turnout %	Candidate	Party	Votes	%
67,219	93.4	C. Healy	Nationalist	32,717	52.1
		F.G. Patterson	Conservative	30,082	47.9
				2,635	**4.2**

Stormont Parliamentary Election: 22 October 1953

Londonderry, Foyle[11]

Electors	Turnout %	Candidate	Party	Votes	%
17,379	69.6	E.G. McAteer	Nationalist	6,953	58.8
		P. Maxwell	Independent Nationalist	4,412	41.2
				1,893	**17.6**

Londonderry, Mid[12]

Electors	Turnout %	Candidate	Party	Votes	%
15,798	48.6	P. Gormley	Nationalist	4,134	53.8
		T.B. Agnew	Anti-Partitionist	3,550	46.2
				584	**7.6**

Tyrone, Mid[13]

Electors	Turnout %	Candidate	Party	Votes	%
12,811	63.6	W. Kelly	Anti-Partitionist	4,178	55.3
		E.V. McCullagh	Nationalist	3,376	44.7
				802	**10.6**

Westminster Parliamentary Election: 26 May 1955

Fermanagh and South Tyrone[14]

Electors	Turnout %	Candidate	Party	Votes	%
65,770	92.4	P. Clarke	Sinn Fein	30,529	50.2
		R.G. Grosvenor	Conservative	30,268	49.8
				261	**0.4**

Mid Ulster[15]

Electors	Turnout %	Candidate	Party	Votes	%
66,847	88.6	T.J. Mitchell	Sinn Fein	29,737	50.2
		C. Beattie	Conservative	29,477	49.8
				260	**0.4**

Westminster Parliamentary By-Election: 8 May 1956

Mid Ulster[16]

Electors	Turnout %	Candidate	Party	Votes	%
66,891	89.7	G. Forrest	Conservative	28,605	48.3
		T.J. Mitchell	Sinn Fein	24,124	40.8
		M. O'Neill	Nationalist	6,421	10.9
				4,481	**7.5**

Notes

1. Craig, *British Election Parliamentary Election Results 1950-1970*, p.663
2. Ibid., p.665.
3. *Irish News* 25 February 1950.
4. Ibid.
5. Ibid.

6. Ibid.
7. Elliott, *Northern Ireland Parliamentary Results 1921-1972*, p.63.
8. Irish News 19 July 1951.
9. Craig, *British Parliamentary Results 1950-1970*, p.665.
10. Ibid., p.663.
11. Elliott, *Northern Ireland Parliamentary Results 1921-1972*, p.78.
12. Ibid., p.79.
13. Ibid., p.83.
14. Craig, *British Parliamentary Results 1950-1970*, p.663.
15. Ibid., p.665.
16. Ibid.

Appendix 5: Election Results 1956-1963

Stormont Parliamentary Election: 20 March 1958

Armagh, South[1]

Electors	Turnout %	Candidate	Party	Votes	%
17,343	43.1	E.G. Richardson	Independent Nationalist	3,698	49.5
		M. Traynor	Independent Labour	2,306	30.9
		J. McParland	Independent Nationalist	<u>1,470</u>	<u>19.6</u>
				1,392	**18.6**

Down, Mourne[2]

Electors	Turnout %	Candidate	Party	Votes	%
16,106	84.7	J. O'Reilly	Nationalist	7,139	52.3
		Mrs C. Calvert	Unionist	<u>6,506</u>	<u>47.7</u>
				633	**4.6**

Down, South[3]

Electors	Turnout %	Candidate	Party	Votes	%
17,257	74.4	J. Connellan	Nationalist	6,686	47.7
		J.Y. Thompson	Unionist	4,065	30.0
		T.J. Kelly	Irish Labour Party	<u>3,016</u>	<u>22.3</u>
				2,384	**17.7**

Londonderry, Foyle[4]

Electors	Turnout %	Candidate	Party	Votes	%
18,029	67.6	E.G. McAteer	Nationalist	6,953	57.0
		S. McGonigle	Independent Labour	5,238	43.0
				1,715	**14.0**

Tyrone, East[5]

Electors	Turnout %	Candidate	Party	Votes	%
16,211	89.1	J.F. Stewart	Nationalist	7,336	50.8
		G. Forrest	Unionist	7,100	49.2
				236	**1.6**

Tyrone, Mid[6]

Electors	Turnout %	Candidate	Party	Votes	%
12,811	63.3	A. Blevins	Unionist	3,949	48.7
		T.C. Gormley	Independent	3,013	37.1
		F. McConnell	Nationalist	1,149	14.2
				936	**11.6**

Tyrone, West[7]

Electors	Turnout %	Candidate	Party	Votes	%
15,347	81.9	R.H. O'Connor	Nationalist	6,750	53.7
		A. Stewart	Unionist	5,813	46.3
				937	**7.4**

Stormont Parliamentary Election: 31 May 1962

Londonderry, Foyle[8]

Electors	Turnout %	Candidate	Party	Votes	%
18,744	75.7	E.G. McAteer	Nationalist	8,720	61.4
		S. McGonigle	Independent Labour	<u>5,476</u>	<u>38.6</u>
				3,244	**22.8**

Tyrone, Mid[9]

Electors	Turnout %	Candidate	Party	Votes	%
12,520	81.9	T.C. Gormley	Nationalist	6,297	61.4
		A. Blevins	Unionist	<u>3,957</u>	<u>38.6</u>
				2,340	**22.8**

Notes

1. Elliott, *Northern Ireland Parliamentary Results 1921-1972*, p.63.
2. Ibid., p.70.
3. Ibid., p.72.
4. Ibid., p.78.
5. Ibid., p.82.
6. Ibid., p.83.
7. Ibid., p.86.
8. Ibid., p.78.
9. Ibid., p.83.

Appendix 6: Election Results 1964-1969

Stormont Parliamentary By-Election: 30 June 1964

Tyrone, East[1]

Electors	Turnout %	Candidate	Party	Votes	%
16,883	89.7	A. Currie	Nationalist	8,223	54.3
		A. Blevins	Unionist	6,927	45.7
				1,296	**8.6**

Stormont Parliamentary Election: 25 November 1965

Armagh, South[2]

Electors	Turnout %	Candidate	Party	Votes	%
17,606	33.5	E.G. Richardson	Nationalist	5,223	88.5
		P. McSorley	Independent Republican	682	11.5
				4,541	**77.0**

Down, Mourne[3]

Electors	Turnout %	Candidate	Party	Votes	%
16,202	77.7	J. O'Reilly	Nationalist	6,793	54.0
		Mrs K. Forde	Unionist	5,791	46.0
				1,002	**8.0**

Down, South[4]

Electors	Turnout %	Candidate	Party	Votes	%
17.474	58.0	J. Connellan	Nationalist	6,907	68.1
		I.C.W. Hutchinson	Unionist	<u>3.227</u>	<u>31.9</u>
				3,680	**36.2**

Londonderry, Foyle[5]

Electors	Turnout %	Candidate	Party	Votes	%
19,607	62.2	E. McAteer	Nationalist	7,825	64.1
		S. Quinn	Independent Labour	<u>4.371</u>	<u>35.9</u>
				3,454	**28.2**

Stormont Parliamentary Election: 24 February 1969

Armagh, South[6]

Electors	Turnout %	Candidate	Party	Votes	%
18,140	69.3	P. O'Hanlon	Independent	6,442	51.2
		E.G. Richardson	Nationalist	4,332	34.5
		P. Byrne	NILP	<u>1.794</u>	<u>14.3</u>
				2,110	**16.7**

Down, South[7]

Electors	Turnout %	Candidate	Party	Votes	%
17,486	54.0	M. Keogh	Nationalist	4,830	51.2
		F. Woods	Peoples Democracy	<u>4,610</u>	<u>48.8</u>
				220	**2.4**

Londonderry, Foyle[8]

Electors	Turnout %	Candidate	Party	Votes	%
19,875	81.4	J. Hume	Independent	8,920	55.1
		E.G. McAteer	Nationalist	5,267	32.6
		E. McCann	NILP	<u>1,993</u>	<u>12.3</u>
				3,653	**22.5**

Londonderry, Mid[9]

Electors	Turnout %	Candidate	Party	Votes	%
16,411	81.9	I. Cooper	Independent	6,056	45.1
		R. Shields	Unionist	4,438	33.0
		P.J. Gormely	Nationalist	2,229	16.6
		J. O'Kane	Republican Labour Party	<u>709</u>	<u>5.3</u>
				1,618	**12.1**

Notes

1. Elliott, *Northern Ireland Parliamentary Results 1921-1972*, p.82.
2. Ibid., p.63.
3. Ibid., p.70.
4. Ibid., p.72.
5. Ibid., p.78.
6. Ibid., p.63.
7. Ibid., p.72.
8. Ibid., p.78.
9. Ibid., p.79.

Bibliography

PRIMARY SOURCES

1. Manuscript Sources: Northern Ireland: Public Record Office of Northern Ireland, Belfast

(A) Private Papers:
Jack Beattie Papers (D2784/22/3/3).
Cahir Healy Papers (D2991).
Anthony Mulvey Papers (D1862).
Patrick McGill Papers (D1726).
F.E. McCarroll Papers (T2712).
Michael O'Neill Papers (D3257).
Eddie McAteer Election Leaflet and Poster (D230/2/6/1).
James O'Reilly Election Address (D230/2/7).

(B) Papers of Nationalist Organisations:
Anti Partition League Branch in County Armagh 1945-1955: Minute Book, Correspondence, Propaganda Material etc (D3184).
Nationalist Party Records (T3062/1-4).

(C) Official Papers:
Cabinet Conclusions (N.I.), 1945-1964 (CAB 4).
Home Office Material: HO/5/33, HO/5/184, HO/5/185, HO/5/186.

2. The Political Collection, Linen Hall Library, Belfast:
Election Manifestos Book 1 and Book 2.
Box 2: Irish Pamphlets Anti-Unionist.

3. In Private Possession:
James Doherty Papers (James Doherty, Derry).
Eddie McAteer Papers (McAteer Family, Derry).

4. Parliamentary Papers: United Kingdom
Parliamentary Debates, House of Commons, 1945-1955.

5. Parliamentary Papers: Northern Ireland
Parliamentary Debates, House of Commons, 1945-1953.

6. Parliamentary Papers: Republic of Ireland
Dail Eireann, Parliamentary Debates, Official Reports, Volume 126 c. pp.1995-2270, and Volume 147 c. pp.161-248.

7. Newspapers and Periodicals
Belfast Newsletter.
Belfast Telegraph.
Derry Journal.
Economic and Social Review.
Fermanagh Herald.
History of Education.
Irish Independent.
Irish News.
Irish Press.
Irish Times.
Journal of Contemporary History.
Listener.
New Statesman.
Tribune.
Ulster Herald.

8. Interviews:
(A) Mr Frank Curran, 2 March 1993.
  Mr Austin Currie, 4 July 1994.
  Mr Harry Diamond, 1 April 1993.
  Mr James Doherty, 16 August 1994.
  Mr Paddy Doherty, 18 August 1994.
  Mr Paddy Gormley, 7 October 1992.
  Mr E. O'Hare, 4 August and 23 November 1994.

(B) Radio Foyle Profile on E. McAteer featuring interviews with F. Curran, J. Doherty and Mr Stephen McGonigle, February 1992.

In addition interviews were carried out in the Derry area with people who requested that they remain anonymous and therefore I have respected their privacy by not naming them.

Finally a number of public figures were approached but they failed to respond to the requests made.

9. Memoirs, Diaries, etc.

Benn, A., *Out of the Wilderness, Diaries 1963-1967*, (London, 1987).

Bloomfield, K., *Stormont in Crisis: A Memoir*, (Belfast, 1994).

Callaghan, J., *A House Divided. The Dilemma of Northern Ireland*, (London, 1973).

Campbell, T.J., *Fifty Years of Ulster 1890-1940*, (Belfast, 1941).

Castle, B., *The Castle Diaries 1964-1970*, (London, 1984).

Crossman, A., *The Crossman Diaries. Selections from a Cabinet Minister 1964-1970*, (London, 1979).

Curran, F., *Derry: Countdown to Disaster*, (Dublin, 1986).

Curran, F., *Ireland's Fascist City*, (Derry, 1946).

Devlin, P., *Straight Left: An Autobiography*, (Belfast, 1993).

Eade, C., *Victory: War Speeches by the Rt Hon. W.S. Churchill O.M., C.H., MP*, (London, 1945).

Farrell, B., *Sean Lemass*, (Dublin, 1983).

Faulkner, B., *Memoirs of a Statesman*, (London, 1978).

Healy, C., *The Mutilation of a Nation: The Story of the Partition of Ireland*, (Derry, 1945).

McAteer, E., *Irish Action*, (Ballyshannon, 1948).

McCann, E., *War in an Irish Town*, (London, 1974), (1st edn).

McCluskey, C., *Up Off Their Knees*, (Southampton, 1989).

McKeown, M., *The Greening of a Nationalist*, (Lucan, 1986).

Oliver, J.A., *Working at Stormont*, (Dublin, 1978).

O'Neill, T., *Ulster at the Crossroads*, (London, 1969).

The Autobiography of Terence O'Neill, (London, 1972).

Shea, P., *Voices and the Sounds of the Drums: An Irish Autobiography*, (Belfast, 1981).

Van Voris, W.H., *Violence in Ulster: An Oral Documentary*, (Arnherst, 1975).

Wilson, H., *The Labour Government 1964-1970: A Personal Record*, (London, 1971).

SECONDARY SOURCES

1. Reference Works

Craig, F.W.S. (ed.), *British Parliamentary Election Results, 1918-1949*, (Glasgow, 1969).

Craig, F.W.S. (ed.), *British Parliamentary Election Results, 1949-1970*, (Chichester, 1971).

Deutsch, R. and Magowan, V. (eds), *Northern Ireland: A Chronology of Events, 1968-1974*, (Belfast, 1975).

Elliott, S. (ed.), *Northern Ireland Parliamentary Election Results, 1921-1972*, (Chichester, 1973).

Flackes, W.D. (ed.), *Northern Ireland: A Political Directory, 1968-79*, (Dublin, 1980).

Flackes, W.D. and Elliot, S. (eds.), *Northern Ireland: A Political Directory, 1968-1988*, (Belfast, 1989).

Walker, B.M. (ed.), *Parliamentary Election Results in Ireland 1918-1992*, (Dublin, 1992).

Ulster Year Book, 1945-1970 (HMSO, Belfast).

2. Secondary Works

Arthur, P., *The Peoples Democracy 1968-1973*, (Belfast, 1974).

Arthur, P., *Government and Politics of Northern Ireland*, (Harlow, 1980), (2nd edn).

Arthur, P. and Jeffrey, K., *Northern Ireland Since 1968*, (Oxford, 1988).

Bardon, J., *A History of Ulster*, (Belfast, 1992).

Barritt, D.P. and Carter, P.F., *The Northern Ireland Problem: A Study in Group Relations*, (Oxford, 1962).

Bew, P., Gribbon P. and Patterson, H., *The State in Northern Ireland 1921-1972. Political Forces and Social Classes*, (Manchester, 1979).

Bell, J. Bowyer, *The Secret Army: A History of the IRA 1916-1970*, (London, 1979), (3rd edn).

Bishop, P. and Mallie, E., *The Provisional IRA*, (London, 1987).

Bowman, J., *De Valera and the Ulster Question 1917-1973*, (Oxford, 1983).

Boyce, D.G., *The Irish Question and British Politics, 1868-1986*, (London, 1988).

Boyce, D.G., *Nationalism in Ireland*, (London, 1995), (3rd edn).

Brady, C., O'Dowd, M. and Walker, B.M. (eds.), *Ulster – An Illustrated History*, (London,1989).

Buckland, P., *The Factory of Grievances: Devolved Government in Northern Ireland 1921-1939*, (Dublin, 1979).

Buckland, P., *A History of Northern Ireland*, (Dublin, 1980).

Cathcart, R., *The Most Contrary Region: The BBC in Northern Ireland 1924-1984*, (Belfast, 1984).

Connolly, M., *Politics and Policy Making in Northern Ireland*, (London, 1990).

Coogan, T.P., *The IRA*, (London, 1986), (3rd edn).

Darby, J., *Conflict in Northern Ireland: The Development of a Polarised Community*, (Dublin and New York, 1976).

Darby, J. (ed.), *Northern Ireland: The Background to the Conflict*, (Belfast, 1983).

Darby, J., Dodge, N. and Hepburn, A.C. (ed.), *Political Violence: Ireland in a Comparative Perspective*, (Belfast, 1990).

Devlin, P., *Yes We Have No Bananas: Outdoor Relief in Belfast 1920-1939*, (Belfast, 1981).

De Paor, L., *Divided Ulster*, (Harmondsworth, 1970).

Edwards, Owen D., *The Sins of Our Fathers, Roots of the Conflict in Northern Ireland*, (Dublin, 1970).

Farrell, M., *Northern Ireland: The Orange State*, (London, 1980). (2nd edn).

Fisk, R., *In Time of War: Ireland, Ulster and the Price of Neutrality*, (London, 1983).

Foster, R.F., *Modern Ireland 1600-1972*, (London, 1988).

Gallagher, F., *The Indivisible Island: The History of the Partition of Ireland*, (London, 1957).

Gallagher, T. and O'Connell J. (eds.), *Contemporary Irish Studies*, (Manchester, 1983).

Greaves, D., *The Irish Crisis*, (London, 1972).

Harkness, D., *Northern Ireland Since 1920*, (Dublin, 1983).

Hastings, M., *Ulster 1969: The Fight for Civil Rights in Northern Ireland*, (London, 1970).

Horowitz, D.L., *Ethnic Groups in Conflict*, (London, 1984).

Kelly, H., *How Stormont Fell*, (Dublin and London, 1972).

Lawrence, R.J., *The Government of Northern Ireland: Public Finances and Public Services 1921-1964*, (Oxford, 1965).

Lee, J.J., *Ireland 1912-1985: Politics and Society*, (Cambridge, 1989).

Lyons, F.S.L., *Ireland Since the Famine*, (London, 1982), (revised edn).

MacManus, F. (ed.), *The Years of the Great Test*, (Dublin and Cork, 1967).

McAllister, I., *The Northern Ireland Social Democratic and Labour Party: Political Opposition in a Divided Society*, (London, 1977).

Mansergh, N., *The Government of Northern Ireland*, (London, 1967).

Moody, T.W., *The Ulster Question 1603-1973*, (Dublin and Cork, 1974).

Morgan, K.O., *Labour in Power 1945-1951*, (Oxford, 1984).

Moynihan, M. (ed.), *Speeches and Statements by Eamon De Valera 1917-1973*, (Dublin, 1980).

O'Brien, C.C., *States of Ireland*, (London, 1974).

O'Connor, F., *In Search of a State: Catholics in Northern Ireland*, (Belfast, 1993).

O'Dowd, L., Rolston, B. and Tomlinson, M. (eds.), *Northern Ireland: Between Civil Rights and Civil War*, (London, 1980).

Pearce, M. and Stewart, G., *British Political History 1867-1990*, (London, 1992).

Phoenix, E., *Northern Nationalism: Nationalist Politics, Partition and the Catholic Minority in Northern Ireland 1890-1940*, (Belfast, 1994).

Purdie, B., *Politics in the Streets: The Origins of the Civil Rights Movement in Northern Ireland*, (Belfast, 1990).

Rose, R., *Governing Without Consensus: An Irish Perspective*, (London, 1971).

Rumpf, E. and Hepburn, A.C., *Nationalism and Socialism in Twentieth Century Ireland*, (Liverpool, 1977).

Stewart, A.T.Q., *The Narrow Ground: Aspects of Ulster 1609-1969*, (London, 1977).

Sunday Times Insight Team, *Ulster*, (Harmondsworth, 1972).

Thayer, G., *The British Political Fringe: A Profile*, (London, 1965).

Thompson, D., *England in the Twentieth Century*, (London, 1965).

Wallace, M., *British Government in Northern Ireland: From Devolution to Direct Rule*, (Newton Abbot, 1982).

Wallace, M., *Northern Ireland: Fifty Years of Self-Government*, (Newton Abbot, 1971).

Walsh, P., *From Civil Rights to National War: Northern Ireland Catholic Politics 1964-1974*, (Belfast, 1989).

White, B., *John Hume: Statesman of the Troubles*, (Belfast, 1984).

Whyte, J.H., *Church and State in Modern Ireland 1923-1979*, (Dublin, 1980), (2nd edn).

Whyte, J.H., *Interpreting Northern Ireland*, (Oxford, 1990).

Wichert, S., *Northern Ireland Since 1945*, (Harlow, 1991).

3. Articles

Bing, G., 'John Bull's Other Island', *Tribune* 1950.

Beckett, J.C., 'Northern Ireland', *Journal of Contemporary History*, Vol. 6, No. 1, 1971.

Delargy, H., 'The Man Who Outlived His Memory', *New Statesman* 5 September 1975, p.274.

Farren, S., 'Unionist-Protestant Reaction to Educational Reform in Northern Ireland, 1923-1930', *History of Education*, 1985, Vol. 14, No. 3, pp.227-236.

Farren, S., 'Nationalist-Catholic Reaction to Educational Reform in Northern Ireland, 1920-1930', *History of Education*, 1986, Vol. 15, No. 1, pp.19-30.

Heaney, S., 'Old Derry's Walls', *The Listener*, Vol. 80, No. 2065, (24 October 1968).

Horowitz, D.L., 'Community Conflict: Policy and Possibilities', Occasional Paper No. 1, *University of Ulster: Centre for the Study of Conflict*, 1990.

Hume, J., 'The Northern Catholic', *Irish Times* 18 and 19 May 1964.

Kaplin, L.S. and Snydner, S.R. (ed.), 'Fingerprints on History: The NATO Memoirs of Theodore C. Achilles', Occasional Papers No. 1, Lynman Lennitzer Center for NATO and European Community Studies, *Kent State University*, Kent, Ohio.

Kennedy, D., 'Catholics in Northern Ireland, 1926-1939', *Years of the Great Test*, F. McManus (ed.), pp.138-149.

McAllister, I., 'Political Opposition in Northern Ireland: The National Democratic Party, 1965-1970', *Economic and Social Review*, Vol. 6 (1975), pp.353-366.

McCracken, J.L., 'The Political Scene in Northern Ireland, 1926-1937', *Years of the Great Test, F.McManus* (ed.), pp.150-160.

McGurk, T., 'Agony of the 1930s', *Irish Times,* 6 September 1980.

McGurk, T., 'The Anti-Partition Campaign', *Irish Times,* 8 September 1980.

McGurk, T., 'Nationalists 'New Approach', *Irish Times,* 9 September 1980.

McGurk, T., 'New Catholics and Bogus Loyalism', *Irish Times,* 10 September 1980.

McGurk, T., 'Civil Rights and Decline of the Nationalists', *Irish Times* 11 September 1980.

New Statesman, 'A Nasty Smell from Ulster', 3 January 1964.

Phoenix, E., 'Introduction and Calendar of the Cahir Healy Papers', (PRONI), D2991.

Phoenix, E. (ed.), 'Irish News Centenary Supplement: 100 Years of History', (Parts 1 and 2, Belfast, *Irish News,* November 1991 and April 1992).

Purdie, B., 'The Irish Anti-Partition League, South Armagh and the Abstentionist Tactic', *Moriae, Ulster Polytechnic,* (Lent 1984), pp.101-125.

Purdie, B., 'The Friends of Ireland: British Labour and Irish Nationalism, 1945-1949', *Contemporary Irish Studies,* Gallagher, T. and O'Connell, J. (eds.), pp.81-94.

Vinney, M., 'A Journey North', *Irish Times,* 4-9 May 1964.

Whyte, J., 'How Much Discrimination was there Under the Stormont Regime, 1921-1968', in *Contemporary Irish Studies*, Gallagher, T. and O'Connell, J. (eds.), pp.1-30.

4. Theses

Elliott, S., 'The Electoral System in Northern Ireland Since 1920', (Ph.D. Thesis, Queen's University, Belfast, 1971).

Foy, M., 'The Ancient Order of Hibernians: An Irish Political–Religious Pressure Group, 1884-1975', (M.A. Thesis, Queen's University, Belfast, 1976).

McGill, P.F., 'The Senate in Northern Ireland, 1921-1962', (Ph.D. Thesis, Queen's University, Belfast, 1965).

Phoenix, E., 'The National Movement in Northern Ireland, 1914-1928', (Ph.D. Thesis, Queen's University, Belfast, 1984).

Rees, R., 'The Northern Ireland Problem: A Study of the Northern Ireland Government in Context of its Relations with Dublin and Westminster, 1945-1951', (Ph.D. Thesis, University of Ulster, 1986).

Rutan, G.F., 'Northern Ireland under Ulster Unionist Rule: The Anti-Movement Political System, 1920-1963', (Ph.D. Thesis, University of North Carolina, 1964).